William's Gift

One Veterinarian's Journey

DR. HELEN DOUGLAS

GENERAL STORE PUBLISHING HOUSE
499 O'Brien Road, Box 415
Renfrew, Ontario, Canada K7V 4A6
Telephone (613) 432-7697 or 1-800-465-6072
www.gsph.com

ISBN 978-1-897508-37-4

Cover design, artwork, and seals: James McGregor
Cover photo: Louise McGregor
Page design and formatting: Magdalene Carson, New Leaf Publication Design
Printed by Custom Printers of Renfrew Ltd., Renfrew, Ontario
Printed and bound in Canada

Library and Archives Canada Cataloguing in Publication

Douglas, Helen C., 1954-
    William's gift : one veterinarian's journey / Helen C. Douglas.
ISBN 978-1-897508-37-4
    1. Douglas, Helen C., 1954-. 2. Veterinarians--Canada--Biography.
I. Title.
SF613.D68A3 2009   636.089092   C2009-901812-8

To the animals
for all they give us

🐕 🐕 🐕

For my father and brother,
both Williams

If we could measure a life not in time, but in grace;
Not in riches, but in joy;
In love, not sought, but given;
Then we have much to learn from our animals.

CONTENTS

FOREWORD

William's Gift takes us to many places where stories full of humour, tragedy, triumph, and inspiration, both animal and human, unfold as we follow Helen's adventures. Throughout her more than thirty-year journey as a rural veterinarian, she shares her insights into human nature through the world of veterinary medicine. I have been privy to this extraordinary life, witnessing Helen's compassion and commitment to the care of animals and their owners. The lifestyle of being a rural veterinarian has consumed her life in many ways that others cannot comprehend. Her stories capture the essence of that lifestyle—one that is rapidly disappearing.

Helen's story writing began in her early years at veterinary college, where she recorded some of her most memorable experiences. As the years passed, she would occasionally bring out this ratty old rolled-up scroll, which contained a handwritten collection of her personal stories, to read in nostalgia or to write another anecdote when inspired. It was stored in her antique Canadiana hope chest that followed her wherever life took her. For many years following, the scroll remained buried in the hope chest, yet all the while, new stories continued to develop.

Many years of life and practice had passed when we decided to head south to the Bahamas for a well-deserved sabbatical. Shortly after arriving, Helen suddenly became inspired to write the many personal and veterinary stories still to be told. Unprepared for her endeavour, she attempted to search out a laptop or even a typewriter to use for writing—much to the amusement of the locals, as such items were either rare or obsolete. Consequently, she continued to handwrite, as in her scrolls, the stories that are found in this, her first book, *William's Gift*.

It is truly hard for me to say whether I am more proud of the life that has inspired them or the stories, waiting so long, that have finally been told.

Karen Noble
April 2009

ACKNOWLEDGEMENTS

I WISH TO THANK the following people for helping me make this book a reality. Because of them, I have been able to see a long-held dream come true. Thanks to:

Karen Noble, my partner, for her unwavering support and patience, not just with this process, but for travelling these paths with me.

My mother, Edith Purdy, who has supported me my whole life in the finest sense of these words.

My sister, Carrie, and her wonderful girls, who have shared many equine adventures and misadventures with me. Carrie, a treasured constant, has been there for the whole journey.

James and Louise McGregor, who, despite the tragic loss of their daughter Molly, found the time and generosity of spirit to provide editing and computer and graphics assistance, but more important, the friendship and encouragement needed to help me finish my book.

Judy Tullis for typing all my messy handwritten notes and Morgan for the Glossary.

The staff at Valley Veterinary Clinic for their loyalty and interest, and everything they do every day to make this a real story.

My first and finest mentor, Dr. Eric Pallister (posthumously). He practised for fifty years with no modern gadgets and taught me how to be an intuitive veterinarian. A true gentleman and horseman, he instilled in me my lifelong love for veterinary medicine.

ONE

STARTING OUT

THE PLAIN CHESTNUT GELDING rounded the last turn of the mile-long steeple-chase track at Keeneland well ahead of the pack. At 15.2 hands, he was a good deal shorter than most of the impressive, well-bred thoroughbreds he ran against. With the humble name "William," no one had expected much of the little New Zealand-bred horse, and he ran at nine-to-one odds. I had noticed him in the parade, and as his name was the same as my father's, thought he was worth a wager, if only to give me a horse to hope for.

The spring day in Kentucky was perfect for the horses and for the first day of the meet, with a light breeze keeping the animals cool and the turf good and dry. A cloudless blue sky and the scent of the apple blossoms made the day magical. The atmosphere was vibrant as the field neared the last hurdle, an impressive four-foot brush. With no exception, we were on our feet and cheering them on. I threw my hands in the air and shouted wildly. My little horse, the undisputed underdog, was coming in first.

Suddenly, disaster struck as William caught a toe and somer-saulted over the last jump landing hard and throwing his rider wide. A pause; inconsolable silence, as disbelief washed over the crowd. He didn't get up. The buzz of whispered conversa-tion began as the emergency black barrier was erected around the fallen animal. The ambulance drove onto the field, and, to a person, we waited.

An unexpected grief overcame me, and tears started to pour down my cheeks. I stood experiencing deeply and with no inhibi-tion the depth of William's sacrifice. As a seasoned veterinarian,

I had been witness to many tragedies and much loss in the animal world. I had long ago cultivated the ability to stay calm in emergencies, to act and not feel when I needed to most. I had dealt with many such events in a cool professional manner, serving over and over the owners and their pets with no reflection on my own feelings. Now I wept like a baby, and the cumulative pain took my breath away. A tidal wave of repressed emotion knocked me off my feet.

How did I get to this place?

🐾 🐾 🐾

I had always known I wanted to be a veterinarian, simply assumed I would be, from my earliest introduction to the idea of choosing a career. This had relieved me of the angst of most of my adolescent friends, who changed their future plans as often as they did their clothes. In the end, they had to draw something out of the hat as graduation neared. I carried on, not even having made a second choice, taking the necessary courses and spending my free time getting the all-important experience with which one had to be armed to apply to veterinary school. The fact that I was female had, thankfully, ceased to be a deterrent by the time I came in front of the interview board. Although the idea of a woman veterinarian was still novel in the late sixties, the obstacles were insignificant compared to even a decade before, and I was lucky enough to have had only support and encouragement along the way.

In the summer between the third and final year of veterinary school, students usually sought employment with a practice specializing in the area of veterinary medicine in which they were interested. This four-month period was considered to be an important internship for those of us who wanted to go into practice. We looked forward eagerly to doing some of the procedures we had been trained for and to taking more responsibility. Of course, it was a bonus if the job could be found in a part of the country where one wanted to be, so I was thrilled to get an affirmative answer from a mixed practice in Nova Scotia. I had spent my childhood summers at our seaside cottage there. Not only is this a wonderfully quaint and hospitable province, it is a place where veterinarians are known to be less cautious about letting students tackle things on their own. This may be due to the easygoing nature of most Nova Scotians, who are still less inclined to litigation than many Upper Canadians. Whatever the reason, I had certainly heard of students being allowed to do very exciting and varied things there and eagerly accepted the position.

I set out in early May, somewhat anxious about the long trip alone, with just my young Dalmation for company. It was a thousand miles to my destination, and I had never tackled such a road trip on my own. Although my car was sound enough mechanically, I was apprehensive. I knew the long journey was the first of the summer's challenges. The warm sun, the first green colours of spring, and the miles slipping by were hypnotic. We were a team—my dog and I, on a grand adventure, and when I arrived in Bridgewater, I felt more than two days older.

I knew of a family that had moved to Bridgewater from my hometown years before, but I hadn't contacted them in advance of arriving. Hoping they could help me find a place to stay, I arrived at their doorstep and was pleased to find that they remembered me.

It was one of the best things that happened to me that summer, finding the Glens. Mrs. Glen led me around to the front of their classic white Lunenburg County home. It had been a sea captain's house and was quite magnificent, with lawns sweeping out to the water. Off to the side of the property, with a little strip of beach all its own, was a small guest cottage. White with green trim, it had a fireplace and a front porch complete with rocker, and within an hour of my arrival, I had taken it for the summer.

The few days before I started work were spent exploring the area. Mrs. Glen explained some of the history of the people living on both sides of the LaHave River. A German boat had gone aground in the Lunenburg area two hundred years before, and the descendants, who stayed, with their Lutheran religion and hardworking ways, became the backbone of the Lunenburg culture and economy. The mailboxes along the north side of the LaHave, as I followed it down to the sea, were inscribed with many variations of the one or two original names. It was amusing to see the Whynots followed by the Whynottes and the Veinottes followed by the Veinots. By the time I had crossed to the south side on a small ferry, I had passed through East LaHave, West LaHave, Upper and Lower LaHave. The boxes on the south side had more French names, and I drove as far out as the lovely village of Petite Rivière.

Following the winding river the ten miles back upstream towards my cottage, past the fishing boats and neatly stacked traps, I felt completely enchanted by the area. White wooden seafarers' homes proudly sported the Lunenburg bulge, an architectural feature creating a vantage point above the front doors from which the women could look out to sea for the returning vessels. The homes were well cared for and most had lovely cottage gardens. The area was fantastic, rich in culture and history and natural beauty. I looked forward to my time in this place.

Many of the people who came to the practice were backwoods people. I learned something about their strong, stoic constitutions my first week on the job. Dr. Read, my employer, had warned me that people often came in without appointments, it having been impossible to convince them of the need to call first.

A rough-looking man in hunting clothes came into the clinic during a quiet time one afternoon. His large hound had a nasty, ragged wound on its side that required immediate attention. We were worried that there had been a lot of blood loss, perhaps even bleeding into the chest, as the dog was pale and in shock. While we hooked it up on intravenous fluids, the owner sat patiently in the reception area. When Dr. Read finally felt the animal was out of danger, he returned to tell the owner to go ahead home. The dishevelled fellow said, "I'll just go on to the hospital, then," and peeling back his jacket he displayed a nasty shotgun wound in his own upper arm, which must have been causing him no little pain. He had waited to find out about his dog before looking after himself.

Dr. Don Read was certainly not of the old school of Maritime veterinary surgeons I had heard about who would, reputedly, turn their practices over to you. He was careful and conscientious, and I was only gradually allowed to take on appointments and minor surgeries. But by the second week, I was forced to treat an emergency on my own. Dr. Read was on a country call and couldn't be reached.

The front door burst open and a young woman with two crying children in tow frantically thrust a small dog writhing in convulsions over the counter into the arms of the receptionist. In this case, the diagnosis was fairly easy to make, as the dog exhibited the hyper-reactivity typical of strychnine poisoning. It was worsening rapidly, and any sudden movement or sound would start a new episode of convulsions. With difficulty I administered an intravenous injection of anaesthetic into the moving foreleg and was rewarded by seeing the animal relax immediately. We lavaged the stomach, trying to remove all toxins that might be left, and administered charcoal powder.

For two days, the little sheltie cross lay under deep sedation. Every time she came out of the anaesthetic, she started convulsing again and had to be given more barbiturate. The nursing care was considerable, as she had to be turned frequently to avoid pressure sores and pneumonia. Maintaining her intravenous treatment was complicated by the constant paddling movements she made. The owners, though fisher folk and not well off, wanted to continue with treatment as long as there was any hope at all and came around regularly to see their pet. When, on the third day, we knew we had won, they came to pick up their uncoordinated but recuperating "Sally." They brought with them enough fresh scallops for all of us to take home.

🐎 🐎 🐎

The area around the mouth of the LaHave River was an intricate network of islands and coves. One group of these was called the Bush Islands, and practically everyone who lived there was a

"Bush." Many of them had no heat other than their woodstoves and no electricity. Each small island boasted several brightly coloured, shingled houses, all with lobster boats and traps at the moorings. Dr. Read was an avid yachtsman and invited me out with his family several evenings, skillfully manoeuvring his cruiser through the mazelike channels between the islands. The boating was tricky, with unmarked channels, sudden narrowings, and dangerous hidden rocks. I felt privileged to have a glimpse into a life seldom witnessed. On each of these outings I gained entrée into a secluded world far from the usual tourist routes. On the most special of nights, we watched the sunset turn the surface of the still Atlantic water from pink to dark purple before we headed in under the supervision of the ever-watchful gulls.

I had been looking forward to doing some scuba diving in the Atlantic, and Dr. Read arranged for me to go out with one of the elder Bush fishermen. A friend who also wanted to dive arranged to come to the South Shore the same day so I could have a buddy. We headed out shortly after sunup, the mist still hanging on the water, which was eerily still, slate gray, and looked very cold. He put down anchor three times for us, and we did shallow dives just off small islands so we could descend gradually. The large, purple starfish, sea anemones, and rock coloured lobsters were spots of life on the sandy ocean floor. We each came up with a large scallop on our last dive, proudly hoisting our net catch bags over the side of the boat. I was taken aback when Mr. Bush opened one with his knife and carved it up into several pieces. Thrusting one of them at me on the end of his knife, he assured me that scallops were best eaten raw. I was surprised to find out that they are as delicious and delicate in flavour as an oyster.

Later that summer, I had another remarkable diving experience. Ray Patton, my diving coach at Guelph, was spending two weeks in Nova Scotia with friends and intended to do a couple of dives with a biologist from Dalhousie University. The scientists had a summer research program going in St. Margaret's Bay, where they had impounded a dozen bluefin tuna, some weighing up to 600 pounds and reaching lengths of ten feet. They were conducting trials on digestion that necessitated feeding the large fish pieces of tagged bait, and divers had to swim out to the large, netted compound regularly for these feedings.

I was invited to dive with them, and they got together enough scuba gear for me to go along. We swam out along a guide rope and descended into the cold, dark green water with our baskets of raw fish. Nothing could be seen as we adjusted our buoyancy, so we could hover easily at thirty feet below the surface. Suddenly they appeared, silver and flashing they swam by us, eyes as large as bottle bottoms, dark blue stripes down the middle of their sides . . . beautiful fish! They took the bait out of our hands, swooping so close we could touch them. It was breathtaking to see these giant creatures so close to us that their yellow eyes seemed to be looking right into ours. I felt unafraid. I had been blessed with a privileged moment. At the end of the summer, they were released.

One Saturday afternoon, we were just finishing up a hectic morning of appointments and looking forward to going home when a man from Liverpool, an hour away, telephoned in a panic. He had discovered several lumps on his dog's abdomen that he was certain had just appeared. The animal simply had to be seen, as waiting until Monday would be too distressing for the owner. Reluctantly, knowing that the dog was otherwise in fine form, we agreed to see him as an emergency. When the man hurried in and put the dog on the table, he assured us that these lumps had not been observed previously in the two years they had owned the dog. It was one of the funniest moments of the summer when we told him that it was perfectly normal for a male dog to have nipples. Beet-red, he couldn't get out of the clinic fast enough.

On the weekends there was never a shortage of things to do. The Glens had taken me under their wing, and I was included in Sunday dinners, nights around the television, and invited on many outings. They had a small stable and allowed me to use one of the young horses on a regular basis that summer. Ben, the huge Percheron cross gelding I was given to ride, had a heart as big as his dinner plate-sized feet. So I'd feel I was helping out, the exercise was called "giving the young horse some mileage"—but it was sheer pleasure for me. I had been an enthusiastic rider since, at the ripe age of seven, I was bribed with lessons in order to modify some undesirable childhood behaviour.

I had been really unhappy at the thought of spending the entire summer away from the beasts and my favourite pastime. In the evenings I would explore the hills and lumber roads stretching away from the river with their seventeen-year-old son Michael, on his horse. Some of the hilltops were cleared, and we could see far out along the river to the sea ten miles away, glinting blue in the distance. We could canter our horses up the grassy track of an abandoned farm to the top of a hill, scattering daisies and dragon-flies, and be rewarded with a panorama in all directions.

On other occasions, Mrs. Glen and I would go exploring the antique and junk shops that opened every summer for the tourists. Mrs. Oickle's at Green Bay was an old house whose every room overflowed, until finally the house itself spilled out onto the lawn. Hours could be spent inspecting the piles of books, rugs, postcards, old clothes, and every other sort of Maritime memorabilia. Several rusty school buses on blocks housed collections of tools and car parts.

These outings would often end with a trip to the Turkey Burger, a once-white shanty in the middle of nowhere. This canteen was run by an ex-navy cook, who would pile more food on every plate than could possibly be eaten. The lineup outside the door of the flat-roofed, dingy building often straggled well out into the parking lot. Once inside, clients had to choose from a menu that was handwritten on pieces of cardboard and posted on every available flat surface. The chowder was so thick you could stand your spoon up in it. The side salad was piled into soup bowls till they overflowed. It was always fun to sit in different seats on return visits, because I was then confronted with parts of the menu previously hidden from view. The friends who visited me that summer were always taken aback when I pulled up in front of the dilapidated Turkey Burger after telling them I was taking them to the best restaurant in town. For good food, it had the others beat by miles, so the unique and colourful character of the place and its patrons was just a bonus.

Since Dr. Read had taken over the practice, the emphasis had gradually switched from large to small animals, so we didn't get many country calls. When we did, it was a pleasant change from the usual routine at the clinic to go out to a farm. Some of the calls involved long drives on back roads, more visits to homes and parts of the province I would otherwise never have seen. Many of these small family farms were being run by elderly people, as the young people had not been interested in taking over and had gone off to the city or to Upper Canada.

In much of inland Nova Scotia, small farms were being deserted and sadly lay overgrown. On some of the remaining ones, I was fascinated to see the men still using methods that had scarcely changed in a hundred years. Hay was often raked with a horse-drawn vehicle and loaded by fork for transport to the mow. Many farmers still plowed the small, rough fields with a team of oxen. These oxen were prized possessions and were often exhibited in the local fairs; with their brass-tipped horns and ornate carts, they were an important part of the parade. On the country calls I was able to go along on, I met some of the most interesting people of that summer. Many of them had never heard of, much less seen, a woman vet.

One such call was to a cow with a prolapsed vagina. We arrived at a farm with a low frame barn, and I followed Dr. Read into the dimly lit interior, carrying my share of the equipment we needed. Cobwebs hung about my head and neck. Some minutes later, a stooped, very wrinkled, and obviously nearly blind farmer entered the barn. He watched the fairly simple procedure to replace and secure the prolapse without much comment, and I busied myself, also quite silently, holding the cow's tail. When we all emerged into the sunlight, the gentleman realized for the first time that I was female. My coveralls and scarf certainly contributed to a total lack of femininity, and with his posture and poor vision, my cover had been complete. As I stood with my arms in a bucket of hot soapy water, he contemplated me for a moment. Then without any formalities or introductions, he came right to the point with his query: "Shouldn't you be a nurse?"

🐄 🐄 🐄

In midsummer, I adopted a kitten. A child had found her under a hedge, wet and shivering, and brought her to the clinic. The mother and the rest of the litter were nowhere to be found. The tiny tabby fit into the palm of my hand and was almost too young to be fed solid food. Yet she had an undeniable will to live. I decided to take her on and fed her from an eyedropper until she learned to lap. She looked perilously small and fragile curled up on a red hot water bottle in the big cage. Eventually I christened her LaHave and took her home to my cottage. That made three of us to sit on the porch admiring the river in the evening.

The last week of summer had been slow around the clinic. I was getting organized to leave for Ontario that weekend, feeling entirely satisfied with what I had learned and done. On the second-last evening before my departure, Dr. Read asked me if I would do office appointments by myself for the last hour. These after-dinner appointments usually consisted of vaccinations, flea allergies, and ear infections—things I could handle on my own. A look at the book confirmed that only routine problems were booked, and so at 6:00 p.m. he left for an important regatta at the yacht club.

Happy that things had gone smoothly, I was just about to put the answering service on when the phone rang. True to Murphy's Law, the second calving call of the summer came in when the veterinarian was out on a boat, having left his student in sole charge for the first time all summer. With a surge of adrenalin, I told the farmer I would be right there. The young woman on reception was willing to help me and thankfully knew where most of the necessary equipment was kept. We rounded it up and put on our coveralls with false bravado. If I had known then what complications lay ahead, I would have been doubly nervous. Luckily I didn't, and beginner's luck saved me.

We drove up to the large dairy farm shortly after dark. The farmer was a Dutchman who greeted me at the door to the milk-house with poorly disguised disappointment. He led Pam and me into the barn, where his wife and daughter stood by the straining cow. I tried to look confident as I laid out my equipment and put together the calf-jack. The farmer gamely tried to hide his regrets about not having the "Doc" and even ventured a good-humoured crack about "Ladies' night."

My examination quickly told me the reason for the delay in calving. The calf was breeched, and only the tail could be readily felt. But it did not seem too large, so I was optimistic about correcting the malpresentation. Standing on a bale of hay in the gutter, I spent ten minutes revolving the calf forward until finally a hind leg could be grasped and carefully brought up and out so the foot was visible. The other hind leg took about as long, as it was farther down in the uterus. When the calf finally arrived on the barn floor, we were all terribly disappointed to see that it wasn't alive.

I had started to wash up my equipment when luckily something triggered a vague memory about the connection between breech births and twins. I sauntered back to the cow, explaining that a final exam should always be done on the mother for tears in the womb. And there it was, another tail, pushed now into the identical position of the first calf. It was smaller than the first, though, and in no time was lying on the straw at our feet. To my great disappointment, it, too, was dead. After examining the mother to ensure she was fine, we packed our gear somberly and said goodbye to the family. It was not until I was in the car that I let myself experience the full range of my feelings: excitement and happiness at having been up to the job . . . relief at not having missed finding that second calf . . . and sadness at their both being stillborn.

Leaving Nova Scotia was bittersweet. The next time I pulled a calf, it would be as a veterinarian.

TWO

AN ELEPHANT
COMES TO VISIT

MY FINAL YEAR WAS the epitome of the axiom "work hard, play hard." For myself, and most of my 120 class-mates, it might be argued that the "play hard" part won out, but perhaps that is just what is remembered most easily. The riotous goings-on were a necessary outlet for the tension building up as exams approached. There was the additional pressure of job hunting, and it was the first time most of us had looked for a full-time job. Leaving the university and friends we had known for six years was frightening. The pressure to find and choose the right job seemed overwhelming and more competitive than I had anticipated. As our time to join the real working world loomed nearer, our partying grew more exuberant, as if we intuitively anticipated the huge responsibilities that would await us when we left the sheltering walls of the veterinary college.

We had been required to sort ourselves into groups of four or five people who were to remain together throughout the year. The process whereby that number of people arranged themselves into teams would have been amusing if so many people hadn't been hurt by it. It took almost two weeks. It was the same feeling of discomfort that I experienced as a child when the captain had to choose a team one by one from a gang of kids. Some of us were invited to join more than one team, while others were totally left out. Subtle yet complicated negotiations preoccupied us for days until finally a list was presented to the professors—just in time for the first rotation.

I was lucky enough to find myself in a group whose interests complemented each other's perfectly. On some rotations, my interest in horses proved to be of value, and on others Gord's or Sue's knowledge of cattle pulled us through. The fourth member was the most scholarly of our group and intended to become a small animal practitioner, so we were well rounded out. All of us were easygoing and more or less inclined to pull our weight. Not all of the groups stayed so harmonious throughout their time together.

Our final year was organized into rotations of two weeks. Small animal medicine and surgery were two of the most important. It was critical to make the most of the short time we had in surgery and seemed equally critical to make a good impression on our evaluating professors, though in retrospect we were all doctors already. In comparison, the two-week poultry rotation or the study of epidemiology never caught anyone's complete attention. The small animal devotees went into these surgery rotations with fervour, while our large animal types couldn't wait to get into the barns.

Our two-week surgery rotation had four procedures scheduled. We were all to be given a chance to be surgeon, then assistant surgeon, anaesthetist, and finally instrument person. Our patients were Humane Society dogs and cats we were charged to neuter, and it was imparted to us with great gravity that we were lucky to have this opportunity, as other veterinary colleges had not had live surgical patients for many years.

The fellow who was to do the first surgery had a cat to work on, and his hysterectomy took well over an hour. All of us were terrified. As he cut into the pale midline, I felt a hot flash, and the blood drained out of my head. I was precariously close to fainting. I felt panicky—perhaps I could never be a surgeon, and therefore never a vet! How could this be? A feeling of total dejection overcame me as the week proceeded and my own surgery day approached. I tossed and turned all the night before in a cold sweat, envisioning my first incision over and over, almost as a nightmare. I was sure I couldn't do it.

The surgery went beautifully from the first application of scalpel to skin. I felt totally at home and found that tissue handling came quite naturally to me. Surprisingly for someone who has never been able to sew on a button without personal injury, when it came to surgery on animals, I was right at home. My mark wasn't outstanding, but my relief and happiness could not be measured. I would be able to perform surgery after all; it was just getting past that first cut. From there on, I was sailing and had found a new and seemingly familiar element in which to perform. Surgery day couldn't come fast enough.

🐎 🐎 🐎

Every few weeks, there was a party given by a drug supply company in an attempt to draw our attention to their products. There were often wine and cheese parties, and we nodded in the direction of the tables of brochures and displays as we made our way to the refreshments. The most notorious of these was an extravaganza thrown for each graduating class at one company's headquarters, an hour's drive from Guelph. Buses were supplied for the occasion. We all trouped obediently around the factory and the product display before we were shown to the large banquet room. Rows of tables had been set up for us, and a buffet steamed in readiness. The crowning touch was the unlimited supply of wine that made this annual event what it was.

The evening started on a formal note, with speeches of welcome followed by speeches of thanks. As more and more of the inexpensive Canadian bubbly was consumed, decorum was abandoned. Comedy acts were followed by yodelling displays at the microphone. Suit coats and ties were shed. A team of salesmen competed with a team of students in a wine-drinking competition. In a moment of total absurdity, the most retiring fellow in our class was carried from the shadows on the shoulders of two of the huskiest class members to receive some sort of contrived award. Not surprisingly events deteriorated rapidly. As we staggered back to our bus, they were prying one of their sales managers out of a lavatory stall where he had become lodged. And one of my classmates was found the next morning sleeping in his car with his head on the steering wheel. Thankfully he had never turned the key.

My sister visited me often in Guelph. Anne is two years younger than I am, and we have always shared our interest in horses. As teenagers, we boarded horses near home and were able to get out to see them most days after school. As soon as I got my driver's licence, I took over my parents' role as stable shuttle. All through high school, we continued to ride regularly, even in the worst winter weather. Even after six years away, I still missed riding with her. Anne enjoyed coming to stay with me for weekends in Guelph, despite the six-hour drive. Being part of the activities around the university was a great break from being the youngest child and the only one left at home. I kept my horse, a reliable cob type, with friends who ran a boarding stable, and there was always a spare horse for her. There was also a communal cutter and a set of harness I could use on Clunker, my reliable buckskin schoolmaster.

One weekend after Christmas, Anne needed a change of scenery and drove down to see me for a few days. There had been a lot of snow that winter, and the country roads were in perfect condition for sleighing. This crisp night, the moon was full, making it as bright as daylight, and we decided to go for a spin around a country block in the cutter. I overloaded the contraption by asking along two good friends from school. It was extremely cold, so the four of us bundled up well. The three of them sat crowded together in the seat swaddled in heavy blankets, while I knelt in front of them in my old raccoon coat, driving the horse, my fingers quickly numbing from the cold. It was almost surreal, the bright moonlight creating distinct jet-black shadows from each tree branch across the silvery road and highlighting every graceful sweep of snow. The cutter slipped easily along on the crunchy surface, and the sleigh bells jingled to the rhythm of the fast trot.

The final downhill stretch ended at a "T" intersection, where we turned left to go the half-mile to the farm laneway. I eased myself out of kneeling position, almost paralyzed with cold, and prepared to pass the reins to one of the others. Not being part of the bundle behind me I had suffered the most from the biting wind and simply had to move. As I jumped out of the cutter to jog a few steps, I scared the now walking horse. Or perhaps he simply pretended to be scared, as he was never one to bypass an opportunity for a lark. Before Anne could organize the reins, he bolted down the hill, leaving me behind on the road. It was funny even then. The three humans swaying in the rickety little seat were so well wrapped up that they couldn't extricate themselves. Even if they had, there wasn't much they could have done but jump. The reins were now flapping in the breeze. It looked like a caricature of a Currier and Ives print. Clunker gaily took the corner at full gallop, putting the left runner up on a large snow bank. The cutter deftly deposited its occupants in the centre of the intersection, with their rugs and wineskins. By the time we reached the farm lane, Clunker had taken a short cut across a field and left the sleigh behind him on a log pile. Neither it, nor any of us, suffered damage, and Clunker looked too proud of himself to be chastised when we found him standing in the barnyard waiting for us.

From then until the end of February, I tried to apply myself to preparing for my final exams. There were three oral exams as well as the written ones. The prospect of oral exams had all of us worried, since we had never been required to confront our examiners in this manner before. Certainly it would be the first time that we would have to be so honest about what we didn't know. I found it almost impossible to sit still and concentrate, evening after evening. My two roommates and I would alternatively take delirium breaks, stopping to play one side of a record at full volume or just rampaging around the house trying to engage one another and create distractions. As a last resort, there was always housework, and our humble students' quarters shone as never before. There were incredible volumes of material to be memorized, as each species varied in its makeup and consequently its diseases and treatments. All three of us passed our exams, as did the other members in my rotation group. So I sailed into my last few weeks of elective rotations feeling relaxed and on top of the world.

We had a young elephant to examine when I was on a last week of radiology. The circus man who owned him had arrived at the school with three of the creatures on his truck. He had been forced to make a detour from the show because one young male, a yearling, was lame. The other two beasts were a mother and her calf, which was covered with long spiky bristles of hair. With its long ears and trunk out of proportion to its body, the calf was a delight. The event caused pandemonium inside and out. While the trainer supervised the young male inside and tried to get him into position for an x-ray of his foot, the other two were tethered by iron ankle chains to the pavement. The elephant inside was confused and excited by all the strange equipment and the break in his routine. He forgot the meanings of all his normal commands and first bowed, then sat up and begged instead of lying down. He was trying every trick he knew to accommodate his trainer, but it was all too much. Thousands of dollars worth of radiographic machinery were at risk.

Meanwhile, outside, hundreds of students had gathered. One girl couldn't resist touching the baby and was soon swept off her feet and suspended ten feet in the air wrapped in the angry mother's trunk. She was put down seconds after, unharmed but considerably shaken. Unfortunately, all the commotion was for nothing, as the cause of the lameness could not be found. The trainer was obviously relieved to get his charges reloaded and gone without any more serious problems.

In early February, I travelled to Ottawa for a job interview. The position advertised would involve mostly small animals, but I could do whatever horse work came in. The interview went well, and I had an affirmative answer the next day. Once I knew I had a job secured after graduation, I started looking at new cars. The Rusty Duster had served me well, but it was to be turned over to Anne. Three weeks before the end of classes, I signed a bank loan for a full-size Chevrolet station wagon. It was a huge gas-guzzler loaded with options and adorned with wood panelling, and I was absolutely thrilled with it. I was certain it was exactly what I needed and would pull the horse trailer to shows that summer. It hadn't occurred to me that as a junior vet I wouldn't get many weekends off to go to shows. Then, to break it in, I decided to drive to Kentucky.

There was a group of girls in our year who were full of life and always game for a lark. Many of them had been on the hockey team together for several years. I had only recently gotten to know them better when I joined them for a few games. There was a tremendous corps d'esprit among them, and they were usually at the forefront of class affairs and pranks. One night after a hockey game, the subject of my ostentatious new vehicle came up, and before I knew it, four of us were planning a trip to visit horse veterinarians in Lexington. Somehow, we convinced our professors on the merit of this idea, although I suspect they had already given up trying to hold us.

We hit the road on a Thursday afternoon in early April, spring fever running high. We got to the American border at dusk. The atmosphere in the car must have been infectious. We even had the officer at the border laughing when one of us politely asked him to "tell us the way to Kentucky." As the car carried us along through the Ohio night, the air became warmer and the music changed to country and western. We saw the sun come up as we were crossing the river in Cincinnati. During the night, we had entertained ourselves composing eight verses of words for an Ode to O.V.C. to the lilting tune of *Farewell to Nova Scotia*. The weekend lived up to all our expectations as we sampled grits and gravy, admired the splendid thoroughbred breeding farms, and enjoyed the spring sunshine. And the song was an equal success when it was presented to our class the following week.

Since it was known that I had a vehicle capable of transporting multitudes, I was asked to be a driver to our final graduation party. The class officers had booked a posh resort north of Toronto for a weekend. With many of the spouses along, it was a sizeable group, and we were well able to fill their dining room, swimming pool, and tennis court. There was still ice on the lake below as we were running back and forth in our bathing suits from the steaming pool to the sauna. The last night started with a perfectly cooked five-course meal to be followed by a nightclub gala. We were to be entertained by Bobby Curtola, a fifties crooner who hadn't been heard of in years. The few senior townspeople who had paid for admission were annoyed with our overly enthusiastic partymaking, and at one point the manager bluntly invited us to stop disturbing the show. But it was impossible to contain us. We all knew it was the last time we'd be together before our lives changed. By the end of the night, even Bobby Curtola had given in. He was last seen on the dance floor doing the bump with the group of ladies from the hockey team. I haven't seen some of them since I let them out of my car the next day.

Within a few more days, I had all my belongings packed. I pulled out of the laneway of the farmhouse where I had spent three years and tried not to look back. I was off to a new life as a doctor of veterinary medicine in the Ottawa Valley.

THREE

PIGEONS, BUDGIES, AND OTHER LIFE LESSONS

I STARTED WORK FILLED with confidence and enthusiasm. I didn't know that in the next six months, my innocent optimism would steadily deteriorate until finally I would begin to wonder if I were in the right profession at all. I knew I would have to endure a steep learning curve, but little did I know that I would lose confidence before regaining it, or how humbling it would be. But gradually, clients started to ask for me, difficult cases worked out, and I began to develop a new, more realistic sense of confidence as I gained experience. I wish I had been warned that most newly graduated veterinarians suffer from this same feeling of inadequacy when they begin to practise.

The well-equipped suburban hospital was run by an ambitious young veterinarian. I was one of a string of new graduates he had hired, and some hadn't worked out too well. It wasn't long before I realized that I was being watched very closely. The fact that Dr. McKay was the kind of man who almost never forgot anything and scarcely made a mistake only made my inexperience more obvious and embarrassing. My plaster casts fell off because they were too loose. My surgeries took twice as long as his. During office hours, there were clients to see every ten minutes, and I found it difficult to write up the details of each animal's history as I examined them. So I lagged further and further behind. By the end of the first month, I began to feel so inept that I began having difficulty with even the more simple procedures such as finding a vein for an intravenous injection.

Dr. Warren McKay, who had turned the practice into a successful business, was a perfectionist. He simply couldn't stand the thought of any of my cases going out the door without his stamp of approval—a position not hard to understand, as he was responsible for it all. He was exacting and a good teacher, but all that constructive criticism was sometimes hard to accept. He maintained some personal distance from his staff, and we all called him "Dr. McKay." He obviously kept himself coolly aloof from most people in his outside life as well. Once I heard him comment on a good friend's leaving to live in another city by saying, "Guess I'll have to get myself another friend." Although he was intimidating to me, I respected him greatly for his veterinary skills, and so did the clients.

One of Dr. McKay's clients was an older lady who travelled a considerable distance to see him and had done so for years. She had an aged mixed-breed dog that had a history of kidney disease and could be fed only an expensive therapeutic diet. The woman was very aware that at any time her pet's kidneys might cease to function altogether. Unfortunately, Dr. McKay was away on holiday for a week when Fluffy was presented with an emergency of a different kind.

Pyometra is a serious condition resulting from the introduction of infection into the uterus. In some cases of pyometra, the volume of nasty-smelling purulent material accumulating in the uterus is so great that it drains through the cervix and out the external genital opening. In other cases, called closed pyometra, the cervix remains closed and the infection "hides" in the animal, creating a life-threatening emergency because the developing blood poisoning can lead to shock. Any dog with pyometra is an anaesthetic risk, but an older one with ill-functioning kidneys presents a grave problem. Surgery is the only solution.

Mrs. Evans was not at all happy to see me enter the examining room instead of Dr. McKay. It was quickly evident that Fluffy had a nasty pyometra and there was no possibility of waiting until Dr. McKay's return to make a decision. At the moment, she was still fairly bright and had not gone into shock, but her colour and blood counts showed she had early toxemia. I explained to Mrs. Evans that her only chance was to give her vigorous intravenous fluid and antibiotic therapy followed by an emergency hysterectomy. As I spoke, the owner's face reflected her complete lack of confidence in me and her terrible concern for her pet. She reluctantly handed her over to my care and went home to wait by the telephone.

One of my favourite older veterinarians, a horse doctor, always said: "Emphasize the worst that can happen and then people will be happy if things turn out well." Unfortunately, because I was so anxious to give the lady some faith in me, I didn't paint a dismal enough picture. The surgery went well and I was pleased to be able to telephone Mrs. Evans to report that her dog had woken up and all looked well. But the next day, Fluffy was obviously becoming more depressed rather than brighter, and I quickly saw that she was not maintaining her hydration. Before I had even had a chance to check her blood urea level, she had vomited, and I knew with a sinking feeling that she was starting to go into kidney failure. Despite large volumes of intravenous fluids, her condition deteriorated, and within forty-eight hours of surgery she was dead.

The distraught client blamed me entirely for her pet's death, not believing that she might well have died even under Dr. McKay's care. On his return, he was confronted with a lengthy letter of complaint, including a refusal to pay even a portion of the costs. He looked rather grim about it but didn't make any comment. My confidence sank even lower, and I became reluctant to take on any serious or complicated cases. I was convinced that I was taking one step back for every two steps forward. Thankfully, it was only a short time later that I had a chance to prove my abilities — mostly to myself.

The first major surgical emergency that I was forced to undertake on my own after Fluffy was a gastric torsion. Bloat, or gastric dilatation, is a condition manifest in large, deep-chested breeds of dogs that comes on with horrifying suddenness. The dog may just jump or play with a full stomach, and the pendulous organ can swing. Within minutes of the stomach rotating, gas begins to dilate it, causing strangulation of the circulation to the organ. In less than an hour, the animal can be in shock or dead. Immediate decompression by stomach tube or by large-bore needle is crucial. The male Rhodesian Ridgeback that was presented to me was in a fairly early stage of bloat and was able to walk into the clinic. I was hopeful that I could pass a stomach tube to let off some of the gas before I entered his abdomen.

But once he was anaesthetized, I found that, secondary to the torsion, the esophageal entry to his stomach was too tightly constricted to allow passage of a tube. Reluctantly, I thrust a needle into the most dilated area of his now drum-like side. With the release of some of the pressure, I felt I could begin the surgery to correct the torsion. The stomach and spleen were both involved, and it was a formidable task sorting out the direction and degree of the rotation. It took an hour to get everything back into its normal position and suture the stomach to the abdominal wall. By the time I closed the incision, it had been almost three hours since I started the intensive work on Tag. I was ecstatic to see his colour returning to a normal bright pink, but afraid to be hopeful too soon. The next twenty-four hours would be crucial, as the stomach wall can become devitalized and necrotic if the circulation has been impaired for too long. Some dogs never recover from the endotoxic shock that develops after a bloat, and still others need more surgery to repair a damaged stomach. I felt optimistic, as he had not been in distress for long before we got him into surgery. I was so anxious for him to recover well that I was on pins and needles for two days. When he walked out the door five days later, no one was happier than I. The owner's sincere appreciation was important to me, but more so was the step I had taken towards regaining my self-confidence.

On one of my first nights on call for my new job, proud and excited to have an emergency pager on my belt, I got one of the most disturbing calls I ever had to deal with. I was riding my horse when the pager went off, and hurried back to the tack room to return the call, wondering what was ahead of me. Some teenagers were soaping tack and ended up eavesdropping.

I returned the page and contacted a youngish woman with a very thick French accent, who sounded surprised to reach me. She started the conversation by saying she had just acquired a new dog, a year-old black Labrador male that she was experiencing behaviour problems with.

"I don't know what to do, he keeps jumping on me," she complained.

"Well," I offered sympathetically, "that's fairly normal for a dog his age. You'll have to start by taking him to obedience school. Is he neutered?"

"What is neutered?" she asked.

Frustrated by the language barrier, I struggled to explain this professionally in front of the now intrigued adolescents.

"He'll have to have his testes removed," I said; adding help-fully, "this will curb some of the unwanted masculine behav-iour."

"But what if I like it?" she answered slyly; then into my stunned silence she injected in lower tones, "I turn down the lights, he comes to me . . ."

I slammed down the receiver, shaking a bit. Was it a joke? What was really going on? Perhaps she had anticipated getting a male vet on the line. I recovered my composure quickly enough, laughing at my own naivety. The teenagers were in gales of laughter, guessing the direction the conversation had taken from my startled, beet-red face.

"Be prepared for everything and anything," said my employer the next day, with a wry smile. "You're not in Nova Scotia anymore!"

Despite being more prepared, I never had to handle a repeat performance.

Dr. McKay had a special interest in exotic pets, and there was a constant parade of wild and wonderful animals into our clinic. We saw snakes with moulting problems, usually brought in "on ice" so that they were moving slowly enough to be handled. We did hysterectomies on raccoons and castrations of rabbits. On one occasion, I even sutured a tear in a bat's wing. Wild birds were frequently brought in with fractured legs or wings and treated "on the house," then released. Our reputation for looking after wild fowl led to one of the more humorous night calls I had that fall.

One Saturday evening, I was paged by a woman concerned about a wild pigeon in her backyard. She claimed it was choking and making odd noises and wanted to bring it to the clinic. She told me she would have to first catch it, then hire a babysitter and take a taxi to the hospital. All this should take about an hour, as she lived on the other side of the city. I went to the clinic at nine, and at ten-thirty was still sitting there, frustrated and fuming. The taxi pulled up just as I was about to give up and go home. The pigeon, wrapped in a brightly coloured child's blanket, was indeed making a strange spluttering noise, but it was bright-eyed and reluctant to be restrained. It and I shared the sentiment that it would have been happier left in the garden, especially since I had no idea whatsoever to do for it.

It was obvious that the lady was genuinely concerned, so I muttered something about the possibility of impaction of the crop or esophagus. I found a tiny polyethylene tube and pushed a few drops of mineral oil into the bird's crop. The woman was quite happy to see something done and didn't bat an eyelash as I added up her bill. Despite the fact that it was a wild bird, I felt I had to receive some compensation for two hours out of my Saturday evening. Even with a discounted emergency fee, the bill came close to seventy-five dollars. With the babysitter and the taxi charges, she had probably spent close to twice that. As I drove home, I couldn't help but laugh, thinking about the pigeon that would have been just as happy left alone and the soft-hearted lady with more money than common sense. To her credit, though, she cared more about the animal than her convenience or pocketbook. I was forced to go beyond that and consider that many people would have no idea how to judge the seriousness of a medical situation regarding an animal. I had a glimpse of how that would impact my whole life.

During afternoon appointments one day, I fell victim to my own soft-heartedness. A dark-haired Scottish lady in her thirties arrived with a kitten that had been limping for two days. She looked worn out and ill herself, and when I told her that the kitten had a broken leg, she could barely hold back her tears. She and her husband had emigrated from Scotland, but he had since lost his job. They had lost another cat, hit by a car on their road. There was no question of having it repaired, as they just couldn't afford it. After talking to her husband on the phone, she told me the kitten would have to be put to sleep. As she talked she became more and more distraught, until finally she broke down and told me that she was being treated for cancer herself. Everything seemed to have gone wrong for them, and the loss of another pet was the final straw.

I was becoming quite upset listening to her and wished I could help her somehow. Impulsively, I told her to come back in the afternoon, and that I would give her my own kitten. LaHave had been suffering from a lack of attention since I started work and I had been feeling guilty knowing she was alone so much. Although I realized after they happily left with her that I might regret my hasty decision, I never did. They kept in touch for a long time, and both my cat and its new owners were very happy with the arrangement. I was, after all, her doctor, and several children doted on her. It was a "go with your gut" moment on my part and it was amazing how well it worked out!

Dr. McKay's interest in birds led to a steady stream of them to our door. I will never forget the day I learned the hard way how stressful it is for a budgie to be handled by a stranger. The consultation was to be a simple check-up and nail trim. Father and Mother had decided to bring along the whole family as an exercise in learning about the care of their bird. Three little children, all with red hair and blue eyes, peered at me trustingly over the stainless steel tabletop.

I gently surrounded the small budgie with my hand and removed it from its cage. As part of a routine physical, we had been taught to listen to the bird's heart and I was at this stage in my examination when the rapid beating stopped completely. It took me a split second to realize that the tiny creature had died of shock in my hand. I looked at the expectant, innocent upturned faces in alarm and then, feeling I had to act quickly, blurted out something about cardiac massage and ran in to the operating room. With one hand I turned on the oxygen and with the other I massaged the budgie's chest between thumb and forefinger. I probably knew before I started that it would do no good but I couldn't bring myself to callously hand back the bird without trying to resuscitate it. I returned to the room and shook my head from side to side slowly. Tears welled up in the three sets of eyes gazing up at me. At a loss for words, I left the parents to explain the death of the bird to their children. Certainly it was not the learning experience they had come prepared for.

🐎 🐎 🐎

Anne had graduated from college the same spring I did and moved back to Ottawa later in the year. That first fall, we had decided to take up residence together on a dilapidated old horse farm out along the Ottawa River. It had not been occupied for some time, and the interior was a mess of peeling wallpaper and paint. What decorating had once been done was unbelievably gaudy, with every room a wilder hue. The mice had installed themselves in every drawer in the kitchen. The cheap carpets bore the evidence of too many doggie misdemeanours and would have to be pulled up. The owner of the farm had put his plans to renovate on hold and agreed to rent it to us for a nominal amount just to have it lived in. Anne and I were thrilled and believed with optimism we could see tremendous potential in the place. It was our first opportunity to have our own stable and look after our horses ourselves. We thought we could get along.

The farm had been beautiful in its day and had been the scene of many horse shows. Along both sides of the long lane were overgrown cross-country fences in need of repair. There were two small barns of traditional Ottawa Valley dovetailed log construction. They were full of someone else's old farm machinery and mouldy hay, but the stalls were still sturdy. All the fences needed work, as the wire was rusted and many of the poles were rotten and falling over. Looking at it, though, we could already picture horses grazing in the fields.

We tackled the work with enthusiasm. The inside had to be made livable before we could start any of the more interesting outside work. We steamed, scrubbed, and chipped away for two weeks before redecoration could begin. The woodwork all had to be scraped and repainted, but the fact that it was our first farm made it all fun and exciting. We were racing winter and had to get on to the outside work quickly so that the barns would be ready before it became unbearably cold.

The great rush to have our horses installed caused more than a few problems. If there are weaknesses in your systems, horses will always find them. I have never since tried to put animals in facilities that were not quite ready for them. The patched-up fences were soon pushed over and the lightweight water troughs lay overturned.

We had been given a poor motley old pony named Bambi that needed a home and would be a good companion for my half-Clydesdale hunter, Lexbrook. We kept them in the paddock that surrounded the barns. In another paddock, with better fencing, we kept two horses belonging to boarders. Unfortunately, these latter beasts had to be transferred through the first paddock morning and night. In a David and Goliath scenario, Bambi created havoc protecting his friend if they were out when this occurred. Trying to get them in first was not always successful, as the pony would never come to us, and we spent hours chasing him around. On other occasions, he would kneel down, get onto his side, and shimmy under the rails, leaving Lexbrook frantic and alone in the enclosure.

One evening, I went out to feed the horses just before dark and found the paddock empty. Bambi and Lexbrook had departed for greener pastures. Since the fence and gate stood untouched,

I could only assume that the pony had crawled under and the hunter had jumped out to follow him. We alerted the neighbouring farms and drove around the country roads until well after dark, but they couldn't be spotted. The police were notified. At dawn the next morning, I went out on one of the boarder's horses armed with an extra halter and lead rope. I headed to the woods at the back of the property and was lucky enough to find hoofprints quite quickly. My dog was with me and seemed to be on the trail. It was nearly two hours later, though, that I found them seven miles away, grazing happily on a small golf course. I fully expected Bambi to be impossible to catch, but the night out had apparently satisfied his urge to wander. They both followed me back resignedly without needing to be led.

After a few weeks of running the farm, Anne and I had sorted out many of the problems. The horses now seemed happy to stay at home, we had become more organized, and things were running smoothly. A Hereford heifer had joined the family and got on admirably with the pony, which made it less of an ordeal to separate him from my horse.

We also discovered Bambi was excellent with small children, so he was finally earning part of his keep carting around little ones belonging to our frequent visitors from the city.

That winter, I enjoyed one of the most beautiful rides I have ever had. It was a weekend, and an all-day storm had kept us inside by the fire. Almost a foot of fluffy, dry powder had fallen by the time the snow started to taper off. After supper, Anne and I decided we needed to get some fresh air. Slipping our bridles over our arms, we ploughed through the drifts out to the barn. There was enough light to ride safely, and a few flakes of snow were still falling. It was an enchanted evening, peaceful, with no one out on roads that were not yet ploughed.

We rode out the lane to the country road bareback, the clouds created by the horses' breath clearly visible. Their spirits were high and they were obviously enjoying being out under these strange circumstances. We rounded one corner to approach a long upward grade with a row of perfect maple trees silhouetted along the length of one side. The road was deep with snow, and not one vehicle had marred the perfect surface. Anne and I urged our horses into a canter, and we rode side by side up the mile-long hill. The snow sprayed up behind us. The horses seemed to feel the magic of the night and stayed together calmly despite their freshness. We were all moving in time to the rhythm of their hooves on the road. Of the many hours I have spent on horseback that is still one of the most memorable.

At Christmas I was on call for the practice, a duty that usually falls to the junior veterinarian on staff. I got an emergency page from a local Doberman breeder of note. She was almost too breathless to speak, but managed to tell me that one of her champion males was convulsing. Would I meet her at the clinic as quickly as I could drive there? She was by herself and had to lift the unconscious ninety-pound dog into the car alone. We carried him into the hospital on a board, his eyes rolling and legs paddling. With extreme embarrassment, she told me that she had done this to the dog herself. Two of her breeding males had managed to get out at the same time and she had heard them fighting from the house. Running out the door, she had grabbed a length of two by four lumber from along the kennel wall. She knew better than to try to pull them apart with her hands. The fight was a fierce one and her shouts and attempts to push with the piece of wood were not deterring them. When she realized that one of the dogs was injured and bleeding she had frantically swung the two by four at the more aggressive dog and watched in shock as he fell to the ground. He had been imported at great expense from England and now lay in our hospital with a severe concussion.

Over the next forty-eight hours, he continued to lie comatose, exhibiting no signs of voluntary movement or awareness of his surroundings. Sedatives had to be given to him to control the paddling movements, along with high doses of cortisone to try to control the inflammation in his brain. In all probability, he was experiencing an intracranial bleed. The petite woman was still shocked that she had been able to do this to such a large, strong animal. Unfortunately, as well as being mortified by guilt, she also had to suffer her husband's wrath. In the end, the dog died without regaining consciousness. It left all of us with a sober respect for the strength that can be summoned out of panic. And, although it represented a serious loss to their breeding program, they decided never again to have two males who might compete for top dog.

I was to leave my first job the following spring—a year after starting there. They were phasing out the infrequent horse work we did do, to become an exclusively small-animal practice. I was interested in doing a lot more work with horses, so I decided it was time to move farther out into the country. By the time I left, the disappointments were not as devastating, the successes not as uncommon or exhilarating. I was just beginning to put into perspective the events that take place in everyday veterinary practice. I was also left with a reinforced desire to have a thorough and a good foundation for small-animal medicine.

I imagine Dr. McKay is breaking in new graduates with the same liberal doses of constructive criticism to this day.

FOUR

UDDER IN THE GUTTER

 I HOPED TO STAY in the Ottawa Valley and anticipated some difficulty finding a job that involved more work with horses yet allowed me to remain in the area. It was to be a matter of good fortune and timing that led me to the next stage of my career. I had only six weeks left before my position with Dr. McKay ended and I still hadn't been able to line up a new job. Then I heard through the veterinary grapevine that a six-month position was available in a small Lanark town, an hour's drive from Ottawa. Though I had hoped for something more permanent than that, it was the first opportunity I'd had to apply for a job that came close to being what I wanted. As a true "mixed" practice, the combination of horses and cows, dogs and cats, pigs and sheep, might be fun to try for a while. It would doubtless be quite different from the year I'd just spent. I realized immediately *how* different when I walked in the door for my interview.

Spring is a frantically busy season in country practice, and manure-stained coveralls lay everywhere, dropped in piles between calls done on the run. A sick calf was tied in the corner waiting to be given IV fluids and pasty, yellow diarrhea spread over the newspapers under him. A dog lay on the floor with a snout full of quills. The phones were ringing off the hook, and no one, it appeared, was going to pay the slightest notice to me.

Jim Lewis was the veterinarian who was going to be staying behind while his partner took six months off to travel. As I would be working with him, he was the one who must approve of me. After he had been pointed out to me, I tried to introduce myself.

On his third hasty pass by me, I planted myself in front of him and confidently said, "I'm here to see about the six-month job position."

"You're happy to do most of the small animal and horse work?"

"Yes."

"Good, you're hired." And with that he was off again. I stood there stunned. I had the job. That was the extent of my interview.

The swinging door behind me opened again, and another man appeared. Unlike his partner, this man made a beeline toward me with his hand extended. "I'm Larry Farrell. I'm the one who's going away." He accompanied this statement with a very firm handshake and a penetrating look from dark brown eyes. A mutual acquaintance had warned me about Dr. Farrell's reputation as a ladies' man, and I felt slightly guilty having the unfair advantage of this advance knowledge. I returned his flirtatious, challenging look confidently and said, "I've just been hired to replace you while you're away."

"Great. Why don't you join all of us for a bite and a brew at the hotel after we close? I'm leaving in three weeks, and we should all get to know you before you start."

I immediately felt at home with all the staff, and we had a casual, fun-filled evening. Larry had everyone up on the dance floor, and there was lots of laughter and ribbing going around. This was going to work out well! I looked forward to starting my new job. It had been arranged that I would rent Dr. Farrell's small house for the period of his absence, which was a great relief, as the hour's drive from home would have been a problem when I was on call. I'd only need to move my clothes over from the farm. But the best news was the mention of the possibility that the job might become permanent. They'd been thinking of hiring a third vet for some time and "well," we'd see how things worked out . . .

Even at that first meeting, it was easy to see how Larry Farrell had gained his reputation. He was tall and fit-looking, with a kind of rugged charm. The impression was that of a diamond in the rough—his casual, outdoorsy appearance at first belying his ability to draw you into engaging conversation. He was attentive and interesting. I wasn't surprised to receive a phone call from him at the farm two nights after we had met.

There was to be an oyster-eating contest at a seafood restaurant the next evening. Larry belonged to a club that met every two weeks to enjoy all-you-can-eat raw oysters. A contest, though, was different. I could tell he was looking forward to the competitive aspect. He couldn't have found a better date, as perhaps not every woman would have welcomed the chance to down unlimited quantities of the raw shellfish as I did. We met several of his friends there, and again I immediately felt at home. We were all supplied with aprons, platters, and oyster knives and set free. When the evening ended, he had finished off eight dozen to my five, but neither of us had come close to the winner's total of fourteen dozen oysters.

I found myself feeling disappointed that Larry was leaving in less than three weeks. After he dropped me off at the farm, I felt really excited about seeing him again. I had forgotten all about the warning I had been given.

Over the next two weeks, we managed to go out together half a dozen times. Each date was different, but they were all full of laughter. I felt I had known him for years, not days. One night we ended up doing the polka to a rollicking Ompah band until we were exhausted. But all these evenings involved what I considered to be refreshingly direct and thought-provoking conversations about life and love. Larry, I discovered, was opinionated and a bit of a devil's advocate. And he professed to "just liking to get to know women well." Our conversations were often quite animated. I hoped he was enjoying our time together as much as I was. I was saved in the nick of time from really falling for him—ironically enough, by his mother.

His parents had come to see him off and to spend the weekend before his departure with him. I went by the house with the excuse of dropping off a few of my belongings, but I was really hoping to meet the Farrells. When I knocked and went in, his mother looked up expectantly at me and smiled, saying, "Are you Jackie?" It didn't take me long to find out that Larry had a steady girlfriend and that she was leaving with him in two days for the six months of travelling and working overseas.

Our last conversation was certainly one of our most animated. I was hurt and angry, because I had been made to feel so special. Yet I had no right to the latter emotion because I had been duly warned. It was just as well that he was leaving in two days, because the long break would give me a chance to cool down in more ways than one. It was for the best, as I escaped a fate of being just one more on a list of broken hearts, and we were to become very good friends when he returned.

🐎 🐎 🐎

Anne was engaged to be married that fall. When I told her that I would be leaving the farm, it was decided that Richard would move in immediately upon my departure. It wasn't entirely to our parents' liking, but they accepted it fairly well, as the wedding date was in sight. Richard had been Anne's high school sweetheart and we all knew him well. He spent most of his time at the farm anyway and had helped us tremendously with the outside work. He had managed over the years to get used to our relentlessly horse-filled lifestyle—or should I say had resigned himself to it. He knew that a life with Anne would mean a life with animals close by. I was glad that my leaving didn't create any problems for her and I could see that the two of them were happy to set about running the farm without me.

For the first few weekends, I returned to help them get ready for a horse show that Anne was going to run on the holiday weekend in May. There was a lot of preparation to do in order to make the jumps safe. We built some new ones as well, and by the time the day arrived, we were really proud of the grounds. The work we had done had almost restored the farm to its former loveliness, and everyone admired the facelift, glad to see the old place saved from ruin.

The morning of the show it was raining heavily. The forecast called for clearing skies, though, and Anne stubbornly refused to cancel. The canteen truck arrived and the loudspeakers were set up, but the writing on the signs was already starting to blur before we had even started. The horse trailers were making deep ruts in the field where they were parking, and we could see that before long someone would get stuck. It was terribly disappointing after all the hard work we had done. Everyone who runs a horse show dreads having such weather, as it can make the competition dangerous, as well as ruin the footing for a long time. It was all the more important for us, because it was our first show and its success would ensure the return of exhibitors to the next.

We delayed getting started for as long as we could, but the competitors who had braved the day were soaked through, cold, and wanted to get going. Miraculously, just before lunch break the sky cleared, and by early afternoon there was some warmth in the sun. More people had arrived, some of who had shown there years before and had waited at home for the rain to stop so they could come and ride over the same fences again. The footing was a little slippery and deep in front of the jumps, but there weren't any accidents. Many of the trailers had to be pulled out by the neighbour's tractor. But in the end, it was a great day, somewhat steeped in nostalgia. People made the best of the situation, helping each other out by sharing dry clothing and steaming mugs of coffee. We were all glad to be out again, enjoying our horses after the long winter. It was the first of many shows Anne held there and they became well known for being fun and friendly.

☙ ☙ ☙

Working at Brentwood Veterinary Clinic was as different from working for Dr. McKay as I had expected it to be on the first day. For one thing, the clients themselves were very different. Country people are generally less emotionally involved with their animals than city people are. Perhaps that is because they often have more of them, or because they are more realistic about life and death. They are also more familiar with natural phenomena, with health and illness and the difference between them. So the emergencies we had were usually true emergencies. It was difficult to get used to seeing the offspring of the farm animals, as cute as any puppy or kitten, being treated as economic units. In many cases, the owners just couldn't afford to pay for medical care for them. So I had to relearn my approach to both my new clients and their animals.

I also had to start at the bottom again in a professional sense, as I was a greenhorn when it came to cattle work. After the struggle I'd had with my self-confidence the previous spring, it was disheartening to experience that "new graduate" feeling again every time I arrived at a farm.

The first milk fever I treated really gave me cause for alarm. Milk fever is a fairly straightforward emergency to deal with if there are no complications. In dairy cattle, calving results in a great rush of calcium from the bloodstream to the milk forming in the udder. As a result, the blood level of calcium can fall dangerously low. Because this mineral is essential for muscular contractions, the affected cows cannot stand, eructate, or eliminate. In the early stages, they appear uncoordinated but still bright. Eventually, they become totally "flat" and can die. I had seen Jim administer the usual dose of two bottles of a calcium-glucose solution into a cow's vein recently, and within moments she had responded by getting to her feet. I felt sure it was a situation I could handle.

When I got my first call to a downer cow, I almost looked forward to treating her. With clean coveralls on and my two bottles of calcium in hand, I headed out to the farm. It was one of our better-run farms, and the farmer prided himself on his purebred cattle. I examined the cow for other complicating conditions such as mastitis and couldn't detect any.

" This is one of my best cows," he said proudly.

I had the farmer tie her head so I could find her jugular vein, and started running in the first bottle of solution at the speed I had seen Jim use. I had just started giving her the second bottle when suddenly she threw her head back, stiffened horribly and collapsed sideways to lie wedged, spine down, in the gutter. Both the farmer and I were momentarily speechless. My heart was hammering.

"I think her heart has gone into palpitations," I said when I had sufficiently recovered. "Go out to the field and get a couple of your boys to help us get her back up."

As he ran out to his truck to go for help, I frantically looked for the barn telephone. Thankfully it was easy to find on the bright, newly whitewashed wall. I got Jim on the phone and he reassured me as best he could, "Well, she'll either live or die. Probably live. Nothing you can do but wait and hope for the best."

I returned to the site of the disaster wondering yet again whether I was cut out to be a vet. The cow blinked at me and tried weakly to right herself. By the time the farmer had returned with his sons and rolled her, she had recovered sufficiently to hold herself in an upright position. I tried to act as if collapse was a common occurrence when administering calcium and said offhandedly, "She'll be up and around soon," as I departed.

As I drove out the lane I felt scared and a bit discouraged at the prospect of starting all over again. Obviously, more pitfalls loomed in front of me, and my hard-won confidence felt quite fragile. Another steep learning curve! Could the clients withstand it, much less myself? This time, however, it didn't take me so long to get into the swing of things. Within a few weeks, I was feeling completely at home in my coveralls and finding Lanark County just as fascinating as I had found Lunenburg County.

FIVE

"THEY'LL LET ANYBODY BE A VET THESE DAYS . . ."

IT WAS THE BACK ROADS of Lanark that really won me over. Each new call led me to discover another winding, up-and-down road that delighted me. Even after driving them dozens of times, I never took them for granted. I would often find myself wishing I could show it all to someone or share the visual banquet I experienced while finding my way around. The early mornings when the mist was still lying on the low ground and the spring evenings when the setting sun cast long shadows over the green and gold world were particularly beautiful. But the most special time for me was after a snowfall. The roads in the wilder regions of Lanark were narrow and twisty, with miles of split rail fences snaking through the rocks and trees that bordered them. When there were six inches of fresh snow sitting on the fences and weighing down the tree branches, I felt as if I were driving from one picture postcard to another.

I discovered that there were two distinct types of landscape and that this had resulted in the evolution of two entirely different lifestyles. One part of the county was flat and its rich soil supported prosperous corn and dairy farming operations. I had to learn where each farm was located on the well-laid-out concession roads. The other part of Lanark was hilly and rock covered, with so little topsoil that most of it had never been cropped. Here and there, small clearings were used for grazing sheep and beef cattle, but the people had to supplement their incomes by driving buses or selling wood. It was this part of the countryside that fascinated me.

The use of square cedar logs in the building of homes and barns is part of the heritage of the Ottawa Valley. Most of these dwellings were built in the mid-nineteenth century and many still remain in good condition. Smaller cedar trees were used for the endless miles of fencing, along with tree stumps and the omnipresent rocks. The style of house that was built was quite consistent, a simple one-and-a-half-storey building with a central peaked dormer above the front door being the most common. The logs were dovetailed by hand at the corners so they fit as neatly as those of a fine cabinet. The spaces between the logs were filled with rocks and wood before being plastered with a lime mixture. The effect is lovely, and nowhere else in Canada can so many of these historic buildings be found.

It shocked me to find out that there were still hillbillies living in the woods within our practice area. They lived in everything from rundown log shanties to old buses. Many of them owned heavy draft horses that they used to pull logs out of the bush in the winter. Although these people seemed rough and old-fashioned, they were hardworking and so unaffected that, once they had accepted me, they were a joy to know. It took a little while, but accept me they finally did.

When I got my first call to draw blood for mandatory lab testing from four heavy horses belonging to such a woodsman, I was eager to get there and introduce myself. I admired the draft horses with their wonderful combination of strength and gentleness. I wanted these people to get to know me and use me to look after their horses. It hadn't occurred to me that even here, far from Nova Scotia, this man and most of the others would never have met a lady veterinarian.

When I pulled up to the small house, no one came out to greet me. There were doghouses everywhere, with lean hounds on short chains regarding me skeptically. I wandered over to the group of ramshackle barns through the spring mud.

A voice from nowhere said dryly, "I see they'll let anybody be a vet these days."

I stopped in my tracks, surprised and a little hurt. A tall, thin man in dirty work clothes surveyed me from where he leaned on the fence. Much as I longed to make a witty retort, none came into my head, and the moment was lost. I didn't know whether to continue or turn back. But he gestured and moved towards the barn, so I followed him into the dark interior.

Four magnificent Belgians stood tied in standing stalls, their coats gleaming. I found out later they were his pride and joy and he often won pulling contests with them at the local fairs. It seemed wisest to ignore the fact that he might not want me there. I tried to act relaxed and sure of myself as I took the blood from the horses in turn. I asked him about their ages and show careers, thankful that I knew how to "talk horse." When I had finished with the last tube and packed up my kit he said, "You're not afraid of them, are you?"

"No," I replied

"Well, I guess you're all right, then." I took it as the approval I had been hoping for.

I worked many times for this man over the next few years. He had two brothers, each of whom kept horses with him inter-mittently, and so they appeared at some of my visits. They were completely different from him and from one another. Bill was overweight and jovial and perpetually out of work, but it didn't seem to bother him. Howard was excitable and a little simple-minded. He talked constantly at high volume and was almost uncontrollable in an emergency. They all lived at the farm on and off with their mother. I knew I had truly been accepted when I was asked inside for tea. I enjoyed that tea, sitting around a table piled high with dirty dishes, the floor covered with cages of young chickens, as much as if I'd been having it with royalty.

As the months went by, I realized how lucky I had been to find the clinic. Jim was a fair and generous boss and always encouraged me through the rough spots in my cattle work. I knew he was always there to back me up. I had managed two simple calvings one night, when I came up against a problem I hadn't previously encountered. I was already exhausted when the third call came in.

It was raining, and an exceptionally thick fog made driving difficult. The call to a third cow having difficulty calving came in just after midnight, so I had the additional problem of finding my way to a new farm with visibility nil. To top it all off, the farm was an hour's drive away in normal driving conditions—on the very edge of our practice area.

I loaded up the car with all the equipment I anticipated needing. My eyes were tired and I felt tense when I finally found the place. The small Hereford heifer should never have been bred. She was far too young and small to have a calf. She lay in a box stall that hadn't been cleaned out for some time, but I convinced the farmer to throw a bale down behind her so I could examine her without kneeling in the muck. It was readily apparent that the calf was dead. Its swollen head and protruding tongue looked macabre, and I knew it wasn't going to be a good night. She was straining hard, and I had to administer a spinal anaesthetic to continue my investigation of the problem. I could only repel the calf a little way back into the vagina, but it was enough to ascertain that the front legs had both been retained. They were firmly lodged, far from reach.

I struggled for a long time trying to push the calf back farther and grasp an elbow or a forearm. But the now half-hearted straining continued to work against me, and my arms were bruised and exhausted. I was frustrated and knew I wasn't accomplishing anything. Reluctantly, I had to telephone Jim for help. The farmer was good-natured about it and tried to make me feel better by preparing a sandwich and coffee for me as we waited for Jim to make the difficult drive.

When Jim arrived, he didn't waste much time manipulating the calf. Within moments, he had frozen the cow's side with local anaesthetic and started clipping and scrubbing it for surgery. I tried to prepare the area around the cow with more straw so we would have a more suitable place to work and lay out the instruments. All of a sudden everything seemed all right, almost cozy, in the old barn, as the other cows chewed their hay contentedly around us, and the rain fell outside. Jim's presence and experience had salvaged the situation, and we felt confident that the cow would have a fighting chance after all. Within ten minutes, the fetus was lying on the ground. I held the uterus so it could be sewn up quickly. Half an hour later, he was finishing the last skin suture.

We walked out to our separate vehicles in silence. I started to apologize for having had to call him out on such a night. But Jim gave my shoulder a squeeze and said, "It's okay. That was a tough one. You'll be able to do the next one on your own." His kindness made me all the more determined to pull my own weight.

Not long afterwards, I had the opportunity to do my first solo Caesarean section on a cow. I had mentally prepared myself for the time when I would have to do one, going over the preparations and procedure in my head. Luckily, this time another vet had done the exhausting work of trying to manipulate the calf and had called us to do the section. A friend of mine who had been an operating room nurse had begged me to call her if I ever needed a hand with surgery in the country, so I picked her up on the way to the call. We walked in with crisp coveralls and headscarves, feeling efficient and in control.

This time, the barn was clean and brightly lit. The entire procedure went off without a hitch, and explaining it all to my assistant made it almost fun. My friend couldn't believe how much blood was lost during the initial entry into the abdomen or that I wasn't concerned about it. Her attempts to keep the surgical equipment sterile and organized were futile. The shoulder-length plastic gloves that I handed out to all my helpers were a source of great amusement. The calf was alive and well. I passed it up and over my shoulders to waiting arms. It blinked its eyes as if astonished to have been brought into the world by this unnatural route.

Although physically tiring, it was a rewarding moment for me and, as always, I felt overwhelmed by the joy of new life. It is consistently and indescribably moving. It never grows old or stale to be the expeditor of a miracle.

In late fall, Larry wrote to say that he'd like to extend his trip until after Christmas. Once away, he was finding it hard to contemplate settling down again. And returning in the dead of the Canadian winter from a warm climate wasn't making the thought any easier for him. Jim and I had a long talk about the future, and I was pleased and flattered when he asked me to stay on. Certainly there would be problems to iron out—I knew already I wouldn't want to do cattle work forever—but for the time being I considered my new job and my new lifestyle to be more satisfying than I had ever expected.

I was doing most of the small animal work for the clinic by the time Christmas neared. Jim was happy to be relieved of it, and each of us was enjoying concentrating on our particular areas of practice. Many days he would be out on the road from morning until night, only making brief stops at the clinic. By the time Jim had dropped his dirty coveralls and equipment in piles and pulled out all the drawers to find what he needed to take out again, it looked like a hurricane had struck. Usually this loading and unloading procedure was carried out at the same time as an animated telephone conversation or two, pacing with the extra-long phone cord. Then he'd be off again, leaving us to recover our sense of order and get back to work.

Most days were fairly routine in the small animal department, as indeed they are in any job. I might have several dogs or cats to spay or neuter in a morning. Sometimes there were teeth or ears to clean or porcupine quills to remove. We saw a range of dogs from the mangy, neglected hounds that lived their lives tied to their houses, to pampered lap pets. The hounds had certain special problems one might call occupational hazards. We treated them frequently for lacerations of the feet and infected wounds incurred fighting with wild animals. Sometimes their injuries would be as a result of getting caught in other hunters' traps.

One such case was Clyde, a large, languid, bloodhound male who had been missing from home for two days. The owners found him, hungry and in pain, with his hind foot caught in a trap. Unbelievably, when they released him he hobbled twenty feet only to get his front foot on the same side caught in another one. They brought him to us with severe damage to the hind foot and more superficial damage to the front.

Examining the worst foot, I was extremely worried about saving it. Although the bones weren't broken, the soft tissues were crushed terribly and the footpads were swelling from lack of circulation. I told the owners we would dress it and hope to save it, but we might not know for two weeks if collateral circulation would take over. If it didn't, the foot would develop gangrene and the leg would have to be amputated. They wanted us to try and they came regularly to hold him for the bandage changes, but the foot looked worse and worse. The front paw was healing adequately, but it appeared that one of the large pads was going to slough off it as well. The unfortunate fellow was getting around on two legs.

He was a remarkable dog, and his stoic nature allowed the owners to take over the dressing of the wounds themselves. I told them to bring him back on the fourteenth day and we would make a decision then. When I peeled off the smelly bandage I wondered how lay people could have coped with such a sight. Clyde was losing the whole foot, and they knew when they saw my face that we had no choice other than to amputate.

The surgery went well, and I was able to remodel the front foot at the same time. By the time Clyde had his sutures out, he had grown entirely used to his handicaps and was back to wandering off. The family was in the process of building a run for him, as there was no more leeway for tangling with traps. They paid their substantial bill in regular monthly installments without complaint. There was never a question of whether the right decision had been made, as it was plain to see that Clyde was well adjusted and happy. I also learned that one can never attempt to judge who will and who won't go the extra mile for their animal.

Amputation of limbs is a difficult issue for pet owners and one that is hard for them to decide on. It's strange the way that similar cases often come close together in practice, as I had another such problem to deal with shortly after Clyde. This time, the family was extremely reluctant to consider amputation as an alternative. The medium-sized shepherd female had been hit by a car and her left femur was shattered into so many fragments that it couldn't be repaired. She had a wonderful temperament and was so good with children that they didn't want to let her go. After two days of indecision, I tried to push them towards the surgery option, as I wanted to get on with doing something to resolve her plight. I thought that I had convinced them that everything would be okay. Halfway through the surgery, they called back again—this time to have her euthanized. They had changed their minds. They were afraid that they couldn't deal with looking at her defaced body.

If it had been today, I would have complied, because I have been forced to realize that the service I am providing is to the owners. Back then, I was altruistic enough to feel that I could put the dog's life first and answer to the owners later. I completed my surgery and called them back.

"We don't know if we want her like that," said the father.

"Well, from what I've seen she should do well," I said. "Other dogs I've done have adjusted well and been running around within two weeks."

There was silence on the other end of the line.

"But we feel we're being cruel to her," he replied after a moment.

All I could say was, "I think she'd rather be alive with three legs than dead." I could feel I wasn't succeeding and beginning to realize I had overstepped.

"What does it look like?"

"Well, it's shaved now, but when the hair regrows it won't look too bad."

It was eventually decided that they would come and visit her after the stitches were removed and see how they felt then. Her recuperation period would take her into the Christmas holidays. I would be on call for the holidays as junior vet, so I took her home with me for several days. We all got used to the sweet-natured amputee and had become quite attached to her by decision day. The owners couldn't believe it when they saw her walking down the hallway towards them, wagging a happy greeting, fur now covering her incision. She was taken home without further ado and visited for years for routine matters. They have almost forgotten there is anything abnormal about her.

Christmas that year was great fun, despite being on call. I had all my new friends at the Brentwood Clinic. The two women who were the technicians were down to earth and the rare kind of employees that actually cared, as if the business were their own. All of us pulled together to work as a team, helping each other with whatever had to be done. I really appreciated how special the co-operation and friendships were.

There were secretive preparations for the annual Christmas party. It was a potluck held at Jim's. Both Cathy and Lisa produced hilarious joke gifts, pulling everyone's legs about things that had gone wrong in the previous year. I quickly gathered that Jim was the life of the party type, putting as much energy into his antics as he did his veterinary endeavours. Halfway through the evening, he appeared in his "party clothes," a wild-coloured paisley shorts ensemble that no self-respecting tourist would have donned. I learned that this was a tradition, and that they were usually worn at some point or other during every clinic bash. As the years passed, more outrageous articles had been added to the outfit and they all had to be brought along and worn. A pink feather boa topped it all off, and Jim outshone the Christmas decorations.

Unfortunately, the new year brought with it a problem with a long-term horse client that I fell into innocently enough. Between Christmas and New Year's Eve, I went to see a heavy horse that was down in its stall. The man who owned it, Mr. Neal, was a rough Irishman prone to drink and had a reputation for being hard to get along with. The horse was not easy to diagnose, as so many central nervous system problems are indistinguishable. Because of the history I was given, I had to consider rabies as the most likely cause of the problem. For two days, the animal had been staggering and grinding its teeth. The owner had also noticed that it had had difficulty swallowing its food. I gave it several injections, but left them with little hope. The next day, it died. I had to twist Mr. Neal's arm to get him to send the body to be tested for rabies, but he did.

When the positive diagnosis came back forty-eight hours later, the farmer was in a complete panic. He and all his family would have to have a series of rabies injections, as they had all had their hands down the animal's throat when it was salivating. As well, he had never had any of his dogs or his half-dozen other horses vaccinated for rabies, being of one of the old schools that considered their animals "didn't need all that dope." There were cows to do as well. It was a classic case of shutting the barn door after the horse had escaped. Now, however, there could be no time wasted. Because he had balked at the price of the individual small animal doses, I ordered several tanks of vaccine, which would make vaccinating the lot considerably cheaper.

Getting an order in during a holiday took longer than the usual efficient twenty-four-hour delivery time. On the morning of December 31st, I was doing surgery on a cat that had swallowed ten feet of recording tape. I was aware that the vaccine hadn't arrived yet and was steeling myself to call Mr. Neal after I had finished the operation. Unfortunately, he called first, and Lisa explained the situation, telling him I'd be calling the manufacturer shortly to see where our order was. I was going to offer to do them all with the individual doses at the same price as our inexpensive rabies clinics. By the time I telephoned, he was livid and nothing I said could appease him.

"You're obviously more interested in someone's cat than in my horses," he said.

"But Mr. Neal, the vaccine hasn't come in yet. I was just going to call you."

"Well, I think you just can't be bothered to help me. Forget it. I'll get someone else."

I was stupefied, because I did care and had been anxiously awaiting the arrival of the order. Obviously, Mr. Neal did not understand that the vaccine was not a treatment but a preventative. Perhaps he thought that by giving it to his horses and cows he might save others who might have been bitten, hence the rush. I didn't have an opportunity to explain further, as the phone was slammed down abruptly. Over the next several years, no matter how often Jim tried to tell him that I was doing all the horse work, he continued to insist that he never wanted to see that woman vet again.

I was learning that pleasing people was the hardest part of practice. This was a lesson that had never been taught at college. It is a challenge that each young veterinarian must work out for him/herself. As a doctor, whether in human or animal medicine, you can only do the best you can, and even then you can't please every client, simply because people are all so different. Somehow, you must be able to be happy with knowing your best is what you're doing, no matter what the outcome of the case or the reaction of the client. I learned not to anticipate any particular response from people. I also learned to hold a small piece of myself back, separate from my life as a vet, in order to protect my heart. I tried to learn not to take it all home, which was something that took practice and discipline.

One Sunday in the new year, I was puttering around the house catching up on my cleaning when the phone rang. I recognized Larry's voice immediately. "I'm at the airport. I'll be home in about two hours. How are you?"

"Fine," I said, torn between acting cool and enthused. "But I didn't expect you yet."

"No problem—you can stay on as long as you like. See you soon," he said and was gone. I felt very sure he threw out the invitation as a tease. Suddenly I felt very exposed. Larry always knew exactly what he was doing.

In a rush, I started gathering up my possessions. I didn't intend to get involved with him again and certainly didn't relish the thought of sharing accommodations with him. I had not completely forgiven him for hiding what I considered to be fairly important information from me last spring. My reaction to the surprise was strong and unexpected. Now I was faced with having nowhere to go and being on call.

I had passed a motel with some detached cabins on the edge of town. I decided to see if they had a free one. If worst came to worst, there was always a bed at Anne's farm. As I piled my belongings on the back seat of the old workhorse Suburban, I noticed that there seemed to be far more of them than there had been in the spring. My stereo had the position of honour on the front seat between my Dalmation and me. A few house-plants and grocery items ended up on the floor with my vet boots. I remember driving out that day with a head of lettuce wedged on the dash. I left Larry a brief note and set up housekeeping at the motel.

SIX

EVEN CALVES ARE BORN ON CHRISTMAS EVE

LIFE SETTLED INTO a new rhythm as Larry, Jim, and I got used to working together. Each of us was very different, yet we found our own niches and most days worked as three cogs in a wheel. I felt lucky to be part of a team of good-hearted, supportive people. Better yet, there was always time for a joke or a lark.

Larry had come back from his sabbatical with a diamond earring and a handlebar mustache and, with his penchant for riding his Harley-Davidson around town, was seen as quite the character. Jim, on the other hand, had four children and was definitely more of a business and family man, but no less a character. He would fly into the clinic with manure-covered boots and coveralls, and in a few short minutes wreak havoc, opening every drawer in the treatment area looking for that just right plastic tubing or that perfect tool. Jim was a radio talk show addict, and the long hours driving alone in his old turquoise four-by-four truck gained him a knowledge of trivia I have never seen rivalled. His newsy tidbits were punctuated by guffaws as he stabbed the air reeling off hilarious and obscure points. Sometimes Jim indulged in these outbursts as he cracked, peeled, and ate four or five of the ever-present supply of hard-boiled eggs he kept at the clinic. We had all developed an unspoken habit of waiting for the hurricane to be over, then without much fuss putting the clinic back in order when Jim left for his afternoon calls.

Their practice at that time was a very rural one. In fact, it was the only veterinary clinic in a very large area. Our clients were still mostly country people, and my two employers looked after all of their beef and dairy cattle, sheep, and pigs. Small animals were a sideline, to be fitted in somehow. It was fun to be part of such a clinic, busy yet easygoing and not without its humorous moments.

Often small piglets were brought in for us to repair their umbilical or scrotal hernias. One day, three were dropped off and housed in our outside chain-link dog run. One by one, they were masked with a gas anaesthetic, halothane, a process not without risk. Piglets can develop an anaesthetic complication known as malignant hyperthermia and die of overheating and cardiac arrest when operated on. We had repaired two of the hernias and were working on the third. After having inhalant anaesthesia, animals recover very quickly, and the first two were on their feet by the time they were returned to the run. Jim and I happened to glance out the surgery window to see our post-op patients trotting happily down the white line of the busy road in front of the clinic. They radiated glee, looking as if they were on an adventure. Kim, our technician, tore out of the clinic. Rounding them up was riotous, with many cars stopped along the roadside and people trying to help. Bits of plywood and floor mats were used to corral them, squealing, and get them back to safety. The owners never knew.

I struggled with the cattle work. My lack of a farm upbringing made it more problematic and less natural for me than for the other two vets, and although I didn't do too badly, I always felt on shaky ground. Good herd health and nutrition were crucial to the proper management of the large dairy farms, and early pregnancy diagnosis was critical information for the farmers in order to detect problem cows. I left the in-depth cattle work to the more qualified partners and concentrated on small animals and horses, but I was expected to keep up my end on emergency calls. No one was going to let me out of it. Every third night, I took the pager with apprehension. In the spring, we could get several cattle emergency calls every time we carried it.

One night, I got an urgent call from Frank, one of my favourite clients, a gentle, older man, a confirmed bachelor, who lived in a rambling old brick house with a simple fellow whom he cared for. Findlay, in return, helped him with his small sawmill and with a few beef cattle. Frank was a bit of a local historian, as well as a collector of antique farm machinery, and I found on visits there I always learned something interesting. The farm had tumbledown buildings surrounded by piles of wood shavings and different lengths and types of lumber. Old tractors and a few larger log barns added to the general clutter.

On this night, Frank had a shorthorn steer with a piece of wire around one claw, deeply embedded in the flesh between its toes. It was very cold, well below zero, and with a full moon. The barnyard was well lit in the silver and black of the deep midwinter, with extravagant shadows cast from every piece of equipment and pile of lumber. As I pulled up to the small barn and corral beside it, I noticed the steer, blowing spurts of hot steamy breath, was standing on three legs. It had long, curved horns, perhaps the sharpest I had ever seen. The steer looked just as aggressive as its headgear seemed to say it was. Frank scratched his head. "He's kinda wild."

We decided to herd him into the low log barn together, and Frank would lasso him with a rope and snub him to the six-by-six centre post. There was more light outside than in. With great faith, I followed Frank, his rope in hand, and the steer into the dark cavern. I had my injection of tranquilizer ready and was armed with wire cutters and a flashlight, certain we could get the job done.

Thirty seconds later, I heard Frank yell, "Watch out!" and jumped out of the way, narrowly avoiding being knocked over in the doorway. The steer rushed by, snorting and angry, his head down, and it took me a minute to realize Frank was still holding onto the rope. Within ten feet of the doorway he lost his footing on the crunchy snow. I never knew whether he was caught on the rope or just plain stubborn, but he tobogganed around that corral for what seemed like an eternity, bouncing off piles of solidly frozen cow manure on his stomach without letting go of the rope. His shirt and pants were filled with snow. Finally the rebellious animal tired itself and stood still long enough for me to throw the rope still on its horns over a fence post while Frank struggled to get up. I held tight long enough for him to get to the rope and snub the animal. We did get the job done, with no tranquilizer, in that brief space of time while the animal was recovering from his romp, as that all that was needed was one well-aimed cut of the wire between his toes. Frank never complained about his ride or any injuries, but instead, always gracious, thanked me instead for a job well done. I drove out of there realizing that he had found merit in my efforts, even though to me they were barely worth mentioning. To return his generosity of spirit, I simply had to ignore his humiliation by the steer. I was learning the code of conduct of the old-fashioned Lanark County farm people and how to best save face.

That Christmas, my brother Bill, a scholarly and artistic city dweller, with no particular affinity for animals, decided to visit me in my new life as a country vet. I had moved into the first of many log houses that I would occupy in Lanark. My love affair with the dovetailed, square-logged, classic log homes so plentiful in the area had begun. I was so proud of how I had decorated it for a country Christmas, with the woodstove, pine boughs, and a Christmas tree exuding warmth. All was in readiness to have some of my family for the first big dinner in my new home. I made a last-minute trip to the grocery store, and the car was full of Christmas treats I knew my brother would enjoy, as well as the Christmas cake and turkey, when I met him at the bus. Then a call came in.

I picked Bill up at the bus station grinning because of the surprise I had in store. Throwing a pair of coveralls at him, I loaded the suitcases in the car. We had an emergency calving call.

"You'll have to take off your city coat," I said. "We're going on a calving."

It was late afternoon, Christmas Eve, and I could tell he had no idea what to expect. This particular farm was run by a family from England, and they prided themselves on their well-bred Hereford cattle. To the locals, they were hobby farmers, as they both had jobs off the farm. But they were knowledgeable and very devoted to their cattle. They met me at the barn with a bucket of hot water and a stack of towels.

On entering the barn, we found a small first-calf heifer straining badly. Two feet were presented, her amnion had ruptured, and no progress had been made for some time. I washed her up well and examined her internally. I encountered hocks, which identified hind legs and a backward presentation. It was not a breech birth, but would still be a tight pull in such a small heifer, and the calf and birth canal were rapidly drying out.

I assembled the calf jack, an archaic-looking, T-shaped device that fits across the cow's behind under the calf's exposed legs and, once the legs are tied to it, is used to slowly winch the calf out. Applying downward pressure as the cow allowed me, I worked with her straining and used the natural birth arc to help her deliver, pulling the jack towards the ground as I winched. The owners pried back her vulva as she bawled, applying lubrication around the calf as far in as they could reach. Urine and manure sprayed in all directions as the cow's pelvic organs were compressed by the labour. My brother went pale, but gamely helped me with the jack so it wouldn't slip too low on the cow.

After some initial progress, we seemed to have reached a frustrating halt and I knew the cord could well be compressed, depriving the calf of oxygen. I decided to do an emergency episiotomy, to cut the cow cleanly so she did not tear into the rectum, in order to allow more room for delivery. Bill swooned and sat down.

Five minutes later, a bull calf lay blinking on the ground. We happily rubbed him with the clean straw bedding to dry him and treated his cord with iodine to prevent navel-ill—an infection that can travel into the body through the cord. It was a satisfying outcome, and the owners jokingly called him " Bill," a name that stuck. I sewed up the cow, and we cleaned up our gear, happy the delivery was successful.

We were invited in for strong coffee and sherry cakes. For me, it was a great beginning to our country Christmas, and I wondered if my brother was as thrilled as I was at the delivery of a live calf. When we returned to our car, several sad-looking barn cats jumped out of the wagon, having done a good job of destroying both the turkey and the Christmas cake. It was all part of the adventure for Bill, and we laughed as we made our way back to the store.

There were several farm communes in the North Lanark Highlands still associated with the hippie lifestyle and values, but they were becoming more and more difficult to sustain as members and wage earners gave up, times changed, and poverty threatened to overwhelm the spirit of the remaining few. I enjoyed driving up to one of them to treat their Clydesdale horses, a placid team of older geldings. Their handler was a slight man with carrot-red hair in a long braid to his waist, a wispy goatee, and a plaid lumber jacket. The commune needed the horses to draw firewood. Children ran everywhere, excited at my visit. Somehow I admired the members' determination to try to stick it out and hold to their principles, but realized there was also an eerie feeling of loss and sadness . . . that it was only a matter of time before the farm and what it represented would cease to exist. The Clydes were thinner than I had ever seen them and both had terribly sharp, overgrown teeth. As well, they had not been de-wormed in years. I was sure I could improve their condition.

The gelding in the poorest condition was having trouble chewing, spitting out half-eaten bits of hay constantly and thus the reason for my call. On examination of his mouth I found prominent tall hooks on his lower back molars that were so sharp they cut into the gums above when he tried to eat. Without the benefit of modern-day dental power equipment or special training, I had to make a decision as to what to do to reduce the height of those molars so he could eat without pain. Long compound bolt cutters and a flashlight were all we came up with. I perched precariously on a stool as we slung his head rope up over a beam and pulled his tongue out sideways to force him to keep his mouth open. I cut each hook with trepidation—as molars on older horses are known to shatter when cut—then filed down all the rest of the uneven, sharp teeth so they were flat. After de-worming both Clydesdales and giving the owner some nutritional counselling, I left, hoping I had really helped the horses.

I did find out later that the poorest did well by my dentistry and gained weight steadily afterwards, never looking back. It is a common dilemma for a veterinarian to have to carry out a necessary procedure with a high risk attached, but we are never taught about how to deal with the negative repercussions of our unsuccessful gambles. Everything must be learned in the field and on the fly. One would be considered lucky to have a mentor who was patient enough to explain repeatedly what perils might be encountered on any call or with any client and their particular idiosyncrasies. Jim did his best.

Another backwoods call resulted in my unintentionally halter-breaking a rebellious weanling filly. I didn't get many calls up to the Lanark Highlands anymore, but when I did, they usually had the "Herriot" factor and were good for a lark and a beautiful drive. This call seemed simple enough. It shouldn't take an experienced equine vet to vaccinate and de-worm a foal. Why were these folks calling me rather than their regular farm vet? As I drove up, I got an inkling as to why.

The dishevelled farm was humble at best, and the cattle did not look healthy. Money was obviously a problem for this family. The heavy horse cross filly was five months old and solidly built. She stood in a barnyard full of deep muck and cow manure and her abdomen was stuck with manure beads. Ramshackle barns formed an L-shaped courtyard, but the only one that appeared useable had a five-foot door frame and looked like a pigsty.

"We haven't been able to touch her yet," the farmer explained, "but we can get her chased into that barn for you." He pointed at the sty.

"Our neighbour shot a rabid fox, and we want to get her done right away," said the son.

"All right, herd her in there, then," I said. "Have you got a rope and halter?"

I should have left at that point and come back once she had been handled, but it had been a long drive.

The interior of the sty had a couple of low pig stalls on one wall and an open floor area of broken cement covered with a couple of inches of pig slime. It was dark and slippery inside, and there was nothing to wrap a rope around should we catch her. I had a feeling she would put up a good fight. After a few fumbling attempts by the owners to corner her and get a halter on, I could see the filly was getting the best of them. With the filly at about 400 pounds, I questioned whether I should tackle this problem. I put my chances of winning at about fifty-fifty.

I took the halter and rope from the farmer and, after a few moments of trying to corner her, got the rope over her neck. Miraculously, she held still while I slipped the halter on and then we were off. She charged forward, then hitting the noseband hard, threw herself backwards. She zigged and zagged in the shed while my boots became coated with slime. I skied in a tightening circle, all the while afraid I would lose my balance. I was rapidly losing my breath. I put the rope around my waist and held on, leaning back. It was too late to give up, but I knew it could go either way.

In the flash of a mutual pause for breath, we made eye contact and negotiated a truce. The filly exhaled and stood. I stepped back and she followed.

"Hold on to the rope while I get my vaccine and wormer." I passed the owner the rope, not able to tell if he was amused or angry that I had acted so boldly with his filly.

"I guess you won," came the taciturn reply.

The next week, a package arrived at the clinic. The home-made soap and preserves were accompanied by an expensive bottle of wine, a card that read, "Thanks for breaking Ziggy," and payment in full.

🐎 🐎 🐎

Spring was coming on and I had been at Brentwood almost a year. I now knew many of the clients and how to get around the Lanark back roads well. We had many regular small-animal clients whom I knew by name in town, and I felt very much at home at Brentwood and in the area. Gradually my social circle widened. Larry was not in the clinic much, but we all managed to close shop and make a regular event of Friday lunch. Every once in a while, I would be invited out to join a group of his friends for a bluegrass night or an impromptu get-together. He always came up with fun ideas, and I learned to make homemade sausages and joined in late-night jam sessions. Our friendship became more and more comfortable after I knew the score, and I often provided an ear for his wild theories and women problems.

Jim, on the other hand, was having problems at home and spending more and more time at the clinic and at the local pub. We didn't know all the details, but we knew he was often sad or tense, and it hurt us to see him so stressed. He never got impatient or angry at work or took out his troubles on any one of us, and I felt an increasing amount of loyalty to him.

Spring brought lambing season and a whole new element to mixed practice in the Valley. Within weeks, many hundreds of lambs are born in the hills and small barns of Lanark. This is a very intense time for the farmer who has planned lambing times carefully around market demands and whose year-round financial success depends on the outcome of these few weeks.

I was called to a malpresentation one morning just after sunrise. The farm was remote. Mist still covered the fields as I sped up and down the twisting, narrow hills hoping to get there in time. The farmer had a small log house, such as the one I lived in, with various outbuildings—one specifically for lambing. They had been out with the ewe since five in the morning. They greeted me with the ever-present bucket of hot water and a mug of hot tea. Small pens constructed from wooden pallets contained other ewes with lambs. Mostly there were twin lambs and a few triplets, and all were bleating as they trailed after their mothers, bunting at their udders vigorously for milk. Older lambs scampered outside in larger pens.

"I see you've had a good year so far," I said. "What do you think is the problem here?"

"We've tried to turn the lamb," the farmer said, "but it really seems stuck. She may need a section . . ."

The ewe was large enough that I could examine her fairly easily, though sometimes even a woman's hand is too large to deliver a lamb. The problem was obvious: we could feel just ribs, so the lamb was transverse. It was hard to feel which way it was facing across the birth canal, but I followed the little ribs and pulled on the wet skin with two fingers and found an elbow. With great difficulty and after what seemed like a long time, I managed to manipulate the front limb back and cup the knee and foot—one leg was coming! In the end, the lamb and its twin were delivered alive. You never really know the outcome until they breathe, blink, and bleat. And so it was with a mixture of relief and joy I drove out—just in time to clean up and get to work at the clinic.

My confidence was again building with my skills. It never ceased to amaze me that I could really help these people when they needed me, especially when so many had been farmers all their lives. I knew, profoundly and utterly, that I was on the right path.

Rabies clinics at the town hall were part of our summer duties, and this year Jim asked if I would do it with him.

"It's a fun afternoon out of the clinic," he said, "and we'll see a lot of people we would never see otherwise."

I soon learned what he meant. Cats arrived in boxes covered with string and tape, in potato and seed sacks, even pillowcases. We hastily prepared the numerous shots we would need as the animals piled in. Farm dogs covered with mats and tumours, cowering or biting, were presented to us hastily, hind ends first. Often untrained to walk on a lead, each had to be given a needle. We vaccinated the cats through the sacks and the dogs in whatever way we could get at them, sometimes pulling our fingers out of the way just in time.

These clinics were held all over Lanark for no charge. It was a really important service in an area where rabies was still seen regularly in foxes and skunks and it helped vets play a role in the overall health of both people and animals. As well as Mr. Neal's horse, I had seen several dogs and a cow and many wild animals afflicted with the disease and felt committed to preventing it in whatever way possible. The "Wild West" aspect of the day did not, in any way, diminish the importance of our task. Jim took public health and our role in it as partners of the medical profession very seriously.

Neither he nor I probably realized how much I was following his lead, not only in learning commitment to our profession, but absorbing his compassion and open attitude to others. I remember well Jim's remarks when a new vet set up across town, a happening that would usually create negativity and resentment. "There's room for all of us," he said. "Let's have a barbeque and invite our new colleagues over to meet us." It was a sentiment far different than what I had anticipated and another of life's lessons well learned from a great mentor.

SEVEN

THE BUCK STOPS HERE

THE RHYTHM OF THE PRACTICE changed once again as we moved into summer, a time when the amount of small animal work skyrocketed. Most people do not know that veterinary work is highly seasonal. In the summer season, engaging puppies and cute kittens arrive at the clinic for their first checkups and vaccinations in droves, all winning our hearts. Unfortunately, it is also the time when we see the most parasite and skin problems and severe gastroenteritis cases. Skin conditions and allergies start in earnest in mid-July, sometimes as a response to flea infestation and will last almost until the first frost. Our telephone lines are swamped by calls from desperate owners about scratching dogs keeping them awake all night.

This particular summer, a new form of viral enteritis appeared in Canada with startling severity and speed. We had barely heard of "parvovirus" when the cases started coming in, first from shelters and then from kennels of hunting dogs; finally, everyone's dogs were involved. The disease was spreading like wildfire. Lineups of concerned owners, waiting to have their dogs vaccinated with the newly available vaccine, spilled out the door of the clinic and over the lawn.

At one point, we had three puppies with parvovirus in the clinic, all at death's door. We had set up a new isolation ward in the back area where calves usually were put on IV fluids. The pups came in quick succession on one day, each one looking more despondent than the one before. As they were all quite young, we knew them to be in a life-threatening situation, and yet it was frustrating, knowing how little we could do to stop the disease.

Lisa set up ivs in each pup, and blood tests revealed a low white blood cell count typical of parvoviral infection. They lay pale and cold, nauseated and not able to eat, hooked up to the lifesaving electrolyte fluids. One by one, each developed a terrible, bloody, "tomato soup" diarrhea that seemed impossible to keep up with. The smell in the clinic during those days, the never-ending work, the cleaning, the newspapers spread everywhere, was a phenomenon I never saw again. The work and the worry of those weeks almost overwhelmed us, but we pulled two of those puppies through and managed to keep the infection contained so our other patients were safe.

When I remember that summer, I'm aware that the vaccine must not be taken for granted and we should be careful to continue protecting dogs diligently. Thankfully we never had another summer like that, as the vaccine program did prove to be very effective and widely used, at least in North America. Dogs in other parts of the world are often not so lucky.

I had a series of very interesting cases in my first few years at Brentwood, and one of the most challenging came in that summer. A regal, kind, male Doberman about two years old was presented to me by people who had never been to see me before. "Tux" had not been eating well for three days and seemed to be having trouble breathing. His temperature was high, over 104 degrees, and his breathing very rapid.

Perhaps I was expecting a form of lung infection when I x-rayed his chest, but what I found took me totally by surprise. He had a relatively rare condition. "Thoracic empyema" was the presence of a purulent material, caused by infection in his chest, loose around his lungs. A fluid line could clearly be seen in his chest. He had little room to breathe. I had only read about this in books. There was no respiratory specialist in my area, and both Jim and Larry were reluctant to take this on, but I had fallen in love with the stoic dog, and to me, euthanasia was not an option. After reading about the treatments, I decided to give it a try myself rather than send the case to a larger clinic in the city.

Tux had to be clipped on both sides of his chest in order to insert chest drains. With minimal sedation and restraint, he stood patiently on the treatment table while we scrubbed him and put local anaesthetic into the area we planned to drain. First a tube had to be tunnelled under the skin and popped through into the chest cavity and then a one-way valve had to be installed that would let fluid be drawn out but not let air be drawn back into the space around the lungs, which is ordinarily a vacuum. A sample of the smelly, beige fluid was taken to be cultured for bacteria growth. I drained as much fluid as I could from the chest, then flushed warm saline into the tubes and rinsed the cavity, withdrawing the lavage fluid as well. The whole process had to be repeated on the other side and then the chest carefully bandaged so the one-way valves remained secure. Tux endured our ministrations for five days while this painful procedure was repeated, thankfully with less fluid each time. By the time our test results came back and his antibiotic treatment began to take effect, he was eating and happy. He still stood stock-still while we worked on him. It was extraordinary, one of those times when a vet wonders if the animal knows we are trying to help him. Thus started a life-long admiration I have for this breed. They have seldom let me down. He went home at week's end and recovered uneventfully. Only later did I realize how lucky I was to have succeeded.

🐎 🐎 🐎

My weekends were filled with farm auctions and antiquing as I discovered the world of Canadiana. My parents' home had been filled with Victorian furniture, dark and stately, most of it handed down, and I grew up with a love of old things. But somehow they didn't fit with my rustic log cabin. There were farm auctions held every weekend, in fact many to choose from each Saturday, and countless bargains could still be found. Primitive pine furniture, some of it built by original family members a hundred years ago, could be found leaving these homes for the first time. It was a time when originals could be had for relatively little, and city dwellers had not yet started attending farm auctions in large numbers. I would stand for hours, often in the rain, a steaming coffee in hand, waiting for an odd little table or trinket. Tools and rakes, music and books, chairs and trunks—it was worth waiting all day for that special bottle or picture frame, that unexpected treasure. During the week, there was often time to strip or repair these finds and fit them into my household. It was a really fun and eclectic way to furnish my home. I grew to know the dealers and pickers and saw them again and again at the auctions. Learning from them what things were valuable and what was rubbish, I was on the leading edge of a wave of buying that was just gaining momentum.

I regularly did appointments on Tuesday afternoons, and most of these were routine. Usually I didn't have a laboratory or surgical helper in place as I finished up my evening appointments. One night, the last patient was a small shepherd cross, a female dog about twelve years old, who came in flat out.

"She started to vomit yesterday," the owner said, "but she hasn't been feeling well all week."

"Is she spayed?" I asked, as I noted an obvious nasty discharge from her reproductive tract.

"Nope, don't believe in that, changes their personality."

"When did she last have a heat, then?" I asked.

He replied, "Two or three weeks ago, I think. They're not like they once were."

Immediately as I looked at her greyish mucous membranes and felt her tense abdomen, I realized the poor dog had a case of the dreaded pyometra, which was causing toxemia. She was dehydrated and would soon be in shock. In fact, she was barely responding. She needed fluids and antibiotics fast, and ideally blood work, but no technician was at hand.

"She needs an emergency spay," I said, "and even then she may not make it."

"What can you do for her?" asked the owner.

"I'll start treating her for dehydration and shock, and we'll do surgery in the morning when we have a full team—that's if she makes it through the night."

He left, despondent.

I started the IV fluids as our receptionist, Sue, closed down the lights and locked the doors. I tried to gather my thoughts. What could the two of us do? The fellow had refused to take the little dog to the city.

As I stood looking at the little animal in such a tenuous state, my mind played with an idea. A technique called "marsupialization," which I had heard about for gastric torsion and bloat, might work in this case. The bitch was so sick she could barely move, so I might be able to do this tonight if Sue could stay to help. She could.

The idea crystallized as I clipped and prepared her abdomen for surgery, inserting local anaesthetic into the skin and muscle of her midline. I would pull her uterus just enough through the incision, then insert stay sutures in it and make a stab incision into it, draining it tonight. As I opened the midline of the little dog, Sue held her on her side. I hoped I hadn't bitten off more than I could chew. The uterus was readily visible, as it was so enlarged with fluid, but it was an awful purple colour. Should I proceed? The first stay suture seemed to slip a little bit through the fragile tissue, but I managed to keep a small sac outside of the body wall and get another suture in about one inch from the first. A small stab and a fountain of brownish-red pus started to flow out into the little stainless steel bowl, which had to be repeatedly emptied. The uterus threatened to slip out of my grasp, and Sue was trying to hold one stay suture and the dog while I held one suture and the bowl. Was I doing the right thing?

I could either sew up the small tear I had made and tuck it all in or try the marsupialization I had envisioned. I decided to do the latter, which involved pulling the edges out and sewing them to the dog's skin, then closing the muscle and skin around this and bandaging her up with a prayer. I left her late that night with the uterus still emptying its contents and her fluids dripping and went home to get a few hours' sleep.

The next morning, she was on her feet and considerably better. Her gums were moist and pink. Once the bandage was removed, we could see the drainage needed to continue and after cleaning the wound and flushing the uterus with saline, left her until later that day to spay. She never looked back. Proud of myself, I decided to write a short article describing this technique and put it into the "clinical notes and tips" section of our veterinary journal. As a young vet, never involved with research, I didn't realize that a literature search to see what had previously been written should have been carried out first. My paragraph was published and it turned out to be a relatively novel idea and one of interest to quite a few colleagues, some of whom called me. Unfortunately, I never knew if anyone else ever tried it. Likewise, if it had originally been someone else's idea, I never found out.

This is how young veterinarians gain knowledge, far more than from any class or book. We learn through working and reacting to the incredible variety of people, cases, and animals that come though our doors every day. We often have no idea in the morning exactly what will take place that day. We are constantly forced to stretch ourselves, playing our various roles as scientists, counsellors, and inventors.

Things had been running smoothly for some time. We'd been busy, but not too much so. Then a tragic experience every doctor dreads brought heartbreak to our clinic and to a wonderful family.

The MacPhersons brought in their beloved three-year-old black lab, who had been limping badly on her left hind leg. She was radiographed, and it was obvious that her hip joint was severely arthritic as a result of hip dysplasia. There was almost no socket left to the joint, calcium had built up in and around the acetabulum, and the femur was pushed almost out of the shallow joint. It was surprising she could use her leg at all. She must have been in a lot of pain.

Hip replacements had not been perfected for dogs, and the long-term use of painkillers was not common then. There were a few options, and I described them to the family. An excision arthroplasty was a common surgery to treat hip dysplasia. It essentially removed the ball and smoothed off the bone at the end of the femur so that there was no longer a joint, thus no bone-on-bone pain. The animal would develop a callus or "fibrous joint" in the muscle when using the leg, which now floated. It was not a surgery recommended for overweight dogs, but Sadie was a small, slim lab and should do well. We decided to go ahead with the surgery to try to alleviate her pain. I had never done the surgery, but on reading about it, I felt sure I was up to the task.

After Sadie was induced (anaesthetized) and her entire leg shaved, we wheeled her into surgery and began the process of dissecting through the tough scar tissue overlaying her diseased joint. Having never seen anyone perform this surgery before, I had no idea how tough it would be to get enough exposure and to identify the normal structures. I finally got a rather poor look at the joint capsule and incised it over where I needed to in order to expose and remove the femoral head. I had chosen Gigli wire to encircle and cut off the femoral head rather than a chisel, and it was not long before the round piece of bone came off in my hand.

It took a few seconds for me to realize that the surgical site, which looked like a raggedy hole, was filling with blood. I applied pressure several times, but there wasn't anything obvious to tie off. I tried again to pack the site with gauze and to my dismay it still kept filling, perhaps even faster. I was panicking. Trying to sound calm, I said to my assistant, "We must get an iv set up right away," realizing she should have been on one already.

We needed fluid replacement fast, something I had naïvely not anticipated with this particular surgery. Should I open it up more to see if there was one major bleeding artery that could be tied off? Should I turn her over and try to tie off a branch of the femoral artery? It seems almost unbelievable to me now, as I have done many more of these procedures with no bleeding complications at all. Events seemed to be taking place in slow motion. I clearly remember the frozen, yet burning hot, feeling I had when Sadie's heart stopped beating. We tried to resuscitate her for several moments, but could not restart her heart. How could this be happening? I hadn't had time to decide what to do—there didn't seem to be that much blood—but it had happened nonetheless. It was over, and my first healthy surgical patient had died.

I sat in my office with my head in my hands. My face was deep red and my heart beating wildly. It took half an hour for me to be able to call them. Even then, I felt like I was observing myself from above, as though in some strange out-of-body experience. I tried to compose myself and picked up the phone.

I can't remember exactly how the conversation went, but I think I started with something like, "I have terribly bad news: Sadie died under anaesthetic." I was in a fog, but I remember the owner, though extremely upset, was kind to me despite her shock and distress. I tried to explain as best I could. I also remember the feeling of a sense of deep responsibility that came over me that day. Perhaps it was the first time I truly understood the phrase "the buck stops here." I would have to be able to accept that kind of responsibility and live with it comfortably and even to fail occasionally with devastating results, and still find a way to carry on. Words cannot describe how everyone in the hospital felt that day. It was a sobering reminder of the emotional weight we carried.

The next day, I had to do several more surgeries. It was hard to get started, but everything went well. Gradually we all felt better, and things returned to normal in the clinic. Sadie's owner came back in within weeks with two black lab pups.

"We want you to be their doctor," she said.

I was so pleased to see her come through the clinic doors. We both had a few tears before admiring the beautiful pups, a male and a female.

"We'll be neutering them at about six or seven months," I said.

"That's fine, whatever you advise," she replied, "and we are calling the girl Sadie."

I nodded in acknowledgment of both the tribute and the trust.

EIGHT

HANDS AND KNEES
IN THE MUCK

I WAS NOW SEEING horses all over Lanark and developing my own specialties within the practice. Some of our city-type clients owned show horses, but others were still very much the old-fashioned rural horsemen. I started to gain the trust of the heavy horse people over time and did more and more work on these gentle giants. They had common problems like bog spavins (swollen, fluid-filled hock joints) and hernias that I could help them with, but it was actually more general health issues I most wanted to help the owners with. One dealer of heavy horses went to an auction and came back with four yearling colts, all intact male Clydes. He drove his large, rickety, livestock truck up to the clinic one day when I was already fully booked. He refused to make appointments and always walked right into the clinic with his cigar despite the no smoking signs posted everywhere.

"Can you cut these colts today?" he asked.

"I don't know, Roy—I already had my day planned," I said stubbornly, digging in my heels, rebelling at his presumption.

"Oh, I'll just wait with them; thought we could do it here."

There was a mowed area beside the clinic, and I realized it would actually be most convenient, since it was not a busy day, to get it over with and save a drive to his stable later. I changed my schedule around and met him out back with two buckets of hot water. His son was there as well, so we had the three people we needed to drop the colts.

Gelding colts is a very common procedure for a horse vet, and these days it is done most commonly with the animal lying down. General anaesthetic in horses is challenging and unpredictable. First the animal is examined to ensure it is healthy enough to anaesthetize, and a weight estimated before the doses are calculated. A two-step procedure is the most common way to give the anaesthetic. First, an intravenous sedative is given and in a few moments it is followed by a second injection, this time a general anaesthetic, which causes the horse to buckle and drop to the ground. Then the veterinarian has fifteen or twenty minutes to complete the surgery. The only problem is that different horses react very differently to the anaesthetics, depending on their breed, state of agitation, and factors such as anemia or pre-existing disease. The skill of the anaesthetist is in predicting the response of each animal.

One of the first anaesthetics I had administered to a horse when I started at Brentwood scared me. The owner had talked me into giving the horse the anaesthetic in a box stall against my better judgment, because it was raining. The horse was difficult to manage, and the sedative did not relax him very much. I should have given more before I gave the second drug—but I was too cautious about overdosing the young horse. The second injection did not seem to have any effect for at least a moment—far too long—then the horse somersaulted forward with straight front legs with such force we had to run out of its stall. We could not risk getting hurt and couldn't get back to the horse's head. He ended up in the corner with his head down and twisted and his backbone and tail vertically up in the corner as if he was standing on his head. We did get him pulled down and gelded, but I vowed never to do an anaesthetic on a horse in a box stall again—it was far too dangerous for the handlers and the horses.

Years later, I found myself perfectly comfortable contemplating giving four anaesthetics in a row, outside on a lawn. Experience had finally brought me to a place where I didn't feel nervous about it at all. Besides, these colts were Clydes—a quiet breed—and seemed a bit down on their luck and would be easy to get down.

One after the other, we brought them down the truck ramp and induced them. Things went so smoothly that when the surgery was over, we let each of them lie sleeping and went on to the next, until we had four geldings asleep on the lawn. Passing motorists gawked and one even drove around to see if everything was okay. One after another, they likewise stood, as if on cue, shook themselves off, and walked compliantly back up the ramp.

"Oh, give me a Clydesdale to work with any day!" I thought as I carried everything back into the clinic.

That summer, two third-year students came to work with us. Jim was keen on hosting international students, and we often had Swedish or German veterinary students visit while they were travelling in Canada. This year, we had a combination of students who could not have been more culturally different if we had planned it that way. Ron, our vet student from Canada, was a short, dark Israeli who had come to OVC after finishing his military conscription and working on a kibbutz. He was quiet and intense and his interest lay in small animals. The second man was invited by Jim after some written correspondence and was a student from a well-off family in Germany. Gerhard was tall, fair, and ebullient, with a good grasp of English, and he wanted to experience life in Canada. They found a place together and often showed up at work deep in conversation. I wondered when I watched them if the shadows of their parents' generation or the past would affect them in any way but it seemed not to. Time does heal, and there was truly nothing left of mistrust or anger or prejudice in these two special, openhearted young men. It gave me faith in humanity.

We wanted to show Ron and Gerhard something different about our area and give them time away from the vet practice. We booked a whitewater raft trip for our summer party and made the one and a half-hour trip up the Ottawa River. Jim was in high gear, decked out in his paisley party suit. It exceeded all our expectations. We spent three hours traversing six sets of wild rapids, the raft twisting and spinning through chutes and falls, turning sideways, backwards, often filling with water. Most of us fell out at one time or another and got pulled back in, breathless. Between rapids, we had water fights with our bailers and swam and bodysurfed in the small rapids. It was the best of summer.

Ron spent a lot of time with me to learn more about horses. One night, we went on one of the funniest horse calls I have ever experienced to this day. We had been asked to go up into the Lanark Highlands to geld a two-year old Percheron owned by a man I didn't know. I was glad Ron was with me as I found my way along lonely back roads, past ramshackle homes, further into the hills of the Mississippi Highlands than I had ever been. One family obviously lived in a school bus. The owner of the horse, Howard, lived nearby in a small, tin house trailer. His outhouse seemed to be an open-air board affair nailed between two trees. He had a beard to his mid-chest. Huskies were tied to doghouses everywhere, and his two horses, Thunder and Nelly, stood in a two-acre field surrounded by barbwire.

"He's started to bite now. I've got to cut him." Howard said.

"Would you mind getting some hot water before you put his halter on?" I replied.

"Oh, he don't need a halter, he stands when I touch him," said the owner.

Thunder, apparently spooked by the two strangers, trotted away from Howard when he approached him.

"Would you like to get a bucket of feed?" I asked.

"No, he'll stop when I touch him."

Ron and I stood swatting the plentiful June mosquitoes swarming around our heads and trying not to laugh as Howard ran after the horse around the perimeter of the paddock. He looked like a 100-metre racer, pumping arms blurred, beard flowing. Yet he kept it up, around and around the paddock, as the horse cantered, bucked out at him, and veered this way and that, obviously having a lark. Howard kept this up for several rounds while we incredulously watched the man who thought he could catch a horse. All of a sudden, Thunder stopped, turned, and walked right up to his owner as if the game were over.

"It's okay, come on out now — he's ready."

"Could you please put a halter and shank on him now? We'll need it to drop him," I said.

"He'll be okay without it," Howard replied. My patience was getting tested.

"Just give him the needle," he said as he held the horse gently under the chin. He was determined to do it his way, so I approached with the IV sedative in hand. As I gave it, Thunder bit down hard on Howard's forearm, hard enough to break his skin. Howard didn't flinch.

"I told you he was starting to bite," he said.

"Please put on the halter now," I said, trying to sound forceful while swatting the worsening mosquitoes. We had compromised enough, and now I somehow had to get control of the situation in order to do my job.

"Old Doc Hanna used to do them standing," he said.

My patience was just about worn out and I snapped back with, "Well, I'm not old Doc Hanna." Howard reluctantly shrugged and nodded that we could go ahead my way. Such was the dance I often had to do with woodsmen who had never seen a lady vet.

🐎 🐎 🐎

I lost my beloved dog that summer. She had been with me from my student summer in Nova Scotia, through vet school, until now. As she faded into kidney failure and ill health, I decided to ask Jim to give the overdose of anaesthetic while I held her. I found it unbelievably hard, even though I had euthanized many other animals. As I held her close to keep her vein still, she wagged her tail trustingly, and I felt as if I were committing the ultimate betrayal rather than trying to spare her further discomfort.

Is this how other people feel? I can't believe how awful it is, I remember thinking.

I was despondent. I found it took weeks to stop grieving and months before I stopped missing her—but I had a new under-standing of what my clients were feeling as I carried out this all-too-common service for them. The ache in my heart taught me a lot about our bond to our pets and why so many people said they would never have another animal after going through this loss. Losing my own dog helped me to gain the empathy I needed for those times.

Ron was working with me one day when a true emergency came in. A small white terrier had been run over by a car. Whitey's front feet were destroyed, the bones crushed and exposed. There was massive soft tissue loss, and gravel was ground into what tissue remained. The owner had no money, and told us so right away, but loved the dog and begged us to do whatever we could.

Ron took it on one hundred percent and got truly attached to the little dog as he tried to clean, debride, and splint the damaged feet day after day. Within a week, it was obvious the feet were dying and couldn't be saved. The owner, who visited every day, agreed to have both feet removed, but only because Ron assured him we could design prostheses, and I assured him we would discount the bill so Ron could continue to work on him. Ron just couldn't give up, and I hadn't the sense or heart to advise him to do so. Whitey's incisions healed so he finally had small, pink stumps. We kept him in the hospital to see if he could get along, while Ron experimented with different pads and supports. Soon he began to walk on his back legs around the clinic. He was part of the scenery. I noticed edgily that the owner was visiting less and less often, and nothing at all had been paid on his account.

Ron's world came crashing down the fourth week. The inventions and boots wouldn't stay put. The owner had moved and left no phone number or forwarding address. Whitey was now ours, nothing had ever been paid, and now we were all faced with the grim truth. Could any of us keep him or cope with a dog missing both front feet? I could not and Ron could not take him back to school. It was an extremely hard decision to put him to sleep, but that's what had to be done and probably should have been done earlier. Ron took a day off work, hurting badly. Sometimes we have to know when not to go on, and this was one of those times.

That fall, two evenings of emergencies ended my career with cattle. I had been doing less and less cattle work and found the late-night emergencies stressful and unsettling. One Friday night, I had a call to a calving in the evening, a delivery that went well, but when I came home at eleven, I was nonetheless tired and hit the hay. Shortly before midnight, another calving call came in, and I felt groggy as I drove to the second call, twenty miles away. It was hard work, and my arms were numb and bruised as I lay on my side working to correct the malpresentation. The cow lay straining in the gutter, and I was working uphill. I had to remove the dead calf's head to get the two front legs out. Finally I resolved the messy situation. I drove home now covered with manure and blood and jumped in the shower.

At two in the morning, I had just gotten to sleep when the phone rang again. It was a calving. I actually cried. I couldn't face it and called Jim. The cow needed a Caesarean section in the end, and there was no way I would have had the strength to do it. It was for the best, and Jim didn't mind, as I seldom asked him to bail me out. I was constantly questioning my ability and desire to continue doing these cattle emergencies.

The next night, I had a call that made up my mind. I went to see a downer cow. She was in a large, free-stall barn. To get to her, I had to slog through manure over my ankles. I perched my kit on the edge of her stall near her hindquarters and opened it, wondering if she had milk fever, mastitis, or even ketosis. I took her temperature first. While waiting for the thermometer, I ran through the possibilities in my mind. Suddenly, the cow next to her stepped into the gate separating them and it swung forcefully over behind me, knocking over my kit full of needles and bottles first, then hitting me. Without knowing what had happened, I arrived on my hands and knees, just a nose above the deep manure in the aisle with all my gear scattered around me. Bottles and needles were sinking into the muck.

It was at that moment that I decided cattle practice wasn't for me. I was going to have to find a way to tell Jim. He had so much stress already, what with the business and problems at home, and he seemed really down. I certainly didn't want to let him down, but I just didn't want to do it any more. Larry was also spending more and more time away from the practice, so I knew all the cattle work would be on Jim's shoulders. He took it well, though. He had seen it coming. I hoped we could work it out, and we did for a while, with everyone just doing what they were good at and helping each other get by. I didn't know it, but the writing was on the wall. We all couldn't both continue to be on call at all times.

NINE

NEVER DRINK AND DRIVE YOUR HOUSE . . .

I HAD JOINED THE LOCAL Drag Hunt with my friend Mary. The riders were an enthusiastic group of people who got together twice weekly to gallop cross-country and jump, following a dragged trail of fox urine. There was a comfortable clubhouse where everyone could meet after riding and a well-loved pack of American Foxhounds that were the pride of the Hunt Master. We were lucky enough to have hundreds of acres of land to use, and over the years, many jumps and trails were constructed and maintained for the use of the hunt. The landowners were an important part of the picture and were invited to the meals and social events with the riders.

Though improbable now, I managed to ride almost every Wednesday and Saturday afternoon with the Hunt. Perhaps it was because I didn't own the practice, but it was also because Jim was an extraordinarily kind and accommodating man. Then there was all the riding in between to keep myself and my horse fit. I felt a confident rider and often took Mary's second horse to the meets, a young, flea-bitten gray mare that was quite strong—yet we forged a partnership.

There was a lot of ritual involved, including the red and black Hunt coats, the sherry served on silver trays before we rode, the blast of the hunting horn, and the excited horses. It really didn't matter to us how we looked to others. The thrill was so great and the feeling of galloping and jumping cross-country and being a team with a horse, as we made split-second decisions on timing, jumping, or pulling up, was exhilarating. The draw to ride was far stronger than any voices in my head about "stuff and nonsense." Many of my friends made fun of us for playing at hunting or dressing up to ride in what they saw as a pretentious charade. I knew the element of pretension was due in part to the British aura and in part to the fact that we followed the hounds as they chased a laid trail of fox urine—not a real fox. Early in the day, two or three energetic people, usually patient spouses or people no longer able to ride, spent hours laying the scent through field, bush, and across ditches. They tried to set an interesting course to follow, and there was emphasis on how the hounds would work and test their hunting skills.

Sometimes the scenery alone was worth all the effort. In the summer, the meets were sometimes a bit tedious, with heat and flies and rock-hard ground to deal with. But the fall was glorious. All senses came alive as the riders struggled with strong mounts and the smell of the lathered horses mingled with the subtle tones of the foliage heated by the afternoon sun. The skies alone were so breathtaking that to canter along the field with thirty other horses alongside, watching the vista change from blue and yellow to the purple and brown of late afternoon, felt sometimes as if we were in a magnificent eighteenth-century painting. The horses loved the fall too, and we could gallop for longer, through cut corn, across mown hay, and through narrow trails in Technicolor maple forests. We went home exhausted, smelling of horse sweat and covered with mud. It was always a heady rush.

At the Hunt parties, I met a couple that had purchased land near the Hunt and wanted to build a house and barn there. There was a small log home on the property and the reclusive older man who had lived there for years had just been moved to a nursing home. They wanted the house demolished or preferably moved and used. My mind started to spin. Could I do it? What was involved with moving a house? Well certainly I had to get land first and find out if this house even could be moved. After confirmation that it all could be done, I purchased the house where it stood and twenty-five acres of land near the Hunt, where I would move it in the spring. There were permits to apply for and all sorts of preparations to be made before then.

At Christmas, my mother visited, and I took her to see the house I was going to move and renovate. It was dark and cold. The little house was truly depressing, if not disgusting, that day. The horrible furniture, the garbage—even the old man's clothes—remained. Not to mention cat dirt, mouse dirt, and years of grease and grime on all the walls. On top of that, I explained to Mum, I would have to deal with removing the brick façade and the summer kitchen before moving it. All she could say was "Why, Hon, why?" I could see she was totally upset by what I was undertaking.

With much help from friends and a lot of brute physical work, I was ready for the move the next spring. We had already spent days removing the porch and summer kitchen by mid-May, the day the load restrictions came off the roads. Both the old and new sites were prepared for the event. A large flatbed was backed under the little house where it stood on four corners of its former foundation, and down the road it went. Accompanying it were hydro and telephone crews and police. All went according to plan as it pulled onto the new land, at the end of a dead-end road. The house sat on the truck poised to move into place by noon, and the moving crew knocked off for lunch.

The two friends who had taken the day off to be with me suggested we go for lunch to celebrate. We were all giddy with excitement at the undertaking and had been up since early morning. A large bottle of champagne was produced by one of them, and off we went to the nearest house to make sandwiches. Undoubtedly we would have been better off to have crashed the bottle onto the house to baptize it than to drink the champagne. After much toasting and excited banter, we were all feeling tipsy and giddy and had to make a pot of coffee to straighten up before going back to the site. We had taken far too long. Even dealing with the work crew again seemed like a big task. I was already exhausted, and the champagne hadn't helped.

When we got back to the site, close to two hours had passed, and the workers had given up waiting for us. This was before everyone had a cell phone and they hadn't known where I was—so they simply moved the house into the place they thought I wanted it and started blocking it up. Unbelievably, it had been put down in the wrong place, facing north instead of west. I had planned to face the front windows towards the sunset. After all the planning, how could such a thing have happened? There was no turning back. Because of a magnum of champagne and a careless hour, I had to crane my neck to see the evening sky as long as I lived there. Later, I told the story of the move many times and was thankfully able to laugh about it.

🐎 🐎 🐎

Anne and I had continued to own a horse together and we kept her at Mary's. She was an old hunter mare with good bloodlines and now had advanced asthma, a condition known as heaves. We decided to have her bred, as she could no longer be ridden. The summer I was working on my house she foaled in mid-June. She had been leaking colostrum, the precious early milk that contains life-saving antibodies for the foal, for about two weeks. It was a worry, as it could deplete the antibodies available to the foal in the first few hours after birth, which would then compromise the animal by weakening the immune system and thereby leaving it more open to a life-threatening infection called septicemia.

As the time came, I camped out at the barn and was present when the foal arrived in the early morning hours. I called Anne, who raced over in time to see the foal still wet behind the ears—it was a chestnut colt, lovely, but small and thin. Undoubtedly, the mare's problems breathing, which had really worsened in the past few weeks with spring pollens, had decreased the oxygen supply to the foal. When the foal did not get to its feet within the usual time, I started to worry. I knew too much to pretend everything would be okay.

When by four hours after birth the foal still hadn't nursed, I milked out the mare and administered the vital colostrum to the foal by nasal tube. He put up little resistance and seemed cold despite the warm June day. About twelve hours after he was born, I was deeply worried, yet trying to remain calm on the surface so as to not let Anne know how concerned I was. He had stopped trying to get to his feet and had a weak suckling response. I had no stall-side kit to check his blood globulin level but I knew he probably had far too few antibodies in circulation. Was this a dummy foal, deprived of oxygen, or a foal with an infection before or at birth? In any case, it seemed likely he was now suffering from septicemia.

For the next forty-eight hours, we struggled to save him. We had no commercial antibodies to give intravenously, no special neonatal facilities, no waterbeds or blood gas machines. We got oxygen in a small cylinder from the hospital for a nasal tube, put the foal on fluids, heated, tube-fed him, and turned him. Even when his colour finally turned brick red, then blue, and his heart stopped, I still couldn't give up. I was performing cardiac massage through tears when Anne finally said, "Stop; it's over. It's okay."

We sat outside against the barn wall shocked and speechless. I tried to understand that the eleven months of anticipation had ended this way. I vowed to improve my ability to help such helpless, fragile little foals. It could be attempted at the big veterinary hospitals, but even there, the success rate was low. How could we do better in the field? Trying to save a critically ill foal is still one of the biggest challenges a horse vet faces, and losing a foal the most intense experience a horse owner can have. I had had both happen at once.

Anne and I gradually recovered and resolved to have a foal one way or another.

We could accept that nature makes choices we cannot always influence. We purchased a lovely weanling that fall, a bay thoroughbred colt that was healthy and vigorous. We had great success showing him at local hunter shows on the line, and then he won as best junior colt at the Royal Winter Fair in Toronto. There is no way that anyone—other than another horse breeder—watching us receive that ribbon could fully understand the blood, sweat, and tears that preceded it. Many highs and lows and so much work and money spent all contribute to that rare moment of winning for any animal breeder.

🐎 🐎 🐎

I was doing more and more horse work at Brentwood and, although it was rewarding, I was starting to feel the frustration of being under-equipped and without an equine mentor. One case that brought it home was a longstanding lameness problem in a race horse's hind leg that I was trying my best to diagnose properly. I had done some diagnostic nerve blocking, a process where parts of the leg are frozen with lidocaine so that the area of pain can be identified. When the horse's lameness disappears, one knows that the area of pain has been found and eradicated, as he'll trot sound. I tried hard to freeze the three joints of the young horse's hock. I had never been shown how to do this and I wondered, as he moved around and threatened to kick at me, if I was getting the lidocaine into the joints at all. But his lameness diminished, so I must have succeeded in getting some in after all and I was able to identify the problem joint.

I set up my outdated x-ray machine, with some of the knobs taped and dials missing, and took several views of the joint. The x-ray cassettes that held the film were of the same vintage as the machine. I suspected there was early arthritis in the joint, but to be thorough, I sent the x-rays to my radiology professor at vet school to get an expert's opinion. I hoped he would pronounce a clear-cut diagnosis and treatment.

"The x-rays simply aren't good enough to get a diagnosis," he said. "They are far too blurry and underexposed. What kind of equipment do you have?"

What a disappointment it was to have spent so much time, put the horse through so much, and have charged the owners for an involved lameness study that resulted in no answer. I was forced to refer the lameness to a neighbouring horse vet with more experience and top-notch equipment and to cancel the bill. Again, I found myself frustrated and vowing to do better. Should I try to talk Jim into getting newer equipment for me or should I go spend time with other equine veterinarians just to find out what I needed and how to improve my techniques? I desperately wanted to move up a level in my horse work.

🐎 🐎 🐎

I was preoccupied that summer with building my house. First, the house had to be emptied of the previous owner's garbage and then plaster and lathe removed from the walls and ceilings, a filthy job. One weekend, ten of us took to the walls with crowbars and masks and eventually filled two great bins with debris. Finally, the house was stripped down to log walls and pine floors, officially "gutted." We were ready to sandblast it all. My friends were intrigued with the project and amazingly, generously, helpful. They all came, on and off, to lend a hand and watch the progress as the little house was put back together. My vision of what it would look like when it was done kept me going at an ungodly pace. I worked every day before work, at lunchtime, and after work late into the evening, as well as every weekend.

One regular visitor to my building site was Keith, a married man from the Hunt Club who had taken a great interest in my project and in me. He was known to be flirt and had a loose arrangement with his wife; he was obviously interested in more than just the house. He first brought food and drink, then started showing up with lumber and building supplies. I had never anticipated having such help with the house and it was hard to turn off his attention or his generosity. I endured lots of teasing about my unsolicited "Sugar Daddy." The weekly visits increased to almost daily. Keith was starting to advise me and take over parts of the project. I now had to balance all this with work and was getting lots of counsel from worried friends.

One day, Mary and I were riding to the Hunt along a path that would take us right in front of the log cabin. Workmen were sitting on the roof putting on the shiny new tin, probably wondering how I could take time off to do something as extravagant as ride to hounds. They raised their hammers as I yelled "hello," and Mary and I picked up a canter to cross the field in front of them. We were late; however, it must have seemed like we were showing off. My mare was fresh, and I wasn't paying enough attention when she suddenly saw demons and spooked sharply sideways out from under me. I was deposited on my behind right in the middle of a juniper bush in front of the three guffawing carpenters. It seemed unspeakably embarrassing at the time, and although I forgot about it, they apparently didn't. Years later, I hired a carpenter for another house, and he started with, "Do you remember the day when . . . ?" He had been sitting on the roof that day.

I was dying to get into the house by snowfall, and the exhausting schedule I had set myself was telling on me. I was short-tempered at times and barely able to concentrate at work. Things were already going way over budget, and now I was faced with a big expense I hadn't bargained on. The entire septic system had to be built above ground on the unforgiving bedrock, and a septic pump installed to pump the effluent up from the basement. Eight or ten thousand dollars' worth of fill was needed to cover all this up and blend the house and foundation into the new "mountain" it created.

The solution came in an unexpected way. As I was driving over to work on the house one day at lunchtime, I saw a truck full of dirt fill leaving the Hunt Farm kennels nearby. I stopped the driver, whom I knew.

"Where's this fill going?" I asked.

"We have to take the entire kennels three feet down. They have to redo the runs because of hookworm infection in the hounds, I think," he said. "We are just dumping it."

"Could I have it?"

"Sure, but there'll likely be ten or twelve trucks full," he replied. "Do you want it all?"

"Do I!" I replied, scarcely able to believe my luck.

By nightfall, I had enough fill dumped around my house and weeping bed to solve my problem, and in a half-day later that week, a small bulldozer made the whole area and house look as if it had always been there. Things had a way of working themselves out. With the new landscaping, tin roof, and windows installed, the vision was becoming a reality. All we had to do was chink all the spaces between the logs and we'd be weathertight and could start to work inside.

I had another regular visitor to my building site that summer. Angela had been a client at Brentwood for some time, and we had met when I looked after her dogs. After her first visit, when she dropped by just to see what I was doing, she became another contributor of everything from sandwiches to ideas, obviously intrigued by what a woman and ten friends were accomplishing. She seemed to have a lot of time on her hands.

Angela was a bit wild and crazy, obviously more than a little bored, and in quite an unhappy marriage. She would show up at odd times, convertible top down and music blaring, bearing always-welcome food and drink. Angela was used to being the life of the party, but there was always a hint of sadness or loneliness if you looked closely enough. Sometimes she would come to laugh and take part in whatever was happening. Other times she would be upset, agitated, and preoccupied with problems at home. I would always stop what I was doing and listen. Both the happy times and the times I was a sounding board were important to me — a distraction from what was becoming an overwhelming obsession for me — my house.

Winter came, and life was an ongoing series of projects. Now indoors, I was learning about framing, wiring, and plumbing as I worked alongside the contractors cutting, soldering, gluing, insulating. Winter was a quiet time at the vet clinic, so I could stay at the house, working on it and learning. I was eagerly looking forward to moving in. My friends were hanging in there, but obviously had less time and interest for the project than they had started off with, and the jobsite seemed lonely and cold. Time was punctuated by visits from Keith and Angela, although I never knew when they would appear.

Somehow, without my knowing how or when, my personal life started to preoccupy me and take more and more of my energy as my house neared completion. Angela was descending into a worsening private crisis, not just because of her marriage, but also because of family demons not dealt with and money problems—the accumulation of all of it threatening to overwhelm her. Sometimes her visits would be full of laughter, but more often they were full of tears, a person in distress still trying to be a funny girl. I was becoming more and more emotional about her situation and determined to be her one safe haven.

One night, Keith appeared at my door late, in a snowstorm. He'd had a few drinks and was over the moon. The team he coached had won the hockey championship. He had no sooner gotten his coat and boots off, grinning while I put the coffeepot on, than the phone rang. It was Angela, sounding stricken and in some sort of trouble.

"Can you come get me? We had a terrible fight at home and I left. I put my car in the ditch. I have no one else to call. I'm at a telephone booth," she said.

"I'll be right there. Where are you?" I said.

I started putting on my coat and boots without explaining.

"Where are you going right now? I can't believe this . . . I just got here, I want to celebrate," said Keith.

"Angela is in trouble. I have to go."

"I'll always be second to her," he said bitterly. "You seem to forget about me whenever she calls or comes by."

I didn't reply, but I wondered if he wanted to add, "after everything I have done for you." He didn't wait for me to get back.

Angela had become the emotional touchstone of my life. I rode the roller coaster of her highs and lows from joy to despondency with her. I became focused on helping her. Always a people pleaser, I was turning into a people saver. It took me years to figure out what was happening to me back then. Without my knowing how or when it occurred, my interest in one person and all the drama had surpassed my interest in my house and work. I worried about her far more than I should have and missed her when she didn't come.

One night, Keith and Angela both showed up together, a rare event, as he was coming less and less often. We decided to go to supper at a nearby restaurant. It turned out to be one of the oddest evenings of my life. I sat and listened to them debate, grandstanding over who was more important to me, who had contributed more to my life and my project. I sat quietly, painfully aware of the small role I played in their larger lives and that neither could, nor would, change anything for me, really. I was important, but only in my own time slot, like entertainment or diversion. As their riotous claims were put forward, somewhat tongue in cheek, I felt flashes of anger and confusion. I knew that in their humour was a lot of truth. I felt terribly lonely. What was I really to them?

"People are starting to talk," Jim said one day. "It's a small town."

He was as concerned about me as I was about him. Both of us looked worn and tired and seemed to be struggling just to get through each day. "We both have problems, don't we?" I said.

We sat, not knowing what to say next.

"I'm not feeling too good these days," I volunteered, not sure how far to go.

"Neither am I," he said. "Are you getting the help you need? I am and I think I'm finally coming out the other side."

Angela actually changed the course of it all. Perhaps she had scared herself one too many times, had come to me for help one too many times, or was just plain getting too attached to me . . . scared about where it was all going.

"I want to make my life and my marriage work," she said, more serious than I had ever seen her.

"I thought you said you'd have to leave him . . . this town . . . start again to get healthy," I remember saying.

"No, I'm determined to make it work here. I *will* make it work here . . ." she said.

"But you said—"

"That was then, this is now. Goodbye. Good luck. And thank you for everything. I will be okay."

She turned and walked away, taking the laughter, the music, the distraction, the sadness, and the need with her. I didn't see her again for two years. I often wondered, looking back, if I would have cared so much if she hadn't needed me. I had to go through a very difficult time before I would learn more about it all, or about myself.

Soon after that, I descended into a period of worsening sadness and ever-present fatigue. My head, heart, and body were burned out entirely as I hammered, painted, scraped, and toiled my way through my house project. I became driven to organize and execute everything perfectly and on time. My friends came around, obviously worried about me, but they didn't really know what to say or how to help anymore. It was late winter, and the half-built house was lonely.

I didn't realize then how depression can come on, get its hooks into you, and prevent you from thinking clearly. I once read an article describing depression as something hovering around you, as if you were sitting at a bonfire with wolves circling in the cold, black, darkness at your back, threatening to pull you into the dark with them, away from the warmth of the fire. I didn't realize the sadness, the sleeplessness, the obsessive working, and the feeling that I was looking in at my life from the outside, were all signs of an impending depression. And no matter what advice was offered, I simply couldn't snap out of it, or stop hammering. I was exhausted.

After a year of living in my new house, I really wasn't feeling much better. It had become an unpleasant and vicious circle, where I didn't feel like my old self at all. Every day I felt like a hamster on a wheel, never able to finish everything I needed to do. Some days I just felt like I had a big, black, cloud over me; or I was desperately sad all day. Jim once more suggested I get some help.

"There are counsellors out there who know far more about you than you do about yourself," he said.

I laughed. I definitely didn't believe him, but decided to give it a try anyway. What I remember was what the wonderful, motherly woman I went to for help said: "You aren't trained to help anybody. You probably weren't helping Angela and you certainly weren't helping yourself. In fact, I suggest when you see a person with problems you run in the opposite direction as fast as you can."

It hit a spark. I was going to help myself.

One day at work, I sat down and cried. I couldn't get up and do my work.

"Jim, I don't know what's wrong or how to fix it, I'm so sorry," I said. "I'm going to have to take time off work."

"It's okay; it's a good idea for you to take some time off," he said. "We all go through rough patches, and you have to do whatever you have to do to get better."

It took only a few days for me to decide what to do and where I would go to rest. The house would be easy to rent out, and I would just have to let it and a lot of other baggage go and put myself first. I needed time to think and I knew a perfect place for it.

I set off for England to live with my friend Peggy, a wonderful older English lady whom I had met many times when she visited Canada to teach riding. She had offered her home to me anytime, for as long as I wished.

"I'll visit horse vets and I'll see some of England," I reassured my family.

"Just don't be *too* busy. We want you to get better," they said wisely.

And I was gone, flying into London on Guy Fawkes Day, small bonfires visible throughout the countryside as my plane approached Heathrow airport.

Many people asked me how I could leave the little house that I had worked on so hard and lived in for such a short time. I answered that I had no choice. "It will be there when I return," I replied.

Others asked me if I was running away. But still I had no answer and no choice. I had to go and sort through it all somehow; after all, I had learned over and over that time heals. Through the pain of my depression, I felt a glimmer of optimism as the plane touched down in England. Just knowing Peggy would take care of me for a while helped.

What I didn't know was that I would never live in my little house again.

TEN

AWAY

THE FIRST FEW WEEKS in England, I walked for many hours each day. Sometimes Peggy would drive us to the heath, or to an overgrown park with mossy, damp, walking paths, or to the seaside. Other times, I would just set out on my own and walk around the quaint little town. I had never been to England and found it to be far more different from Canada than I had imagined. The twisting country lanes lined by hedges, the ancient brick and Tudor buildings, the thatch-covered barns all were like a feast for my eyes and soul. I felt so at home, I must have been British in another life. We settled into our new routine quickly.

Peggy and I had babysitting duties to do one weekend. Her son lived in a nearby town and needed us to stay with his young son and daughter for several days. It was a lovely country home, three hundred years old, and its heavy Tudor beams, low ceilings, and Victorian garden made it seem like I had stepped into a postcard. Everything around me was different, especially in the kitchen, where the family cooked on a unique iron stove called an Aga. The children took great delight in asking me to speak Canadian all weekend and I translated boot to trunk, bonnet to hood, petrol to gas, and jumper to sweater. I hadn't realized how North American I was, and our differences were the source of much laughter. To the disbelief of the children, I had never heard of Marmite, and the laughter reached fever pitch as they watched me try to choke down the thick, black, salty paste spread on my bread.

Peggy knew I loved riding cross-country and went to great lengths to arrange a Hunt for me with her friend, Alicia, in the Berkshires. This, however, was to be the real thing—they hunted live. We arrived at her farmhouse after a drive of three or four hours through the famous brownstone villages of the area west of London. Alicia and her family were farmers and were therefore considered working class in the area the Hunt used. They were not the grand lords and ladies of the manor houses we had seen spotted infrequently around the countryside, but hardworking cattle drovers and dedicated horsemen. They had a large, plain-stuccoed farmhouse in the centre of an open yard. Stables with Dutch doors ran the length of one side of the ancient cobblestone court, and the cattle operation was off to the other side. The house was full of manure-covered boots, various bits of tack, and innumerable Jack Russell terriers.

I had one day to ride with Alicia before the meet. She gave me a dun-coloured gelding, not much bigger than a racing thoroughbred. I was disappointed not to have been able to ride one of the big gray Irish hunters they owned, but after following her around her humble cross-country course, I began to change my mind. My horse was delightful, surefooted, easy to handle, and took good care of me no matter what the obstacle. Our two-hour ride tired me out, but not Alicia or her two horses, which were very fit for hunting season. I had no idea what was ahead of me the next day.

The Hunt met at noon at an imposing gray manor house. The entire picture was truly one from a painting. The horses were absolutely gorgeous, the setting old-world, and many of the ladies rode sidesaddle in full costume, with face nets and skirts. It was clear and sunny. Some sixty strong, we set out trotting down a narrow, paved lane. I was a bit nervous, but my mount was behaving. It was the only live hunt I had ever been on, or would ever be. There was no sign of the "anti's" that day. In fact, no one spoke to me of the growing opposition to the Hunt, or the political forces that would soon end fox-hunting for good during my stay at Alicia's.

The pack of dogs turned into a lane, narrower than the last, then through a gap into a field and took up the chase. The horses set out at a gallop as if they were one unit, and in the next half-hour we traversed obstacles no one at home would have considered. We galloped up hills and down, squeezing through winding lanes and jumping out of hock-deep mud. We galloped on pavement, sparks flying from the horses' shoes. We leapt through hedges into wet fields of clay. One by one, the sidesaddle riders came off, and finally I met the ground as well. My horse caught a wire hidden in a hedge and somersaulted into the red clay of a ploughed field, narrowly missing landing on me. As it galloped off I trudged after it, boots covered with heavy, slippery clods of clay, covered with orange-ish mud from head to toe. Alicia brought my horse back, and I set off again, boots slipping in the stirrups. I felt exhausted, and we were only just beginning.

I lasted three hours with them. Finally, when I realized I was so tired I wasn't really riding any more but was simply a passenger who had become a hazard to my kind horse, I asked to go home. Some others had pulled out before us, and Alicia had chores to do, so it worked well for her to depart and leave the hard core of the field to ride until dark. Once again, I had been surprised by how different things were here than at home, where drag hunting now seemed so safe and controlled. There was no get-together afterwards, as everyone went home to look after their horses. Peggy and I left for home the next day.

I had already met numerous horse people and now, for some reason, I needed contact with veterinarians. It's a draw, a passion for most of us that is always there beneath the surface. I screwed up my courage and called the two largest horse practices in Newmarket and asked if I could spend time with each of them. Newmarket is world famous for racehorses, and, in my world, famous for horse vets of the highest calibre. They were courteous and explained they often had international vets visit to observe. In fact, they recommended a B & B where I could stay. I could come right away, as no one else was visiting. I was off on the train for my next adventure. Waving goodbye to Peggy, I promised to be back in plenty of time for Christmas.

🦊　🦊　🦊

Newmarket is set up, as are most small towns in England, around a High Street, where the majority of the small shops are concentrated. One of the practices was at one end of this main street, right in town, and the other practice was at the other end. What seemed remarkable was that the stables were downtown as well. The racing stables had "yards" with young horses in training scattered through the small town. Each morning, hundreds of young thoroughbreds were ridden out at sunrise along gravel paths where one would expect a sidewalk to be. The quiet parades in the half-light were beautiful young animals sporting multicoloured Newmarket quarter-sheets, babies going out to the heath for a gallop. The yards were three-sided affairs with a gate to the street and a centre courtyard for bathing and walking out. The brood mare operations were out of town on magnificent acreages with double board fences and manicured hedgerows, where expensive mares and foals stood knee deep in straw so clean a person could lie down in it. I was in the heart of British racing country.

During my stay in Newmarket, I witnessed the inner workings of the stables and the lives of the devoted equine veterinarians. When it was quiet, I would talk to the assistants, wells of knowledge themselves, or peruse the shelves of medications, copying recipes. There were libraries to take advantage of as well, but usually I travelled with the vets, trying to be useful to them as I watched—exchanging ideas, sharing information. One practice was very different than the other, being more conservative and less surgically inclined, as its founder had a more "wait and see, give it time" approach. The other had a three-bay surgery suite and had recently developed new techniques for joint and throat surgery. In fact, one vet there lectured on throat problems all over the world. I knew I was absorbing valuable veterinary information daily in such a rarefied environment. On top of that, I had the rare privilege of being allowed to enter stables housing the most valuable racehorses in England, some belonging to the Aga Khan or the Queen. It was what I needed most: a reminder of how much I loved veterinary medicine and an opportunity to refocus—and it came with a refreshing lack of responsibility.

One can feel when one wears out a welcome, and I realized it was time to move on and give these working people their space. They had been very patient and welcoming, yet I knew how tiring a string of volunteers and questions could be. It was time to think about my next step. The December rains were pounding England mercilessly, and I found the cold, gray, damp oppressive. I went back to Peggy's and planned a trip to the travel district of London, one famous for offbeat and adventure travel. I had a two-week trip to the sun in mind, perhaps Spain or Portugal. But something far more exotic caught my eye.

There are two streets in London renowned for travel shops. Signs shout out: "Discount travel!" "Exotic travel!" "Adventure travel!" to all possible destinations. Spain began to appear a mundane choice as I perused brochures on Nepal, South America, and Africa. If not now, when would I ever make such a trip?

I brought all the brochures back to Peggy's on the train and we pored over them excitedly. She also had been an enthusiastic traveller in her day, and we had fun debating the destinations, the pros and cons, the budget needed. My interest had been piqued by a six-week trip across India and Nepal. With a group, I would travel from Bombay to Kathmandu. There was seating available on an Air India flight with a group leaving in two weeks, if only I could get the inoculations and visas needed in time. It was affordable, even cheap. As an adventure tour, we would camp at night, with a few exceptions for city stays, and cook our own food daily. It completely intrigued me. I would be able to see much of India and the Himalayas with a built-in group of friends. The visas could be obtained in London at the embassies. It could be done. I called my mother.

"I am leaving for India in two weeks."

"I can't believe what you're saying!" she replied. (I heard echoes of "Why, Hon, why?" from so long ago.)

"It's true! I'll go with thirteen other people, so I'll be safe. Our driver has done it many times," I reassured her. "I have all my shots and I'm getting my clothes and equipment ready. It will be amazing. I'll see the Taj Mahal, the Himalayan mountains," I babbled on excitedly.

"How will I know where you are?" she asked, starting to cry.

"There are addresses you can write ahead to. I'll send you our full itinerary and I'll write you all the time." I signed off.

I flew to Bombay just before Christmas, by myself and totally unprepared for what was about to happen to me.

I flew on Air India, a flight of twenty hours, landing once in Istanbul. Gracious stewardesses in saris served us samosas, rice, and chapattis. In Istanbul, several men in Muslim dress with wound turbans got on board. Many women were travelling stoically alone with several children, often with one on the lap. The smells, food, and music were exotic and thrilling. We landed in the dark in Bombay.

The airport was chaos, but outside the airport was a scene of even more disorder. Welcoming relatives shouted, taxi drivers beckoned, and purveyors of goods and hotel rooms crowded the sidewalks beckoning to me. For some reason, unknown to me now, I had no reservation, no hotel room awaiting me. A man with a wool cap and striped knee-length tunic over cotton pants steered me towards a taxi.

"Hotel room, hotel room, take Krishna hotel, good, reasonable rates," he chanted.

"Take this taxi, reasonable rates," from another vendor.

I approached someone who appeared fatherly and low risk. "Will you take me to a safe hotel?" I asked, exhausted and confused by the chaos.

The cabbie nodded, wagging his head jovially from side to side. He repeated "Hare Krishna Hotel, open," and we set off.

We drove though the late-night streets. I caught glimpses of people crouched around fires, seemingly camping on the streets, and many dogs. Loose cattle wandered everywhere appearing suddenly in our headlights. We passed the occasional bicycle rickshaw. The smell of smoke filled the air, strange in such a big city, a smell associated with wood stoves and winter at home. Finally, we pulled up in front of the Hare Krishna Hotel, which had smoked glass doors and a dingy grey lobby. A monk in an orange robe showed me to my room.

I lay on my bed, reeling with culture shock. How had I possibly thought I could do this alone? The room was acceptable, but subtly, disconcertingly unfamiliar. Two cots with thin mattresses were set side by side in the small room. The bed coverings were worn wool blankets, the sheets grey and rough. The bathroom had a tile floor and walls, with no tissue evident and the shower sprayed into the room at large, rather than into its own cubicle. Everything seemed damp. The light switches and ceiling fan were grimy from pollution.

Despite my apprehension about being in such a faraway and different place alone, I fell asleep quickly.

The next day, everything seemed worse—the light of day revealed to me a world I could never have imagined. Putting on a brave face, I started out on foot to find food and coffee, as there was no coffee shop in the Hare Krishna Hotel. I got a map and headed out, hoping I could find someone to speak English and to give me direction or encouragement. I walked for hours, trying to take in what I was seeing. Piles of garbage rotting on every corner were obviously the feeding places for the many loose dogs and cattle. Brahmin cattle wandered languidly, and the foot and vehicular traffic worked around them and the lumbering ox and donkey carts. There were people everywhere, as I had expected. But they all looked as thin, dark, and wiry as I felt oversized: a soft, fat, pink slug carrying all the excesses of North American society on my frame.

A woman dipped her teapot into a puddle for water, and at the other end a cow drank. A young mother knelt to milk a water buffalo that had stopped to eat discarded produce. Small vendors cooked samosas in black pots full of bubbling oil and put them out on newspaper to sell, where flies assailed them. A little boy with a metal rack offered me hot, sweet tea, "chai," from his tally of six steaming glasses. Soon children gathered around me, pulling at my sleeves, looking up into my face. "Rupees, rupees?" they asked as they followed me along. In lieu of a coffee, as no restaurant had materialized near the Hare Krishna Hotel, I had "chai" and a hot, unidentifiable pastry and retreated to my room. I wasn't sure I could cope, and felt unsure of what to do.

I decided, almost in tears, to telephone the hotel slightly north of the city where we were to meet as a group before our departure two days away. Yes, I could come now, early — they had a room, and other members of my tour had started to arrive as well. I took a taxi, past miles and miles of shops; low, grey concrete apartments, many seemingly half built and never finished; and then slums beyond description. Children stared at me as I stared back at them, trying to take in what I was seeing: houses of fabric and cardboard as far as my eye could see, people relieving themselves in a field, others lined up at an overflowing pipe for water. I felt heavy, exhausted, upset, my heart hammering hard in my chest. We pulled through some yellow stucco gates into a courtyard, and I heaved a sigh of relief. The owner came to greet me with hand outstretched and in English welcomed me. He took me to my room overlooking the grassy courtyard on one side and the Indian Ocean on the other. Several blue tents had been erected on the grass below me, and shortly a few Australians pulled up in a bicycle rickshaw. I met the first of my twelve companions for the next six weeks. That night, I slept well under my netting and . when I woke the next morning and looked out over the sparkling water, things did not look so ominous or feel so threatening.

Our group gathered there over two days — nine Aussies, two Brits, two Americans, and myself. Several others were alone. My instant band of friends was youthful and entertaining. We forayed out by taxi often and came back to our enclosure at night after feasting on wonderful, spicy, inexpensive food. One of the most beautiful sights I saw in India was the flower bazaar in Bombay. We wandered tiny, narrow alleys that proffered nothing but flower shops. Wreaths, sprays, necklaces and bouquets hung from the walls and ceilings of the small, dark booths and outside them, under canvas canopies, crisscrossing the street over our heads. Vendors sat inside the shops, cross-legged, on mats, shoes off, working with their flowers. Block after block of these alleys twisted and turned, and we felt lost, our senses overwhelmed by smells and colours. On the way home with my small group, my nerves were jangled by the cruel incongruity of our happiness against the sight of beggars on almost every street corner, some of them lepers, some reaching into our taxi to implore us for rupees. I had gone, within moments, from the beauty of the flower bazaar to witnessing absolute despair.

We pulled out of the courtyard on a Sunday, three days before the New Year. Our large Mack truck was outfitted with two long benches and a canopy and pulled a wagon with our suitcases and tents. Cook tables were fastened to the sides of the truck and food staples were stored under the benches. Simon, our valiant driver, had done this trip many times and reassured us he could do everything from change an axle to negotiate our way out of trouble.

"Do not under any circumstances lose your passports," he warned us, "or even I can't get you home. They'll ask for them at checkpoints as well, and you need them to leave the country."

I patted the moneybelt under my T-shirt, reassuring myself.

We climbed all day, gradually away from the sea and reached the plateau that began to define the southern tip of the Rajasthan Desert by nightfall. Hot and dusty, we ran off the road into the sandy plain about a kilometre and set up our first camp.

Simon explained the drill to us: we were to dig latrines and garbage pits. We could shower with a portable unit that one pumped up and then held over one's head with one hand, bathing with the other. And each day, two people would cook all three meals and two other people would clean up. The day before, the cooks would receive a food allowance and shop in whatever town we passed through for the next day's meals. Seemed simple enough. What I didn't know then was that many days, we would live on bread and peanut butter, supplemented by the dehydrated food under our bench seats.

It was cold at night, even in the desert, and I cursed myself for bringing such a thin sleeping bag. But my tent mate, Vicky, a nurse from Australia, was easygoing and friendly, so that was a great bonus, and I could always borrow a blanket from her.

The first three days were a good introduction to India, as bumping along in the dusty truck was interspersed with visits to the cities of Jodhpur, Jaipur, and Udaipur. We saw the Raj castle built on an island and the Red Fort. No one was ill yet, and we got a kick out of the continual game of chicken Simon had to play negotiating the narrow roads. All approaching traffic, especially the wildly decorated Tata trucks, forced us off the pavement onto the shoulder, dust flying, as Simon attempted to miss the oxcarts and pedestrians in our path.

On the evening of the third day, disaster struck Vicky and me—and it was my doing. She ran every night, a few kilometres, no matter where we were, and I guarded her moneybelt. That evening, as I sat on a low stool with her moneybelt under me and enjoying a cool drink, several men with bicycles approached our group. We had already realized that within minutes of setting up our camp, village people would start to arrive and watch, but this night two men had blankets to sell. I had had three miserable nights shivering in the little tent and was very interested in buying one. I swear to this day I didn't stand up, but somehow, in leaning forward to look at the blankets, I exposed the moneybelt, and when they left they took it with them. When Vicky arrived back from her run, she had no money, passport, or plane ticket.

What it amounted to was that we were as close to New Delhi as we would ever be in our tour. We would have to leave our group the next morning to travel there alone and attempt to get it all replaced. Simon, our leader, shook his head.

"With the New Year's holiday, the embassies and airlines may not be open," he said. "I doubt if you will make it back to the group again; you'll probably have to fly home from there."

Because of my carelessness, both of us would miss the whole trip. I cried on and off all night, feeling guilty and anxious. My companions made an impressive effort to search the area with flashlights in case the belt had been discarded, but no luck. Vicky did not show either her distress or any animosity towards me, staying calm and very quiet.

The next morning, we were put on a bus for the four-hour ride to Delhi. It was the day before New Year's Eve.

Simon left us, saying, "On Saturday night, we will be in Agra visiting the Taj Mahal. If you can get back there with Vicky's paperwork, meet us at Lauries Hotel. After that, you won't be able to find us until Kathmandu. Good luck."

Imagine how despondent and alone we felt leaving them. And now we were both living entirely off my funds. When we got to Delhi station, we asked a taxi driver to take us to the Central Tourist Camp, as Simon had advised, and were driven around and around through smoky streets. Later I found out we had been taken far out of our way. Our eyes and noses stung from the diesel fumes that hung over the city. We stayed in a cabin that looked like an outhouse. It barely had room for the two small cots inside, and the floor was muddy cement that had been mopped but hadn't dried. There was no bedding, a single light bulb hung from the ceiling, and there were plenty of rats scurrying around outside.

"I guess you get what you pay for," I said, as it was only four dollars nightly to stay there. We choked down a ghastly supper and retired, not knowing what else to do. We lay side by side, terrified but trying to put on a game face, and formulated our plan for the next few days. I'm sure both of us were awake well past midnight.

"What a unique way to spend New Year's Eve," Vicky joked gamely in her strong Aussie accent. I felt a wave of relief that she was capable of a moment of levity.

The saga of the next few days is long, and I'll forego all the details, but suffice it to say we worked very hard at our task, taking many taxis, waiting in many lineups and literally pushing our way into bureaucratic offices. Even to use the phone required standing in line for hours to be handed a phone with a crackling line that might or might not stay connected. We had to get paperwork stamped and notarized—usually far from where it had been issued—and we had to wait and wait. Finally, by Saturday at noon and through sheer, unbending determination, we had everything replaced, including Vicky's traveller's cheques. We could rejoin our group.

Elated, we taxied to the bus station to book an express bus to Agra. A booth outside the bus station with a sign saying "Lion Travel" advertised deluxe, air-conditioned coaches to Agra, leaving at 6:30 that night. Feeling more relaxed, we splurged on the tickets and returned to our cabin to pack up. But it wasn't to be that simple!

When we returned, the booth was gone. It had simply disappeared. One of the men appeared and, seeming agitated, told us that the bus was to leave from the Red Fort, several miles away, not the bus station. He wrenched our packs from us and shoved them into a taxi, so we got in with the two men, feeling very shaky. At the Red Fort, we were asked for money to buy our bags back and unceremoniously dumped out. There was no bus. I was so upset and angry I found myself yelling at him, and then a policeman and a crowd gathered. It was now close to six p.m. We had to get to Agra, four hours away, that night, or we would miss our friends and the rest of the trip.

We were rescued by a Sikh taxi driver who simply took pity on us. He was genuinely kind, spoke excellent English, and took care of us until we got onto a local bus, even standing in line to buy our tickets. We had been warned to hold onto our belongings, so we sat in the crowded seats with our bulky knapsacks on our knees bumping along through the night. There were no more bus stations, but people seemed to get on and off randomly, and at each stop we asked, "Agra, Agra?" Finally a man nodded "Agra," and we got out into a dark road in a residential area of a town we were not even sure was the right one.

A bicycle rickshaw pulled up and in voices getting ever more weary and disconsolate, we asked "Lauries Hotel?" He nodded and within ten minutes had us there. We pulled into the gates at eleven and saw our truck and our friends. The relief both of us felt was beyond describing. We laughed and told stories well into the night and pulled out with them at six in the morning, not caring that we had missed seeing the Taj Mahal.

The rest of the time in India went without mishap. Often adventurous, sometimes just hot, boring, and dusty, our time was spent exploring the countryside and small towns most tourists would never see. The Australians kept us laughing with their irreverent humour. We saw the bathing *ghats* and the burning *ghats* on the banks of the Holy River Ganges, a sobering yet mystical experience. We tried to absorb what we saw there, as families came to worship and bury their dead in the revered river. We rode elephants in the jungles of the lowland to the north, and then started to ascend the foothills towards Nepal.

It was exhausting—camping every night, taking down and setting up our tents daily. The one or two nights we stayed at small hotels were particularly special times. We were now immune to the grungy rooms and enjoyed the showers, especially if they were hot.

It was on the climb to Kathmandu, a truly magical city nestled in a valley surrounded by snowcapped Himalayan mountains, that I first started to feel joy. Surrounded by terraced rice fields carved into the steep slopes of the green hills, we negotiated hairpin turns for a whole day of climbing. As the sun shone and I listened to my favourite music on my Walkman earphones, we passed Buddhist temples, *stupas* with prayer wheels, and Nepalese teahouses. The atmosphere somehow changed, and the beautiful Tibetan and Nepalese people we passed on foot shyly smiled back at us. Although I had had growing moments of feeling light and happy during the trip, on that day I really snapped out of it. I became myself again. My overwhelming feeling was that it was good to be alive. The cloud had lifted.

Once in Kathmandu, we had a week to explore from the decent hotel where we were based. We were advised to take a trip even farther up and watch the sunset over the Himalayas. I took the local bus to a nearby village one day by myself and wandered the streets feeling safe and enchanted, despite the crowd of raggedy children following me. There were religious festivals daily in Kathmandu, temples to explore, and many travellers and tourists who gathered at night in westernized restaurants to swap stories and give advice. Our tour ended here, and we all flew out at different times, vowing to keep in touch, visit one another, exchange photos. The six weeks had forged incredible bonds. My twenty-four-hour flight home took me to Karachi, Islamabad, and Istanbul before arriving back safely in London. Deplaning and re-boarding in Karachi at gunpoint, I thought to myself, *This will be an adventure to the end*. I left vowing to go back to Nepal in my lifetime. Somehow, unbelievably, I had found my way across several continents and was back safe in my little room at Peggy's. I slept for three days.

🐐 🐐 🐐

Now that I had recovered more of my normal self, the rest of my time at Peggy's was a bit restless. We walked, visited her friends, and explored antique stores, but I felt very much on hold. A job I had been offered in Newmarket fell through, as a work permit could not be had. I started to look forward to going home.

During my last few weeks in England, I attended Crufts Dog Show, perhaps the most well-known dog show in the world. I admired several top winning Dobermans and subsequently arranged to meet their breeders. The dogs were elegant, big-boned, and well socialized. I learned a whole new language of lineages and pedigrees. Before I left England, I purchased a lovely, big, black-and-tan male puppy. Full of promise, I named him Tuxedo in honour of my regal patient of so long ago. Tux and I flew home in time for the spring rush to begin.

As soon as I devoted myself to thinking about my next step, what I was to do became crystal clear. I needed to do what I most wanted to do: work with top horse veterinarians and learn. This was the golden opportunity. My renters would stay on in the house. I applied for and took a job in Toronto at an excellent equine practice. Nothing had ever felt so right since I applied to veterinary school.

ELEVEN

HURRICANE

TORONTO IS A BUSTLING metropolis, in huge contrast to the Ottawa Valley. Traffic, the arts, nightlife, teeming humanity all abound, and the horse scene is just as dynamic as the rest of the city. In a ring surrounding the north part of the city, there are many large and small barns, and there was a thoroughbred track in the city near our clinic. The clinic was in proximity to the track for a good reason: my two employers, partners at Rexdale Equine Clinic, specialized in arthroscopic surgery on race horses. They looked after the race horses themselves, and as I was informed when I was hired, I was to look after primarily the many pleasure and show horse barns farther out of town.

After a couple of weeks of staying with friends, I rented a ramshackle house just outside the spreading suburbs of west Toronto. It was truly falling down, as the property was to be developed for housing, and the house had not been maintained for years. Rain came in under the front door and the window trim and bathroom tiles were falling off, but it was in the country. I just needed my two acres of green to be happy. I could sit on the porch in the evening and see the lights of Toronto twinkling to the south of me, but walk the fields and country roads on the weekends.

The landlady said I could have a horse in the equally dilapidated shed, and I soon had an electric fence set up. I purchased a big, powerful chestnut mare and tucked her in the small garage-cum-box stall. I knew that as long as I could ride, I could feel like myself in this unfamiliar urban world. And, as always, it gave me pleasure simply to have her there and look after her.

Things at the clinic were busy, sometimes bordering on frantic. The two partners spent most of the day at the track looking after patients, but in the afternoons, there was a steady stream of animals to radiograph at the clinic. At least twice a week, the whole afternoon would be booked off for a surgery. At that time, the whole team had to be in place, as the horse had to be clipped, prepared, anaesthetized, and literally hauled into place on the table to be operated on. The recovery took as long as all of this combined, and often it was early evening before we had them on their feet and into one of the padded stalls. Cleanup took place after that. It was mentally challenging and tiring, but I was ready and focused. I was there to learn, straight and simple.

During the first few weeks, I seemed to be professionally scattered and unsure. I made a few mistakes once again and minor gaffes, and they seemed to snowball on me. The clinic was small and overloaded with equipment, and as I rushed, eager to do well or just plain keep up, I managed to drop or bump into things too often, earning the name "Hurricane." The partners called each other respectively "Big Guy" and "Big Guy," and I doubted I could ever be part of that mutual admiration society. One in a string of new associates to have come and gone in that clinic, I was a workhorse and very useful, but not really a part of it. After Brentwood, it was very unsettling.

The really good news was that the clients seemed very happy with my work, and their acceptance helped me get through some of the rougher days at the clinic, where my job was to act as a technician. There was one more aspect of the job that was very different for me. As a horse vet, it was strange to have to spend hours on four-lane freeways getting to calls; indeed, often most of the day was spent driving in heavy traffic. But the lovely horses and well-informed clients provided a balance for that. I felt committed to and pleased with my new job as an equine veterinarian and tried to absorb knowledge like a sponge.

The alcohol swabs provided a flashpoint to emphasize my country background to Dr. Barokov, my boss. I had never used these little square pads in the past, but Dr. B. insisted they were important to the look of professionalism he wanted to maintain at our clinic. We had thousands on hand to be used to wipe our injection sites. It was important that I follow this protocol, and in time it became habit. This seemingly simple little procedure would be a source of unexpected irony in the future.

At Brentwood, I seldom took x-rays because of all the problems I had getting good ones. Now, instead of ten plates a month, I could be taking ten a day and seeing many more brought in by the partners. One day, I had a pre-purchase exam to do an hour west of the clinic. The American purchasing the horse requested all joints possible to be radiographed, so I lugged forty or so x-ray cassettes with me. The horse was restless and had to be sedated for the last half of the radiographs to be taken. When I returned to the clinic I was delighted—the angles and exposures had been correct and I seemed to have a good set of x-rays. But my heart sank as I realized my labelling had been incorrect. Dr. B., looking over my shoulder, noticed it first.

"Why do you have all four ankles labelled as right front or left front?" he asked. "What happened to the hind ankles?"

I realized with a sinking feeling that there was no way the hind ankles could be identified positively. I would have to make the whole trip over again and retake all four ankles, labelling them correctly. This is partly how I learned, moving forward by making mistakes, listening to my new mentors. I thought of it as paying my dues. We all learn from mistakes, and I became a fanatic about double-checking labels after that. Trying hard to get back with a perfect diagnostic set of x-rays with no retakes became one of my biggest challenges.

One service we provided that seemed to be out of vogue everywhere else was the regular tube worming of horses. Gradually, de-worming with pastes and liquids had completely replaced this invasive, old-fashioned procedure, and the results were seemingly just as good. But many of the older vets and trainers still believed in one "good" worming each year by nasogastric tube. I was often sent to the breeding barns to tube brood mares and young stock, sometimes twenty or thirty horses at one time. What a challenge it posed having to restrain yearlings that are young enough to be untrained yet big enough to be hard to handle and dangerous, for such a stressful procedure as passing a tube down their nose to their stomach!

After the tube was passed, they had to hold still long enough to pour medication down the tube via a funnel. Sometimes they would leap forward halfway through the procedure, knocking people and medication everywhere. Even with the older, trained riding horses, the once or twice yearly day allotted for tubing was arduous. The largest barn I did had fifty horses, some of which had to be twitched with a rope or chain around the nose, or sedated; others would lunge or strike out suddenly with a front foot, which called for extra care. Each had their particular evasion, and thankfully the handler knew them all. Those days were exhausting. But as usual, there was an upside. I became quicker and more adept at tubing than I had ever thought possible.

One afternoon at the in-hospital clinic, I had my first injection reaction. The two-year-old colt I was preparing for surgery had to have preoperative penicillin and an IV painkiller before clipping the knee where a bone chip was to be removed by arthroscopic surgery. It had been a relatively smooth day so far, and the receptionist, a knowledgeable horsewoman, came out to hold the colt for his injections. We would be ready on time at one o'clock. Penicillin is a white, thick liquid given intramuscularly, and I gave it in two places in the horse's neck, having done so thousands of time before. Seconds after withdrawing the second intramuscular needle, I saw the colt start to quiver and look dazed, then he backed up rapidly, stiff-legged, and dropped to the ground, paddling rapidly as if galloping. He was seizuring. One of the boards on the front of the stall gave way and a foot came out through the stall front. I knew we had to try to get back to his head as soon as possible to prevent him fracturing his skull by banging it repeatedly on the hard stall floor or injuring his eyes. But it wasn't safe to do anything other than try to hold the stall door closed and wait.

"Hold tight while I go get some tranquillizer. We'll have to get it into him somehow!" I yelled, while Diana held the door tightly.

I ran for my kit.

When I returned, the paddling had slowed and the colt lay on his side, dazed. It didn't look like he had any major cuts or damage to his head. We gingerly picked up the end of the lead rope, worried about setting him off again. I managed to get in and over his neck and administered the sedative in the vein. Immediately he relaxed and his respiration slowed. In ten minutes, he was on his feet. Would Dr. B. still want to go to surgery today? I doubted it, as there would undoubtedly be swelling in the colt's brain. I paged him at the track to tell him.

"It could happen to anyone who gives enough needles. We'll reschedule for tomorrow or the next day," he said. I felt relief flood through me. The "Hurricane" label was a bit of a burden, and I didn't want further fuel on that particular fire. He didn't seem as perturbed by the problem as I had been, and the surgery went fine the next day.

We taught courses at a local community college, and one of the students there needed a room, so I decided to rent one out to help with the expenses. It worked well, as she was horse crazy and didn't mind taking care of Kira, my mare, if I was late or away. Her friends were fun and often came around to play cards or party and their youthful spirits provided me with a lift and, vicariously, with a bit of a social life. One night, I was invited to karaoke with them. It was the first time I had ever seen these machines, or realized how many people played at singing regularly and well. Karaoke was a favourite pastime for a whole group of people I didn't know about. It was hugely entertaining, and they managed to get me up on stage for a group number. I was rewarded by being voted the "best staff member to party with" at the Christmas banquet.

"Best staff member to party with? What on earth have you been doing?" Dr. B asked on Monday morning with raised eyebrows.

I sighed and didn't answer. This would probably breathe new life into the unfortunate nickname. I didn't want anything to decrease my professionalism further in his eyes. "I just get along with the students well," I muttered sheepishly.

Early that spring, a couple that owned an older jumper mare approached me about artificial insemination for her. They had an Olympic-class stallion in mind, but his semen was available only in frozen straws. Frozen insemination was relatively new in Canada and quite difficult, but I was game to try it. We learned together how to get the import paperwork and transportation route worked out. The straws of frozen semen would have to arrive in a container of liquid nitrogen at −150° F and had to be used immediately. I followed the mare's cycles well, and in March we decided to order semen to try the first breeding. The timing had to be impeccable, as the thawed semen is fragile and lacks vigour. The mare had to be checked daily by rectal exam to determine the optimal time for breeding, which has to be done as close to ovulation as possible.

I had set aside a half day to work on this case and got out to the farm at noon, just as the owner was arriving from the airport with the container. "We'll set up in the kitchen," I said. I had brought all the equipment needed for the procedure, including a microscope to assess the semen after thawing it. The mare had a nice, large, soft breeding follicle on her ovary when examined, and the timing was perfect. An injection could be given at the same time to encourage ovulation of the follicle and release of the ovum. I felt confident and well prepared.

We got ready a water bath at 37° in an insulated cooler as per the instructions sent by the stallion centre. Next we were to thaw the three straws for thirty seconds each and invert them gently so the air bubble would move to the top. Then there was the cutting of the one end of the straws, inversion into a syringe, and finally the cutting of the other end to allow the semen to drip into the waiting syringe barrel. The mare had been washed and bandaged and was awaiting us in the barn nearby.

All went well until the cutting stage. I held the first thawed straw up and, moving too quickly and without enough forethought, in front of the two anxious clients, I made the wrong cut in the straw. The precious semen ran out on the counter.

"It's okay—there are still two more," I choked out. And there were. I looked at their faces. They were okay.

We got the other two straws poured into one syringe and then injected into the waiting mare with no further mishaps, but I drove away cursing myself for acting too quickly. What must they think?

The mare didn't catch, and they were game to try again with me in charge, so I went back at it with even more determination. The next cycle, I stayed at their house and tried to time the insemination even more closely with the overnight ovulation. Still she didn't catch. In fact, it took two seasons to get a pregnancy, as she was an older maiden mare. I know now that the mishap with the straw probably wasn't a factor, but it was a moment I never forgot. I vowed to slow down and do my best to live down that bothersome name.

Despite these rough moments and minor problems, my career was progressing in a satisfying way. For all the frustrations of practice, there are in reality far more rewarding moments—horses helped and good lessons learned. Lacerations were sutured, colics were treated, clients were happy, and I had met many nice people. I even had the opportunity to be the vet on call for a week at the Royal Winter Fair. My equine internship was progressing as I had hoped.

After what seemed to be an appropriate time, I mentioned to Dr. B that I would like to scrub in on surgery now and then. Often his partner was late, and I knew the drill well, having watched them many times. Surely we could go ahead on these days. I was dying to be given a chance. It never came. After a few more months passed and my role as a technician had not changed, I asked again, a little more forcefully: "I'd like to be included in the surgery roster."

"The clients who come here really want to see Peter and me do the surgeries," he said.

That was the end of the matter, and there was no further opening for discussion. It was a well-oiled machine that worked, and Dr. B was reluctant to change anything. I hung in there for quite a while afterward, but I must admit I started considering my options. I never asked again, but it was always there, unspoken, and the invitation never came.

🐎 🐎 🐎

I had some outstanding rides on Kira right on the edge of the suburbs of Canada's largest city. There was a massive hydro line near my house, and the cleared land beneath the wires made a good hack-out area. Even better, it allowed me to reach a hidden river valley. It was a miraculous sunken canyon, a green gulch completely out of sight of passersby. The small creek twisted and wound for two miles in a forty-foot-deep carved hole, with foot-paths winding along the lush banks. At one point it was wide enough to canter safely. Mostly I rode there quietly in silent reverie, watching the birds and the occasional otter, delighting in my discovery. I seldom saw another person in my hideaway canyon. Once, a quick, violent thunderstorm came up, and, pelted by rain, I cantered up and out of the canyon across a cornfield and along the hydro line towards home. Crouched over, barely able to see, I bridged my reins and let my horse take me back, where we arrived soaking wet, steam rising from the horse's hot body.

It was a time in my life when I did not ride for social interaction or to get ready for shows or even for fun. It was my solace, after hours spent with people, trying so hard to please. It was my earthy, sweaty, grounding—both an escape and nourishment for my spirit.

Toronto was a great place to be in the summer. There were lots of concerts, both indoor and out. Some of the best were at Wonderland and Ontario Place, and I revelled in all the great music, sharing the energy of thousands gathered under the night sky. I went downtown on my weekends off. Chinatown had endless restaurants and nooks and crannies to explore. Then there were Harbourfront, Kensington Market, Toronto Island, and antiquing on Queen Street. With prices far different than those at a Lanark auction, I could only look and admire.

Unattached, I accepted every invitation and made use of every opportunity. When not on call, I could go downtown late and investigate the night scene. The summer mood there was palpably exciting and infectious. The people-watching was always fantastic. There was so much I had to learn and find out about myself. Both my sense of freedom and enthusiasm for exploration were set on high. I was anonymous in an exciting city for the first time, and it was summer. I was in a far different space than at vet school, where we studied and partied as one. It was also far different from being in Lanark. I was now very much an individual. I felt curious but not afraid, unique but not alone. I needed to explore the essential question, "Who am I when I'm not a veterinarian?" I certainly felt very much alive.

India had changed me in many ways. I not only had a far greater appreciation of where I lived and what we all took for granted—freedom, education, even clean water—I now fully appreciated how lucky I was just to be me. It was a relief to know that my sadness could lift and leave me with a richer appreciation of life.

I had my first serious injury in Toronto. I had been called to do a rectal examination for pregnancy on a young Appaloosa mare. The clients were not regulars, and I was a little disappointed to see there was only a young boy to help me when I drove up to the humble barn. He obliged me and put two bales of hay on their sides behind the mare before I started my examination. He was obviously not very experienced with horses and explained that he was working there to help out with chores.

"Hold her head up well and keep her back to the bales," I said before starting my exam.

No sooner had I touched her tail than she lowered her head and kicked swiftly with both hind feet over the bales. I never saw them coming. One hit my face and the other my chest, and I was thrown across the aisle, cutting my head on a stall door on the other side. I woke up minutes later, a pool of blood gathering around my head from a bad cut on my skull, and barely able to breathe. Was my nose broken as well? The teenager had called an ambulance and I was taken to a nearby hospital. Feeling very alone, I was wheeled in front of the admission desk at emergency, a bloody cloth held to my face.

"What is your name?" the efficient, impersonal receptionist asked.

"What is your address?"

I mumbled the responses slowly, dazed.

"Postal code? Phone number?" she inquired, unmoved.

I answered through the cloth, concussed and having trouble breathing.

"Do you have a contact here?"

I thought hard. Perhaps my student roomie would come, or the friends I had stayed with last year. I was wheeled into a busy observation room where they sutured my head and kept me on oxygen until they ascertained my ribs were not broken.

"You'll have to stay overnight," I was told.

It was a relief, as I couldn't sit up. A large bruise developed on my chest and my nose. In reality I had been very lucky. I could have been killed. I was off work for a week, and somehow my car arrived back at my house before long. It had, however, been a close call. My neck could have been broken. I would have to be more careful.

Business went on as usual at the clinic. We had a steady flow of lameness and surgery cases. I did some teaching at the college and found I liked it very much. But it took an offhand comment from an old friend to change my course once again.

"The only horse vet in the Annapolis Valley died, you know. They really need someone there to do horses, and I know you love Nova Scotia," he said.

My wheels started turning. I was satisfied with what I had learned so far in Toronto. I made a few phone calls and decided the time was right. I made a trip to our family cottage in Nova Scotia and, from there, a foray to the Valley to assess the possibilities. I looked at real estate and approached the bank. With no formal business training, I did no feasibility studies and had no proof such a business could work. It all depended on me. My training, my degree, and my love of horses were the only keys I had to starting up a practice and were all I had to bank on. I convinced the bank manager that my equine experience and willingness to work were the cornerstones of the plan's success.

Nova Scotia might be the perfect answer. There I could stretch and grow in the less uptight climate I knew to exist in Ontario. I had enjoyed it so much as a student and it was my birthplace. Perhaps it would be like "going home." I felt sure I had something to contribute. I went back and told Dr. B. that I was leaving.

TWELVE

BACK TO MY ROOTS

I WAS GOING BACK to Nova Scotia to set up my own practice. It seemed like a dream I had simply spoken into reality, and now the momentum carried me along. There was much to do. I planned to open my business on January first, a symbolic date in my mind—good for a new beginning.

I had to find a house first, one suitable to turn into a clinic with a dispensary, a lab, and a darkroom. It had to be in the area where the most horse action took place—the Annapolis Valley. Yet it had to have a reasonable travelling time to other centres such as Halifax, where there are many large farms. Faxes from the real estate agent came in thick and fast, and finally I settled on a small, beautifully restored schoolhouse in Grand Pré. It had a back entrance and mudroom suitable for loading and unloading gear and where people could come if they needed to buy medications. The downstairs half-bath would make a perfect darkroom. I absolutely loved it. For a Canadiana fan, it was the perfect little house, lovingly restored and with taste. The price seemed reasonable, so I boldly made an offer. After minimal negotiation, I learned it was to be mine on December first. I had enough time to organize the renovations, but only a month in which to get them done.

There was equipment to order. It was frightening to start placing orders for everything from carrying kits to surgery packs, sterilizing equipment to farrier's tools. But it was when I priced x-ray machinery, film holders, and developing tanks that the stakes went up considerably. I had to decide on a bookkeeping system as well and, having no experience in this area, I went with some advice and purchased a manual billing system. Little did I know a computer revolution was just around the corner and soon I would have to replace my manual system.

As my bills mounted, I also found out how to cut corners. I beat the bushes and hunted down a lot of used equipment. I was learning more and new skills. Aware now of the never-ending process of learning life's lessons, I realized I now had the entire world of business to find out about, and yes . . . make mistakes in. It was a portion of the biggest part of the challenge, far more than the medicine.

The trip from Toronto was hilariously funny in itself. I had hired a Western horseman from Nova Scotia to move my household goods and my horse in one sweep. He had a six-horse trailer, and it would be a tight fit, but we should be able to do it. The six-horse pulled into my yard in Toronto at six in the morning, well ahead of schedule, country music blaring. Bruce's mood was volatile, as he had gotten lost in Montreal and had spent hours going around in circles with his large rig. I convinced him to shower and sleep, as my packing crew had not even started yet—in fact, had not even arrived. We shoved all the fragile boxes into the gooseneck. Tropical plants went on top of trunks in the dressing room. We loaded the mare last. We pulled out late in the afternoon and planned to drive straight through.

On our trip, I found out Bruce listened only to country music, ate only hamburgers on plain buns and drank only coke. To be sure of his supply, he had brought three wooden cases of large bottles. As we headed out, the gooseneck door flapped open, and the umbrella plant fell out on Highway 401. Bruce also smoked constantly and spit just about as often. The driver's window wound open every few minutes as we twanged our way down the highway. I heard from him every detail I would surely need to know about the horses and horse owners of Nova Scotia.

I had one month to get ready to open. Renovations did not start on time, and getting to them was clearly not a priority for the carpenters. I felt like an uptight Upper Canadian as I hounded them with worried phone calls. Deliveries came daily, and medications sat waiting for shelves that would house them. Equipment sat shiny and new all over the house in readiness. Had I thought of everything? Two wonderful friends came from Ontario to visit and provide moral support and their company kept to a minimum the fears I heard whispering in the background. Had this really been a good idea? Could I make it work?

I passed my Nova Scotia examinations and paid for my veterinary licence. The darkroom did get completed in time. The newspapers and farm magazines ran my opening advertisements. And on New Year's Day, I got my first call.

"Are you Helen Douglas?" a thin wavering voice asked. "I've been waiting for you to come see my horse."

"Certainly," I said, a little taken aback, as I had predicted New Year's Day to be a holiday there, as elsewhere.

I found out later there was no stopping this mighty and decidedly difficult little lady. Map in hand, I headed out on the crisp winter day on my first call.

"I've been waiting for you to open," she said when I arrived. "I have a little mare here that has a terrible problem and she's had it for almost two years. I don't know if she can be fixed."

It turned out the small Morgan mare, "Lovie," had run into a wooden gateway, and a broken shard of wood had imbedded itself deep into the muscle on the left side of her neck over the vertebrae. After several minor operations, it was still draining, and the mare had difficulty turning her head to that side and lowering it to eat. I could see right away that this was a surgical case. How ironic that my very first call was one I would have to refer on to someone with a surgery.

"Where can I go to put her under general anaesthetic?" I asked. It was a task I wouldn't attempt at this time of year under field conditions.

"There's a doctor near Shubenacadie, I think," Elizabeth said.

"I'll call him and set it up. Perhaps I can go up with Lovie and help with the operation," I volunteered.

We did manage to arrange a date to trailer the mare to the little clinic specializing in racehorses. The veterinarian there was willing to let me assist on the surgery, and it was a good chance to meet him. After we had Lovie under anaesthetic and opened the surgery wound, we found several splinters of wood left behind. They were very deep and wedged between the lateral processes of two cervical vertebrae. We took out all we could find.

"They are very close to the cord," I said. "We'll do what we can."

After the wound was cleaned and flushed well, we partially closed it with a drain in place. The horse recovered well and we were able to take her home before dark. The owner was to flush the area well twice daily, and I would remove the drain in one week. We put a hood and blanket on the little mare, and I left, giving instructions to leave her in until I saw her again. It had been an interesting day. All we could do now was hope for the best. I left Elizabeth with a long list of instructions and headed home.

Before long, my phone was ringing off the hook. Though I took most of my calls in the morning, it often rang late at night as well. Many of the calls the first few months had to do with long-term problems, especially lameness, and the owners hoped I could do something other veterinarians hadn't been able to do. In some cases I could help with the diagnosis, other times make a new treatment suggestion, but in many cases there was really nothing more I could do. It was disappointing for the owners and for me, but sometimes the animals simply would never be sound or healthy again. I was the new kid on the block, representing new hope. It was sobering to see how many times I could not provide a miracle.

As the spring busy season approached, I began to meet more and more horse people. Vaccinations and checkups are traditionally carried out in the spring, and I lived in a whirlwind as everyone tried out the new vet. I drove many miles every day, arriving home tired and dirty. Then there would be x-rays to develop, lab results to call, surgery packs or equipment to clean, restocking and ordering to do. On a quiet night, I attempted to do my books and other paperwork, something I had little aptitude for. Three months into it, I realized I had to have a bookkeeper. Things were rolling and I just couldn't keep up.

The first real emergency I had was a severe laceration in a standard-bred mare. James and Lorraine Weeks had five or six older racehorses running together in their farmyard and had always had some equipment there as well. This time, the running herd had driven one of the horses into a space too narrow to get through and it had impaled itself on the dangerous, dirty blade of a manure spreader. The panicky phone call indicated to me that I should waste no time getting there.

I had never seen a laceration like it. The large slanted blade had gone into the mare's chest on the left side and angling to the outside. Even more, it had come dangerously close to removing her left front leg. I fanned my hand cautiously into the gaping wound. There was a lot of contamination, and yes, I could easily feel the throbbing pulse of the brachial artery in the deepest part. The blade had almost severed the main artery to her front leg! Shaking my head, I picked bits of debris and manure out of the wound.

"This is bad, Mr. Weeks. It's very deep and contaminated most of the way in," I said. "It will be a long recovery; she'll probably never race again."

"Well, she'll make a good brood mare if we can save her," he replied.

I got on a bale of hay and sewed for well over an hour, starting deep in the wound and taking large bites through the muscle. I tried to close the space. Drains were laid in so that fluids could find a way out. I closed the upper half of the incision at the front, but left it open on the bottom.

"The key will be keeping it clean so it can heal from the inside out," I said.

I left him with detailed instructions and departed, wishing them well. The mare had been incredibly lucky not to have bled-out. I could never have guessed that in less than two years the mare would win a race again.

As a student, I had learned every nook and cranny of the south shore. Now, I had a totally new landscape to explore. The area around Grand Pré had a unique topography and history.

Hundreds of acres of farmland had been created below sea level when the Acadians had built earthen dykes to keep out the tides. These dykes were wide enough to drive on and gave a spectacular view of the sea on one side while falling off gently to hayfields on the other. I boarded Kira at a small private barn very near these dykes and often headed off by myself, even in the winter cold, to trot along the top of the dyke walls. Large, brownish ice floes were transported in and out by the tide twice daily, and when the tide went out, there were ice mounds the size of cars littering the sand beaches. It was a sight one might see on another planet, stark and dramatic, quite unlike anything I had ever seen.

The family who had sold me the schoolhouse became my first friends, and I felt lucky to have met them. As fate would have it, we were very like-minded, and in a short time Paul and Suzanne had adopted me, inviting me to supper several times weekly, providing me with a new, instant social life. Their eight-year-old son loved horses and showed an interest in riding, uncommon in young boys, so I began taking him with me on the dykes. As the spring weather came, the farm laneways softened, the wind off the sea lost its bite, and I rode often with him sitting in front of me on a small pad. We enjoyed the experience of seeing the landscape and exploring the beaches together, and I taught him to turn, stop, and move with the horse. Eventually, we would trot and canter together, and the big mare showed no sign that she minded her extra passenger.

A particularly enjoyable tradition in the Wolfville area was the summer pastime of inner tubing down the Gaspereau River. The spectacular little river ran several miles from a dam to the sea complete with stretches of gentle rapids bordered by idyllic green fields. The usual drill was to drop a vehicle off at the bottom, drive all the people and tubes upstream in an open pickup, and launch at the dam. Sometimes there were scores of people, and vendors set up hot dog stands at the top on busy weekends. People even came to camp and tube the Gaspereau. It took over half an hour to go down and it was even more fun with several tubes rafted together. It was a highlight of the busy summer weekends.

Anyone closely associated with a vet—especially one on call seven days a week—soon learns what it is like to live the life of a country practitioner. One Sunday, I was at Paul and Suzanne's relaxing before a big turkey dinner was to be put on the table. A regular client with horses had an old Collie who was clearly on its last legs the last time I had visited the farm. They paged, desperately upset, late in the afternoon.

"Laddie can't get up. We know it's the end. Could you please come out and put him to sleep?" the upset man asked.

"I'll come now and bring help," I said.

I knew that when the time to euthanize a beloved family pet had come, Sunday dinner would have to wait. Paul came with me for the half-hour drive and learned to hold up a vein then and there as I administered the fatal injection.

"Could you take him with you?" the owner asked.

"We'll pay whatever it takes to have his ashes back," they added.

We loaded the big dog's body in the back of the station wagon and drove off. I knew of a clinic with a crematorium and would deliver him there myself first thing in the morning. And then, both of us feeling sadness at their loss and an eerie awareness that we had just ended a life, had to go back and carry on with Sunday dinner. Paul and I were thinking of the call and the dog outside as we tried to maintain our normal routine. It was a first for him, but one of many he would experience through his friendship with me.

🐕 🐕 🐕

There were a few humps in the road that first year. People were a little suspicious of me, being from away. And, of course, I had to prove myself again. The first time I pulled out my little alcohol wipes at Bruce's, he laughed.

"Do you charge more for using those fancy things?" he said.

That sort of sentiment was expressed over and over, simply because I did things differently. It was a large leap from Dr. B's clinic in Toronto to a backyard in Nova Scotia where many owners had never realized horses needed regular de-worming or dental care. Of course there were many educated clients as well, but I got used to the refrains I heard.

"Old Doc Smith didn't do it that way."

"Are you charging more for the surgical gloves?"

"Can we cut any corners, Doc? I don't want that expensive medication."

In Toronto, I had had the advantage of people's assuming we provided top-notch service. Here, I wasn't always sure people wanted it. Gradually, as I figured out who wanted what level of service or medical intervention and gained the trust of the horse community, I found most people welcomed my recommendations. It was very much a proving ground all over again. Introducing new ideas and ways often proved tough.

The first Christmas approached. I had gotten into the rhythm of running my own practice, and business was brisk. It was all very encouraging. I had my first case of serious large-bowel impaction in quite a valuable young warmblood mare. The way the case turned out seemed to cement my reputation as a legitimate horse vet.

Impactions usually occur in winter when a horse doesn't drink or move around much. Such impactions of the large bowel in a horse can cause prolonged abdominal pain or "colic." The pain must be controlled so that the animal does not roll incessantly, causing a worse problem, such as torsion of the bowel. With the pain controlled, one can work to relieve the impaction.

The mare had not passed manure in days, and rectal examination revealed a hard fecal mass almost the size of a foal. I discussed the options with the owner. Her mare could be referred to the vet school in PEI, necessitating a long trailer ride in the winter and a journey by ferry.

"We could try to treat her here," I said cautiously. "It can be done with large volumes of intravenous fluids, but you'll have to stay with her and monitor things round the clock."

"I'll do it," said the owner. "Let's get started."

We moved the horse to a larger barn, as we needed the warmth and the indoor arena. I would set up an intravenous catheter and treatment chart. Large volumes of fluids would have to be administered to moisten the mass and get the bowel moving again. I visited all the neighbouring clinics, rounding up all the bags of fluids they could spare. The mare would have to be tubed with water and oil twice daily and also walked frequently round the clock. The owner could be taught to change the bags of fluids as they emptied. Painkillers would be given via the intravenous catheter as needed. We were set, the plan in place. I would visit twice daily and the owner would call if the catheter came out or she couldn't control the pain.

Two days went by, and we were up to forty litres of fluids. I called the vet school and they encouraged me to keep going. It may take twice that volume, they advised me. I sped up the drip, and soon the mare developed gurgling sounds in her abdomen. At first we got only a few handfuls of manure at a time, but when I examined the horse, I could feel the mass was getting softer. Finally, on day three and with sixty litres of fluids on board, the mare started to pass it all. Within hours, we had wheelbarrows full and laughed that so much joy could be derived from the sight of horse manure.

The owner knew many horse people, and our success was a real feather in my cap. But storm clouds lurked on the horizon.

There was a riding instructor in the area who had tremendous influence on people and had long played the role of a vet advisor to all her students. Unfortunately, she did not welcome my arrival. Slowly, the criticism and gossip she had started made its way back to me. It started off with a few idle comments to let me know there was trouble. It culminated with a client who particularly liked me, inviting me out to lunch to talk.

"I think you should know what's happening," she said. "Someone has to tell you what's being said about you . . ."

Allegations ranged from my having sold expensive and unnecessary drugs to downright negligence — not knowing what

I was doing, not treating horses the right way. The final straw for this decent client had come when she had heard something she knew to be patently untrue.

"If I believed anything she told me about you or your work, I wouldn't have you in my barn," she said.

"I can't believe what I'm up against!" I said, knowing what influence the instructor wielded.

"Don't let it get you down—there are plenty of people here who can see right through it. It's all based on insecurity," she said.

"I'll try not to react," I said thoughtfully. "Perhaps if I don't fight back . . ."

It was not to be that easy. However, as in Toronto, despite the ups and downs and challenges of practice, many more positive things were happening for me. There were horses to vaccinate, teeth to float, castrations to do, and skin conditions to treat. I travelled the province, seeing horses, meeting people, and going the extra mile whenever I could. Life was good, and my roster of clients and cases grew. I started doing a lot of teaching. There were 4H and pony club lectures and night courses on reproduction and nutrition. I was vetting for three-day events and long-distance rides. Slowly, I was carving a niche in the horse world in Nova Scotia. I tried to ignore the rumblings.

I had been there a year and a half when a good client came to me and said "I think my farm would be perfect for you. We're selling this spring."

It was just the right timing for me, as I had been considering looking for a small horse farm where I could hospitalize and treat patients and perhaps do minor surgery. There had been many occasions when I wished I could keep a horse for tumour removal, treatment of a bad cut, or artificial insemination. It might also save me many miles of driving if people could bring their horses in. This little farm didn't have a lot of land, but it had a good, solid horse barn big enough to have a work area as well as some regular stalls. The heritage house was likewise sturdy and workable, with character, yet needed no major renovations. It was close to my little schoolhouse, and the move would be easy.

The sale was easy to arrange, and I would move in early spring. I was moving closer to my dream. Designing the little hospital would be fun, and now I could provide a whole new level of service. With the confidence I had gained from moving my log house, travelling the world alone, and starting my own business, this next step seemed a breeze. I moved forward swiftly.

Right around that time, Elizabeth called me to tell me that Lovie's neck had started draining yellow pus again. The mare's neck had been healed for a long time, and my heart sank. This was the call that I had hoped would never come. Her owner said she had been uncomfortable for some time, but she had not wanted to bother me. Elizabeth told me how the neck had healed then burst again and was draining a foul discharge on the opposite side in two places. All the scar tissue on the left side had made it difficult for the infection to find a way out, so it had slowly developed a new tract.

"It means there were wood fragments still in there, probably between the vertebrae where we couldn't get at them," I said, my heart sinking.

"Is there anything else we can do?" she asked, knowing the answer.

"I'm afraid not," I said.

"I can't put her through this any longer. We must put her to sleep." The feisty little lady was decisive. "The sooner, the better."

This is the kind of case that can really touch a veterinarian—not only had everyone tried so hard and for so long, but the little mare was sweet and stoic. It was hard to say goodbye. We buried her on Elizabeth's farm right under an apple tree in full bloom. At least she wasn't suffering anymore.

THIRTEEN

SNAKES ON A BUS

WITH A CLINIC AT THE FARM, I started to get all manner of visitors seeking veterinary advice. The yellow school bus with the blacked-out windows that pulled up one day was most curious. It was crudely decorated with hand-painted green and black snakes from hood to taillights. Large gothic letters advertised "Rare Jungle Creatures," with a smaller note below inviting one to "Book Your Appointment Now," with the phone number. As I walked across the yard, two heavyset, middle-aged men emerged, their tattooed biceps and emblazoned black vests clearly identifying them as bikers. The oldest wore a red headscarf and sported a graying Hulk Hogan moustache.

"Can you come in here?" he said. "Some of our snakes are sick."

I followed them up the steps into the dimly lit interior, completely transformed into a reptile den. Walls of terrariums lined the bus on both sides of the aisle. As my eyes adjusted to the dark, I saw the snakes, many of them larger around than my upper arm. Fantastic creatures, the largest boa was well over eight feet long. It curled itself sluggishly around Hulk's neck.

"He's definitely under the weather," he said. "We've had this problem before and Old Doc Ainslie gave them chloramphenicol. Do you have any?"

"Well, what are the symptoms?" I asked. "Did Doc Ainslie take their temperatures?"

"They slow right down, seem to have a cold or the snuffles," he said seriously.

"Right, then, let's check the dose in the manuals. If it worked before, it may work again." I suppressed a smile. What the heck did I know about snake medicine? But I was game.

"What do you think they weigh? So I can check their dose, that is."

We negotiated a dose for the several sick animals, and the burly man showed me the correct sites for intramuscular injection. It was a strange sensation poking through the tough scales into the soft muscle below. The snakes did not react to the needles, and the Hulk held them lovingly as they hung limply, wrapped around him.

"See, that proves they're sick," he claimed. I nodded, equally serious.

"The next thing we have to do is warm them up over eighty degrees," he said.

"Be sure to let me know how they do," I said.

"Thanks a bunch! You can get into the show for free any time, Doc."

With several loud backfire retorts, they started up the bus and left, never to be seen again. I walked back into the barn laughing, amused by the slice of life I had just witnessed and hoping I had helped the snakes. I wish I had seen their show.

The renovations at the farm were simple enough, but I was more excited about them than any such projects in the past. My dream was within reach. The area I had gutted for the work and treatment room was the size of six box stalls. It was lined with white plywood and had lots of cupboards, a sink, a laboratory, and a multi-panel x-ray viewer. As well, there were the large, custom-made metal horse stocks that the animals would be placed in for procedures requiring restraint. The final touch was a double-sized stall that could be used, with padding, to drop and recover a horse if needed. The entire front could be rolled back so people and equipment could get in and out easily. The horses could be hand recovered from the outside, for safety, with a system of ropes.

The first patients were literally arriving as the newly minted stall doors were being hung on their hinges. Hadn't I vowed years ago not to do this again? With the proper hardware yet to be installed, we had to tie them in with lead shanks. A mare for a reproductive check and a colt with a bad cut were followed by my horse and a couple of boarders who had arranged to come that day. We had an instant herd of five animals, with more on the way. There was still much to do—fencing, organizing treatment charts, improving equipment—but I was pretty well on track.

When in Toronto, I had met an eccentric older man, a Romanian of reputedly noble descent, completely devoted to his forty racehorses, which ranged from babies to retirees. He was difficult to work for and had trouble keeping help. We had spoken on the phone at length that same spring regarding my leasing his stallion. He called me back. It seemed he had concocted another idea.

"I can support your new facility, give you some cash flow," he said. "With the cost of keeping horses here, it might be worth my while to send you six. Two would be pregnant for you to foal out, but the others could be ridden and sold down there. This might work out well for both of us," he concluded. It was arranged for July first. This would give me time to get the right trainer and horse person to help me. And it would help pay an assistant's salary to have several horses in for training.

I thought I knew the right person. Elizabeth was a horsewoman I had met in Toronto who had great horse experience and medical aptitude. I knew she had been unhappy in her job. I called her.

"Are you interested in being an equine vet technician in the Annapolis Valley?" I asked.

She laughed at the unexpected call. "What would I be doing?"

I told her everything that would involve her or be her responsibility, including the care and treatment of patients and some training of the horses that were coming. Basically she would run the farm while I was on the road.

"I'll do it," she said, surprising both of us. "After ten years here, I'm ready for an adventure."

I felt relieved to have reliable help coming. The two-to-three-week wait would be worth it. The hospital might be bigger and busier than I had anticipated.

The very next week after I opened, while waiting for my new full-time employee, I had a conversation with a regular client that unsettled me deeply.

"Did you know there is a new horse vet setting up just a few miles from here?" Pam asked. "I've heard he's quite a bit cheaper than you."

"No, I hadn't heard," I replied, willing my face not to react—not to show the sudden anxiety I felt. "There should be room for all of us," I continued, echoing Jim's words from so long ago. I wish I truly felt that confident. Hopefully, there would be.

I had a new surgical team to train. Elizabeth arrived, and so did a keen high school student who amazingly volunteered to come any time I needed her and to do chores on our days off. Both of them had to learn to help me anaesthetize animals, assist at surgery, and get them back up on their feet again. We started with the most common procedures—gelding young colts and repairing umbilical hernias. After a few horses, we really were working as a team.

We moved on to doing a few cryptorchids. These male horses have an undescended testicle, sometimes two, and surgery to locate the retained one can be tricky. We were limited by the fact we did not have inhalant anaesthetic, but had to work with the time and safety constraints of intravenous anaesthesia only. The animals were not on oxygen and could only be kept down a short while. I had a run of good luck, because I found the retained testes in the first two ponies one fellow brought me. The drop stall and work area were working well.

We did have an unexpected problem with flies! Sandwiched between a poultry operation and a pig farm, that first summer brought us hordes of them. We almost poisoned ourselves daily with fly spray, trying to keep our treatment and surgery areas free of flies and in impeccable condition.

Count Stano's horses arrived on time and settled in. Things weren't going to be easy with them. They were totally untrained, almost wild, and were going to present a big challenge. It wouldn't be quick. The stallion was the nicest of them, but the others each had problems that would make them hard to sell, even when trained. I wondered what I had gotten into when the shipper said he had been told I was to pay for the transport.

"Ouch, I didn't think it was C.O.D.," I said. Trying to call Stano to no avail, I paid the bill. What would happen when I tried to collect it, and what about the first month's board for six horses? A voice in my head warned me that I was in a precarious situation and might be in trouble, with a new paid employee and six new mouths to feed, if he didn't come through. I tried not to acknowledge the voice.

Then one of the oddest and most dramatic cases I had ever seen happened right in my own barn. A boarder's horse had arrived a few days before, and the owner commented that he hadn't yet been vaccinated for influenza and rhinopneumonitis that spring. I wasn't worried and assured her I would do him shortly; he looked healthy enough. Then disaster struck. As is often the case when a lot of horses are suddenly moved to a new place at one time, a respiratory infection starts to move through the animals. Rhinopneumonitis, a herpes virus, usually causes a respiratory infection like human influenza. Rarely, it causes a fatal neurological infection—encephalitis.

Hawk had appeared wobbly when he was turned out that morning, almost as if he were intoxicated. Elizabeth paged me on one of my calls to tell me it was subtle, but real. Later that day, she paged me in real alarm.

"You've got to come back right away," she said. "Hawk is staggering in his stall and looks like he's going to go down."

I raced back to the farm. I was shocked to see how he was when I got there. Hawk had crashed violently out of the stall, breaking the door, and was staggering around the yard on the end of a lunge line, sometimes falling violently. Elizabeth was barely managing to hold onto him, and I knew if he got loose he could fall into the nearby stream or get out on the road. We couldn't get close to him. It was clearly neurological.

In a panic, I tried to contact the owner, and luckily she was at home.

"Hawk has to be put down right away. He may have rabies or encephalitis. He's in extreme pain and may start to seizure at any moment!" I blurted out. There was no time to be tactful; someone could get hurt.

"Do what you have to," she said in a whisper. "I can't believe this is happening . . ."

Her voice trailed off, and I hung up. When I returned to the scene in the barnyard, the situation was worse. The horse was literally out of his mind, nostrils flared, veins standing up under his skin. The beautiful animal had no idea what was happening to him.

Two strong farmers from next door had arrived to help. All four of us attempted to get the horse pinned against the big barn door and I managed with difficulty to get a sedative injection into him. The high dose of sedation did no good and we never got near him again. One of the farmers went to get his gun and, when the horse next went down, managed to shoot him and end his suffering quickly. We were all in a state of shock, covered with blood, dirt, and sweat. It had all happened so fast. They came back with their tractor to dispose of the body. We all had little to say. It was, and still is, one of the most distressing and acute things that I have seen in my life as a vet.

Within months, it became apparent that Stano had neither the means nor the intention to pay for his horses. As his board and training bills mounted, I started phoning, or adding notes pleading with him to send something towards their keep. One horse was sick and needed medication, two others were difficult and would be slow to train and sell. One day, I got him on the phone.

"You've got to send something," I said, trying to sound firm, "or I'll send them all home."

We ended up in an angry shouting match, something I seldom did, and I pounded my fist on the desk in frustration during the conversation. What had been intended to help my business and create cash flow had become a serious liability. The expense of the move and set-up of the farm, as well as the burden of Stano's extra horses, had, combined with the loss of clients to my new and less-expensive competitor, strained me to the maximum financially.

Paul and Suzanne were still my closest friends and confidantes. We socialized a lot, and now Elizabeth was included. Paul had noticed how much I admired and cared for her. He was the only person I had confided in or with whom I had openly discussed my emotions.

One day, unsolicited, he said "I think Elizabeth would be perfect for you."

"So you have noticed," I replied. "I don't want her to think I lured her down here with some ulterior motive."

"Don't worry—it doesn't seem that way at all. Besides, I think she feels the same way. You two are so happy when you're together," he said.

Elizabeth truly was the person I had been waiting for. We worked so well together, loved the horses so much, and just had this great chemistry. Respect was just an added bonus.

In fact, unbelievably to me, she did feel the same way and we are life partners to this day.

Embarking on such a controversial course in the Valley, a deeply conservative area, provided an additional strain on my new business, but I didn't care. Only then did I realize how lonely I had been for so long. I let myself experience the deep fulfillment of having found my soulmate. We would often forget that other people didn't see us as normal as we lived our so normal, hardworking lives. It happened that Elizabeth walked right into the most financially difficult time of my life. We worked day and night to keep afloat, sure that good intentions would make it all turn out. The dream kept us going, but I knew we were in trouble by the first winter.

FOURTEEN

"ARE YOU BRAVE ENOUGH?"

WINTERTIME CAME and the barn was still busy, but the regular calls had noticeably decreased as I went into my third year. Times were tough, there was a very real countrywide recession, and often the owners of cases I had in the hospital left without paying, and I didn't hear from them for months. One time I was paid in hay, another time with lobster. It was appreciated, but it didn't pay my bills. My bank manager began to notice, as my line of credit mounted. They would not lend me any more money. I was still hampered by five out of Stano's six horses and had received only one minor payment on his account. On top of it all, I had to admit my momentum was slipping.

Many people were trying the new vet, who was very popular. In fact, I heard the sentiment expressed that the horse people were giving him the regular work and saving me for different or difficult cases. My nemesis, the riding instructor, was not only steering everyone to my competitor but heating up her attacks on me, as if sensing I was down. And I knew I would be foolish to underestimate the effect of my personal life on it. I stood in front of the mirror and, in one of the most serious but crucial moments of my life, looked myself in the eye with only one question in mind.

"Can you do it? Are you brave enough?" I asked. Finding Elizabeth had been an important part of finding myself. I would not cave in. I would carry on. I walked away from that moment of self-interrogation stronger, with my head up. I was determined to find a way through this. If I had called it all wrong, overestimated, or wrongly estimated, my business plans or potential, I could adjust, come up with a backup plan. I always had.

Elizabeth went off the payroll to help out and with genuine embarrassment agreed to go apply for unemployment assistance. My mother helped with the mortgage for a couple of months. I decided to go to Halifax and do small animal work for several days each week. It was not at all fun making the long drive in winter weather, and often it was dangerous. But it was familiar and easy to do small animals, and it paid the bills. I met lots of new people, vets and technicians who knew nothing of my troubles. Spring was coming, and we would see what would happen then.

But by April, I could see business really was down. I would have to put Plan B into action. I called Dr. Dick Kemper.

Ironically, small animals—wonderful, reliable, non-seasonal, small-animal practice—would see me through. How thankful I was for that solid grounding in the Ottawa Valley.

Ever since I had come to work in Nova Scotia, I had known of a small, dilapidated clinic in a town twenty minutes away. The owner had retired, but had had no luck in selling it. He had lost interest in it and only went in for a few hours a day. He was on the verge of letting the sole employee go when I phoned him.

"I wondered if you would be interested in leasing your practice," I asked.

"I don't know . . . I really wanted to sell it," he replied. "Maybe we should meet and talk."

"Sure, let's meet at the practice. I'd like to see it," I said.

We met and he showed me the building and then the appointment book. It was initially discouraging, but I could see it had some potential. How much? I didn't want to make a wrong move. The receptionist was a lovely person, and I remember joking with her, wondering if she came with the practice. There would be a lot of elbow grease needed, everything would have to be scrubbed and painted. The hardwood floors were grey. A lot of the drugs were outdated. But we were just sneaking in before horse season began in earnest, and I believed we could do it. Could I have ever imagined last May first when I opened my horse clinic that exactly one year later I would be contemplating opening a new small-animal business?

We settled on a two-year lease, and the rent would include the use of all the equipment in the practice. Dr. Kemper had good surgical equipment and a decent x-ray machine; the rest of what I needed could be delivered overnight. My new friends dug in for me just as my friends in Lanark had almost ten years before, and we were indeed ready on time. Now I was running two different businesses in two different places.

It was a good move, and still very central to most of my horse clients. In fact, I was even closer to the big barns in Halifax that had, in large part, really stuck with me. We now answered all calls at the clinic, getting most of the business calls out of the house. The small-animal practice there was not totally defunct, and I knew it would be possible to breathe life into it quite easily.

I met a few breeders and also the local representative of the S.P.C.A. Within a few weeks, we had started a spay/neuter campaign, and there were often feral or barn cats in the clinic for neutering. Some days were wild when we had several of these poor frightened cats to deal with. Cats frequently escaped through a small crack when kennel doors were opened. Most of us got bitten, scratched, urinated upon, or all three. We had a number of orthopedic surgeries to do early on, and I had a chance to tune up my skills in repairing broken bones. I was rolling now and getting back into stride as a mixed practitioner. Usually I would do small animals in the mornings and horse calls in the afternoons, ending up back at the home farm to do treatments or check mares that were in for artificial insemination. I was amazed at how things had turned out after all my efforts at equine education. One does what is needed to survive, and I was lucky to have the skills and nerve to adapt to the changes that kept confronting my fledgling practice.

At the farm, we were expanding our capability with regards to artificial insemination. We intended to handle stallions there, and by teaching them to collect on a "phantom" or fake mare, we could then ship semen to mares at other locations. The phantom mare was a simple contraption built out of telephone poles and a mattress. It was hidden out behind the barn. We named it "Ever Ready." With a minimum of effort and a mare in heat standing alongside, stallions could be taught to mount this dummy and breed into an artificial vagina. The A.V. was similar to a long can or tube with a rubber lining and a bottle at the end to collect the sample. Some stallions would not use it. A few would not mount the phantom, so there was always problem-solving to do. Once successful in collecting, we would do quality control studies on the samples to see if they were suitable to ship out to mare owners.

One day, we had a magnificent Hanoverian stallion to work with. He was early on in his training for artificial breeding. He was being handled by his owner, and I held the estrus mare. We also had a neighbour who was doing carpentry and a friend visiting from Ontario who had never seen such a process. The enthusiastic stallion was strong and hard to handle and he certainly knew what was happening when he saw Ever Ready.

The reader must picture a 1,500-pound chestnut stallion running out of control at a mattress. The owner, small of stature, gave up on holding him and concentrated on getting the A.V. on the erect penis. The stallion gripped and pawed at the slippery phantom and, inexperienced, simply walked off the front of her. The carpenter had stopped to gape. The stallion owner managed to keep the contraption on the thrusting stallion as he walked willy-nilly around the yard. Finally, though sheer persistence, he got a sample and passed the A.V. off to his laughing audience, including me.

"Well, I got it, didn't I?" he said, slightly abashed.

"It might have been a little unconventional, but you get an A for effort!" I laughed.

The sample was good. It would go better next time. The carpenter was last seen smoking a cigarette.

We were still working on many interesting cases at the farm. We usually had several horses in for A.I., saving me many miles and farm visits. The owners would bring the containers of semen to me from the bus or plane when the mare was ready to breed.

There were challenging cases of colic, and lacerations to repair, and in general I was happy that the clinic was serving a good purpose. We had sold most of Stano's horses finally, just to pay his bills, so I had dug myself out of that mess with very little in the way of support or communication from him.

We had a rare case of pyometra in a mare that summer. The twenty-year-old mare had been bred eleven months before and had approached her birth time with an appropriately large abdomen. One morning, the owner found her draining a long strand of foul, yellow discharge. There was no foal, but a uterus full of infection. We brought her to the clinic, as she would need several days of treatment. We stood the patient old Morgan mare in the stocks, inserted a plastic stomach tube into the uterus, and tied it to her tail, placing the other end in a bucket. It took all day, but we finally filled three five-gallon pails with muck. The mare had been eating and drinking and had a normal temperature. This was truly a miracle with so much infection in her. We had to flush her uterus for days with warm saline, but finally it ran clear, and she went home.

I got "Homer" that summer, an Appaloosa gelding that I traded for an overdue account. He was homely, tall, and spindly, unlike most Apps, but a sharp jumper, and he had an uncanny, almost canine, understanding of humans. He turned out to be one of the most enjoyable horses I ever owned. He was originally intended to be a school horse, but was green and too smart and would regularly run off with the students. I started to ride him myself, and we clicked. Full of pranks, he let himself out of gates, stood in wheelbarrows, and loved cross-country and jumping. Once he got the idea, he would take me over anything, even into water. He became our mascot. We jumped him over picnic tables and even brought him into the house for special occasions.

Life went on in its new form. The horse practice had stabilized to a level I could accept—not enough to live on, but enough for me to be of service to lots of horse owners and patients and treat many interesting cases. My detractor had been somewhat backed off by a formally drafted legal letter pointing out in a reasonable fashion that it would be in both of our best interests to live in peace. Perhaps she realized I wasn't going to give up easily. The small-animal practice grew steadily, and I found I was enjoying it. It had been great to accumulate all the skills and experience I had at both Brentwood and Rexdale Equine. Now they were serving me well. I continued to do horse calls "before work" and into the evening.

One interesting job I had was to geld over twenty huge Russian warmblood stallions one summer. A local entrepreneur brought them back on livestock pallets that had been used to send Canadian dairy Holsteins to Russia. They were housed in Nova Scotia to be gelded, backed, and then sold all over North America. They were too large to drop to the ground easily, so I decided to geld them all standing. We worked our way through the herd, doing three or four each day. It was an opportunity for me to become completely comfortable with the best anaesthetic regime and technique for standing castrations, as well as learning how to handle complications, such as swelling or bleeding. By the time the last of the group was done, I had it really fine-tuned. The young horses didn't even know they had had surgery!

Meanwhile, the group down at the clinic had developed a good rapport. We really had fun working together. One afternoon, I had booked a special procedure on an ailing German shepherd with a cough. I suspected from her x-rays she was bordering on congestive heart failure. Elizabeth had come down to help us hold her for an EKG, which was to be sent via a battery-operated unit over the phone to a specialist who would interpret it and fax back a report.

Sheba was a placid, older female German shepherd and lived alone with her owner way back along the shore. He was a reclusive backwoods bachelor. He had an overactive sense of smell and it distressed him greatly being in the clinic. The smells there upset him so much that he spent the whole time sniffling, grumbling, and even snorting, all the while blowing his nose. As this was distracting to all of us, I asked him to wait in the front room while we hooked Sheba up and ran the EKG.

We put the lovely old dog on the table in lateral recumbency and hooked up the four leads with metal clips to her dampened legs. I dialled the phone, and we turned on the small unit. There was no power. The batteries were dead. Elizabeth jumped into her car and sped the one block to the nearest convenience store. Sheba had been difficult to convince to lie down and so it seemed best to leave her there. I stuck my head out of the treatment room.

"The phone line is busy—we'll keep trying," I said.

The owner snorted, "Well, just hurry up and get it over with." He was desperate to leave.

The phone rang. "The car won't start. I need a boost," said Elizabeth from the store. "I've got the batteries but I can't get back."

We all stared at one another. The receptionist would have to go get her. We put the phones on hold, and the two of us remaining managed to keep the dog on the table and the clips on. The owner was totally unaware that two out of four of us had left the building.

"Hurry," I whispered between clenched teeth. When they arrived back, the receptionist went out front once more and reported, "They've just gotten through," to the anxious owner. The phone rang right through, and we had the transmission done. When the owner left, we all collapsed in gales of laughter. It had been a comical ten minutes, but we had pulled it off.

Sometimes we used the small animal clinic for equine cases. There was a work area there that had been used for both cattle and horses, but it was the gas anaesthetic machine that came in handy for foals on numerous occasions.

I had an Arab foal arrive from two hours away. The flexor tendons on the left hind leg had been severed, and his toe was well off the ground. The referring vet had sent him in a cast. This had been going on for several weeks. The owners were distraught and became even more so when I told them the prognosis was poor, as tendons are notoriously hard to sew and slow to heal. I thought I had an idea, though, that might work.

We anaesthetized the foal and clipped the hind leg. I had devised a plan, an experimental repair technique using some small bone plates we had in the clinic, and they were in the autoclave now. Each was stainless steel, smooth, about one centimetre wide and four centimetres long. I would use them to bridge the clean cuts needed to shorten both the superficial and deep flexor tendons and integrate them into my suture pattern. Perhaps they would prevent the suture material from slicing through the stringy tissue and letting go. One went on the front side of the innermost tendon, and the other went on the back of the outside tendon so they wouldn't rub together. After an hour-long surgery, I sutured up the skin. We had removed two inches of tendon.

We had a special shoe made with an elevated heel to take the strain off the newly repaired tendons. Three months later, however, the foal's toe still tipped up dramatically. The owners sadly decided not to go on. They had spent far too much already. I asked their permission to take the little animal's body, look at the surgery site, then cremate him in our crematorium. It was extremely interesting to see that the tendons had healed well and the plates were well incorporated into the process and causing no harm. Although the tendon attachment surgery had been a success, the stretched structures and joints could not normalize. But this improvised technique for tendon repair might possibly come in handy another time.

We used our aged crematorium for our own euthanasias now, as well as for other clinics' deceased patients and private owners' pets that had died. It took all day to fire up the antique and run it, but it was useful to have, and we often had to prepare the pets' ashes afterwards so the owners could take them home.

One Sunday evening, I was called to an emergency, and we decided to euthanize the large, white Samoyed cross. It was late at night, and I couldn't lift her into the freezer by myself; nor did

I want the owner to see this. I made a decision to leave the poor dog's body on the x-ray table, where we could cremate her early the next morning. When I opened the back door at around eight in the morning, I was almost knocked over by a smell so noxious I can't find words to describe it.

"Oh, no!" I thought, choking my way to the x-ray table.

The dog was bloated to twice her normal size. Rare gas-producing bacteria had multiplied prolifically under the skin overnight and the animal reeked. I touched her and fur came away on my hand. The receptionist, who had followed me in, was gagging and opening windows. We were to open in twenty minutes.

We had to move the dog urgently, but she was coming apart in our hands. Any pressure and a finger would burst through the skin. It was altogether a repugnant mess, and I felt incredibly sorry to have imposed it on my innocent staff member. Gloved and masked, we managed to roll her onto a tarp on a board and get her outside. What a disaster! With all our best efforts to open windows and spray disinfectant, the clinic was still barely tolerable. We cancelled some appointments. We apologized profusely to each and every client who came in that day and I vowed not to make such a careless mistake again.

Months went by, and now seasons, and it was clear that taking on the small-animal clinic had been a good idea. There was a nice mix of time in the clinic and at the farms. And the small-animal clients were kind, easygoing, small-town people. I worked closely with the S.P.C.A. and gradually built the business back up. It was certainly clear that horse practice alone would not have paid the bills.

The second summer of my combined practice, I had an upset with Bruce, the western trainer who had trailered me down so long ago. I did very little work in his barn anymore, but a client there who still called me on occasion wanted me to see her horse, which had severe diarrhea. The horse sounded awfully sick.

"I've seen a few like this, this week," I said when I pulled up, feeling a bit uncomfortable . . . almost unwelcome.

I examined the depressed horse, which was significantly dehydrated and hadn't eaten or drunk for twenty-four hours. "Let's start him on some antibiotics and electrolytes and see how he does over the next few hours. He'll also need some Kaopectate orally by drench syringe," I said, leaving a gallon, "and I'll take this blood work with me."

When I got back to the lab, the blood work indicated a more severe dehydration than I had realized. I phoned Bruce back. "Could you bring him to the hospital for iv fluids and leave him for two or three days? He really needs monitoring," I asked, knowing he had a trailer.

"You already had this planned before you even saw him, you're just trying to drum up business for that hospital," he said. "And besides, the girl can't afford it, or the trailer ride."

"But it could be more serious. It could be salmonella; iv fluids could be crucial. They are the accepted treatment for colitis."

I sounded anxious, as if trying too hard. I felt very strained. It hadn't occurred to me that the suspicion still lingered. I was so absolutely sincere in wanting to do the best for the horse. I said, "Bruce, tell her I'll pick up and treat him for nothing if that's how you feel."

"Nothing you can say will change my mind," he replied. "Treat him here or not at all." "Would you prefer to have the other vet do it?" I asked

"Yes, I would," the answer was clear.

Somewhere along the line, Bruce had lost respect for me; that much was obvious.

"All right, I'll phone the blood work over," I said, hanging up, trying to disguise how upset I was. I put down the receiver and cried for the first time. Some of the stress was obviously getting to me, and I would have to be careful. I knew from past experience how that black feeling could creep in, and I must avoid it at any cost. I had set up the same kind of scenario for stress and exhaustion that had overcome me so many years ago.

🐎 🐎 🐎

The most dramatic case I had in Nova Scotia occurred the following spring. It was a foaling, and the owners had already tried for some time to correct the situation by the time I arrived. The foal was dead and, by the size of its legs, very large. I scrubbed up and examined the birth canal. It was an uncommon and difficult malpresentation, one I had never seen before. The foal's head had gone straight back and only the base of the throat was present. I worked for two or three hours to try to get the foal out. I had to remove one front leg to make room and do an epidermal on the mare to stop her straining, but could not get anything round the base of the neck or find the head, which I might have been able to pull forward or cut off. I couldn't get the foal to budge, and both the mare and I were tired.

"Would you send her to the Island?" I asked.

"No, that's not an option," the owner replied.

"I can't promise you anything, and we will likely lose the mare as well, but I could try to do a section here, in her stall, if you are prepared to euthanize her anyway," I offered. Years later, looking back on it, I don't know where I got the nerve. It was a real long shot. I called Elizabeth at the farm and, telling her what I needed, implored her to come as quickly as possible and be prepared to be the anaesthetist.

"Bring catheters, fluids, drapes, lots of suture material, lots of anaesthetic," I rambled off the list. "Don't forget the surgery pack!"

The barn was cold and dark, and a wind blew down the long aisle, making it a bitter tunnel. We hung trouble lights around the recumbent mare and prepped her. We had laid her against a wall on her back and her head was in the aisle, where our anaesthetist knelt on a blanket. I knelt against her other free side, tucked my knees under her huge body, took a deep breath, and cut. I succeeded in cutting the midline and uterus with no severe bleeding. The owner lay in the bedding behind the poor mare and pushed the foal back up to me slightly against gravity. I found its head was completely over its back. I found its muzzle at his tail-head. The poor foal never had a chance. A group of men

got it lifted out, its length seemed to go on forever as we extri-
cated it from the mare's body. Then I started the intimidating job
of sewing her up.

Elizabeth knelt in the cold all night. At one point she had
to go back to the farm for more anaesthetic. But we carried on.
When the last suture was placed, two men carried me out of
the stall, my legs so numb I couldn't get up. It took the mare
two more hours to get up after that. In all, we had been at it for
twelve hours. Four days later, a foot of the incision herniated.
The owner called me in a panic.

"There's bowel coming out," he said. "I guess I'll shoot
her."

"I'm so sorry. Do you want me to come and euthanize
her?"

"No, I'll just get it over with," he said. I hung up with tears
in my eyes.

Would I try it again? I think not, but that's easy to say. If
we could have driven to the nearest vet school without a ferry
ride—as one can do now—we might have gotten her there.
Sometimes the situation is so difficult to give up on, and the
option of euthanasia so final, that a vet will try against all odds
and good sense to save an animal.

🐎 🐎 🐎

I was approaching what turned out to be a critical decision in
my career. The lease at the clinic was due to be renewed in three
months, and the owner fully expected me to buy his practice.
Although I was really proud of what I had done, I knew I did
not intend to buy it. On the other hand, I found myself in a very
interesting position, as I now understood without a doubt the
horse practice alone could not provide me with a secure income.
So it was mixed practice or nothing. In order to stay, I had to buy
the clinic.

There was the additional problem of overwork, straight and
simple. It is hard to run two businesses single-handedly at the

best of times, but when you have to be on call seven days a week as well, it is a recipe for burnout. I could get some help with the small animals, but not the on-call. It would become a familiar problem.

Elizabeth and I were having dinner one night, with no agenda planned or expectation of talking about such important matters. I blurted out, "Do you think we should stay here?"

"What?" she said, stunned.

"I have to give Dr. Kemper an answer about the clinic soon," I said. She knew it had been on my mind. We both knew that buying it meant moving to the town where the clinic was located and running both businesses there, as going back and forth for two years had been so hard on me. Something had to give, but we hadn't discussed it yet. It had been almost too big a subject to tackle, because the prospect of more change was so daunting. I had finally opened the can of worms.

"It's all so different than what I had envisioned," I said in a matter-of-fact tone, without a trace of bitterness. "And you know we aren't making much above costs."

"I'm not sure it's the right place for us," Elizabeth replied, tentatively, "especially not if we have to move to another town and leave the farm." She had never said anything to that effect before and was now speaking from the heart. I appreciated her honesty.

"I don't think it is. I don't think we will be staying long term, so why get in deeper now?" I pondered, thinking out loud. I had been in Nova Scotia for six years. Now what? Now what indeed?

We looked at each other, almost shocked to have verbalized the possibility of leaving—and after working so hard to survive here. Yet we spoke with certainty, too.

If Nova Scotia was not home, then where *was* home? Would I be driven once more to pursue my dream of practising high-quality equine medicine? I decided I would go for it one more time. But how? Perhaps going back to Lanark should be put on the table, too.

As is so often the case, fate played its hand. The client who had the mare with the large bowel impaction had moved to B.C. and loved it. She was home visiting and told me about an opportunity out West. It was to be the next fork in the road.

"There's a job opening at the clinic I use," she said. "It's the best horse practice in the lower mainland. They do colic surgery for the whole area. It's an amazing place to be part of. You should try for it . . ."

I discreetly arranged to fly out West for an interview.

Perhaps it would all be for naught. It would be such a huge move to make, and of course the farm would have to be sold. I would check it out, but it seemed a long shot. There seemed to be too many obstacles. Yet, it was exciting to think about being in a state-of-the-art facility again. How would I know if I would be treated as more than a nurse? Somehow Toronto and the years of experience since felt like a suitable footing from which to approach another high-powered equine patriarch.

British Columbia was beautiful, and the horse scene and economy were very dynamic. The weather would be much easier than anywhere else I had ever lived. The clinic was top-notch, busy and well equipped. The owner was a very domineering individual, but also very knowledgeable, and I felt, after I had conversed with him, that I could hold my own due to all the experience I'd had in Nova Scotia. I was leery of getting into another peripheral or too junior a position. We both felt I could contribute a lot to the practice. I was offered a job. I flew home with much to think about. For one thing there was the problem of the B.C. Board Exams. British Columbia remained the only province to have separate licencing exams. I would have to look into writing them before I could move forward.

Everything started falling into place quickly from that point on. I found out the exam, given twice yearly, was to be held in three weeks in Eastern Canada. I just had time to get ready. I wrote the exams after studying every evening for three weeks, reviewing material on cattle and swine as well as small animals and horses. I hadn't written an exam in sixteen years, but I managed to pass the two days of testing, so the first hurdle was over. I decided to go for it and listed the farm. I announced to my best clients I was closing the practices and was surprised at how accepting and even unsurprised they were. I let everyone else find out via the grapevine, and before long it was a fact. The farm sold in a month.

We were moving to British Columbia! It would almost be a relief to work for someone else for a while. I started looking forward to seeing another part of the country that I knew nothing about. A neighbouring practice took over the small-animal clinic and bought my equine practice to amalgamate with theirs. Elizabeth and I got down to two horses, Kira's daughter and Homer. They could be left in Ottawa at Anne's farm.

It took four months of work and organization, but I had thought it might take much longer. Although I left Nova Scotia with some sadness, it was with the satisfaction of knowing it was not because I had to, but because I chose to. I was moving on to the next step of my career. We had weathered economic hardship, gossip, and unexpected competition and managed to adapt to it all and survive through hard work and good intentions. The final lesson learned could possibly have been to know when to move on.

From the time I was offered the job to the time we arrived in British Columbia, five months had elapsed.

FIFTEEN

BC, THE SLIPPERY SLOPE

 THE TRIP ACROSS Canada was memo-
rable. Wild and rugged, Northern
Ontario held a few surprises of its
own. A stately young moose in the
middle of the road, passing in the
mist at sunrise, was our greeting one
day. A flash thunderstorm north of
Lake Superior blew our tent over in
the middle of the night, sending us scurrying for cover in the car.
The Prairies unfolded, eerie in their vast flatness, hot and dusty
that year. Stark yet lovely, the scenery mesmerized us as the
miles slipped by. A dinosaur find of huge significance in Eastern
Saskatchewan lured us out of our way. We saw flash lightning on
purple horizons, discovered the back roads and small towns that
make up central Canada's heartland. And who can describe the
feeling of seeing the Rocky Mountains for the first time to someone
who hasn't done so. My excitement grew as we got closer to our
destination. British Columbia was raw, bold, dramatic, and larger
than life.

I had called Dr. Moore from several stops on our trip, and up
to that point there had been no clue of a problem in any of our
previous phone calls. However, when I called from Calgary to say
I was one week out, the response was a bit unsettling.

"I'm right on schedule," I said, "to start Monday."

"Well, er, great," he said. "I'll be going away for the month
of August. You'll be able to drive my truck, as we don't have one
for you yet."

"That's fine. I'm sure I'll know my way around before you
leave," I said.

It wasn't anything he had specifically said, but it was almost as if he hadn't been expecting me. There was a hint of something else, perhaps worry, in his voice. I put it out of my mind.

We arrived in the Fraser Valley with a couple of days to explore. Dr. Moore had located a mobile home for us as temporary accommodation. We could stay there until we got the lay of the land and found a house to rent. Household goods could come out later, hopefully within a couple of months. First we had to become familiar with our new surroundings and find out what was available.

I had only the one contact in British Columbia, and it was a big help and a relief to have her to show us around that first weekend. It turned out the Fraser Valley was set up like a grid with numbered streets running both east-west and north-south. There was heavy traffic everywhere we went. A lot of the stables were on very small lots, one to two acres being typical, so there was very little turnout for horses. Posh, new, private estates mingled with older cottages. Everyone seemed to have security, large gates, alarm systems, and guard dogs. It was very different from Nova Scotia. There didn't seem to be much room to spread out. But everywhere there was evidence that things were booming.

The musty old house trailer had seen better days. The roof was moss-covered, the old shag carpet damp, and it had been empty for a while. We unpacked our few possessions and tried to set up housekeeping with a TV, a microwave, and several suitcases. End tables made of cardboard boxes and a card table and chairs were the only furniture. It was like camping, or early student days. The two dogs, Enya, a Weimaraner, and Punch, a Jack Russell terrier, explored the new digs with glee, snuffing spiders out of corners.

In I, personally, felt no discomfort with all the changes or the accommodation. It was a dynamic and beautiful part of Canada, and in my new job I would be doing exactly what I had wanted. My comfort with our decision to leave Nova Scotia signalled to me that we were doing the right thing at the right time. As it had so many times in the past, I found that life had handed me what I needed next, exactly when I needed it. It was exciting.

The clinic was a square, unimposing building in an industrial park. It was of concrete block construction, with a state-of-the-art surgery suite, a treatment area, and six box stalls. Dr. Moore got lameness and medical referrals from all over British Columbia. As well, his was the only clinic opening abdomens, so we got all the colic surgeries within a day's drive. Because they offered neonatal foal intensive care as another specialty, there were a lot of staff ready to monitor and tend to colics and premature foals at all hours of the day and night. There were now five vets, including Dr. Moore, and his was considered a highly successful practice.

The first few days at the practice, Bill Moore and I travelled together, as he introduced me to clients, showed me how to find barns, and reviewed all the equipment in the clinic and truck. I found things to be really different than in Eastern Canada in many ways. Where there I had seen mostly thoroughbreds and quarter horses as patients, here it would be largely European warmbloods. Most of our clients lived in suburban Vancouver and kept their horses at large boarding stables in the Fraser Valley, where the economy was totally different. Management of the horses was also quite different, from feeding to bedding. High expense and lack of space dictated how the animals were cared for. There was no space for turnout. Hog fuel, or cedar bark, was the common footing for all rings and paddocks. All refuse and manure had to be put in bins and removed at great expense to protect the water table and the salmon-spawning creeks that emptied into the Fraser River.

Dr. Moore had a lot on his mind. He told me there had been two new horse vets arrive in the Fraser Valley that year. Things had been extraordinarily quiet. He suffered from terrible migraines and had had one now for several days. He was really looking forward to his month off and was glad one of the other vets was going on holiday, too. Hopefully, he added, there would be enough for me to do. I signed my job contract during my second week, including a detailed non-competition clause, and was thrown in feet first with a massive red truck, a vet box, and a map.

There was no problem in any of this. I was completely in my element. The three of us remaining at the practice easily dealt with the daily roster of calls. Sometimes I would head downtown, seeing horses in the exclusive enclave of Southlands, a riding and golf club in the heart of Vancouver. Here, owners had small barns in their yards, and common bridle paths led to central rings and show grounds. There was a track and a shared arena as well, and all of it was run by a manager hired by Southlands' board of directors. Other days, I would go across the Fraser River on a ferry and do calls in Maple Ridge and Mission. Those days were fun, although the ferry lineups were long. I had to find small farms hidden in the foothills and valleys of Golden Ears Park. The folks north of the river were a different group. Cowboys, back-to-the-landers, or people who wanted a few llama or ostrich seemed to gravitate there. East of Langley we would start to move into larger, open farmland, and once again the clients changed from uptown and upscale to dairy and crop farmers with kids in 4H and strong ties to the land.

On one of my calls, I met Elizabeth, the lady who would lead me to a house to rent. She was a volunteer worker for the local therapeutic riding group. I overheard her telling a friend about the new house she and her husband were building and their concern about finding the right tenant for their smaller, older house. I didn't hesitate to ask her about it. Was it in the country? On finding out it was on acreage with a small barn, I could hardly contain myself. Trying not to seem over-anxious or pushy, despite the fact I was dying of excitement, I arranged for Elizabeth and me to go for a look at it on the weekend.

I had butterflies as we drove up. The little farmhouse was set on eighty acres with a barn and open fields in the front and woods with trails and a ravine at the back. It looked north directly at the magnificent twin peaks of the Golden Ears Mountains. It was an unbelievable find in an area where land was at such a premium. I almost felt like a kid again, waiting for them to make their decision, and the answer later that day was affirmative. They were relieved, too, at not having had to advertise or interview hordes of people. I knew we had been incredibly lucky, as no one has room to spread out in Langley. Now the furniture and horses could come out. When Dr. Moore got back from holidays, I was really pleased to tell him that not only had calls been going well but I had found a very special and suitable place to live.

All fall felt like back-to-school time for me. Dr. Moore was quick to inform me that a whole new set of dentistry skills would have to be learned. Horse dentistry was evolving, and fast, and the old-fashioned way I had been filing horses' teeth in Nova Scotia was now completely outdated. Dental courses were being given to equine veterinarians in an attempt to bring them to a new level of proficiency so that they could compete with equine dentists, lay people who did nothing but work on horses' teeth. There were new terms to learn: wave mouth, sheared mouth, incisor reduction, and bite alignment, and many more. I studied eruption times, relearned dental anatomy and extraction techniques, and how to cut molars without breaking them. The biggest change of all for me was that they had moved into the era of power dental equipment. Often, I had to use a motorized dremel on a long, flexible shaft with a hand lamp and goggles. I ground off the large hooks that were preventing chewing, enamel flying everywhere. It was a whole new world to me, but the other veterinarians in the area were well versed in the modern equipment and techniques. I had catching up to do.

Dr. Moore was often testy with us, and I thought it was either because of his migraines or the extreme amount of responsibility he had. He had, after all, trained a lot of new vets in a short time and many of these had been new grads; it was a job that took patience. Sometimes I felt the reactions I got weren't fully justified, but I was certain I could adjust to his brusque personality type, one I wasn't used to. After all, I was learning so much. I tried to silence my doubts and worries about returning to a nurse role or the disconcerting pattern I was seeing emerge in our relationship. It was early days.

One day, I was putting in a catheter for a surgery in the afternoon. Dr. Moore passed the stall front and, looking at the catheter in place, made a comment that I found strange, if not unbelievable.

"Good girl," he said, and moved on.

I felt a shiver of disappointment and resentment. Was Dr. Moore seeing me as an equal? Someone who had had their own clinic and knew the score? If so, why had he addressed me as a student? I was very concerned about falling back into such a subordinate role, more because I was aware of the toll it could take on me than as a matter of principle. Yet I knew I had to pay my dues again, having made the decision to jump up a level once more. I tried to put the worry out of my mind, hoping that in a short time I would be familiar with everything and up to speed. Or that perhaps in time, Dr. Moore would learn to trust me. Maybe it had been my imagination. I was being overly sensitive. I had put both Elizabeth and myself through a lot to be here.

We had a severe colic come in one evening and had to call in the whole team of veterinarians for emergency surgery. The ten-year-old grey thoroughbred stallion was in uncontrollable pain and had to be operated on immediately. He was a breeding stallion of considerable value and was insured. We had him on IV fluids, then down under anaesthetic and on the table within an hour. When the animal was opened, loops of gas-filled bowel exploded out of the incision. Dr. Moore used a side-table technique for a lot of colics. A stainless steel tray was attached to the surgery table, and the part of the bowel that was to be worked on could be placed on it for decompression of gas, disimpaction, or resection. There, the surgeon could lavage the bowel with warm saline without contaminating the abdomen, before replacing the abdominal contents. In this case, the stallion had a loop of small intestine twisted 180° and caught through a rip in the mesentery, a fanlike sheet of tissue like a curtain supporting the whole intestine. The entire loop was purple and dying. It would have to be resected (cut out) and the healthy bowel rejoined—an arduous procedure.

I assisted the anaesthetist and monitored the horse. There were some very frightening moments, as his blood pressure crashed numerous times, and his colour remained an unhealthy grey-blue throughout. Bill and his assistant struggled through an intense three-hour surgery. We finally hoisted the animal back to the padded recovery stall around eleven, all of us exhausted.

I was on the phone, calling home, when we heard it. A snap like a whip cracking, or a gunshot, reverberated through the clinic. It took me a minute to understand. Two people ran by me. Bill had immediately recognized the sound of the leg breaking. The anaesthetist ran for the euthanasia solution while two vets held the poor animal's head. It had broken its tibia getting up, slipping on the rubber mats of the recovery stall. It would now have to be euthanized. It was a sound I would never forget. No one spoke and no one cried as we spent another hour cleaning up.

🐎 🐎 🐎

Around Thanksgiving, Paul's son Michael from Nova Scotia drove all our household belongings out in a huge rental truck. It was a job for him, as he was moving out West, and would work out well for us, too. It was so good to see him . . . a touch of home and friendship . . . and we had a couple of fun-filled days with good food and guitar music before he moved on. He was so grown up from the days we had ridden together over the dyke lands of Grand Pré! We started into the task of unpacking boxes and hanging pictures. It was nothing less than wonderful to see our possessions after almost four months. Now we just needed to get a ride for two horses before winter, and life would become normal. We were determined to get them out of Ontario before the snow fell.

I really understood this wasn't a traveller's lark. I was getting too old for that. It had been a big commitment and a serious move. I also really "got" the fact that Nova Scotia was over. It had been such a whirlwind since I flew out here months before for an interview that I hadn't really let myself feel saddened. Now it all

hit me. I had not let myself fully feel the range of emotions associated with leaving my little horse hospital behind. As we settled
into a routine, we often fought homesickness. It was surprisingly
hard to make friends in the Promised Land.

We decided Elizabeth should drive east to get our horses. It
was horrendously expensive to use a commercial shipper. Perhaps
this notion will always be placed in the category of, "It seemed
like a good idea at the time." We purchased a unique-looking,
workhorse of a standard Dodge dual-wheel truck that had obviously served someone else well. It was set up for hauling, and
shortly after buying it, we rented a four-horse trailer for a month.
Soon the plan was in place. Elizabeth was brave and a good long-
distance driver, but there was no way she could do the long trip
alone. Sherry, a delightful lady I worked with at the clinic, was
game to go. She had never been across Canada. After a one-night
meeting, she agreed to go along for the ride to see the country
and help Elizabeth get the horses back. It was to be a three-week
trip with long days and the threat of snow on the return stint. I
hoped they would get along.

Elizabeth set out before dawn on a frosty morning and drove
into the sunrise. Sleeping in the trailer the first night in Banff,
they endured their first bit of minor stress after being kept awake
all night by trains and traffic. By the third day, Elizabeth found
that Sherry wasn't experienced enough to drive the rig, so she
sat and chain-smoked in frustration the rest of the journey. By
the first week, they had run out of things to say. A blizzard in the
mountains on the return trip almost did them in, with slippery
slopes and closed passes and two horses on. Sherry was threatening to jump ship and catch a bus. But made it they did—all in
one piece.

Having the horses in British Columbia was a big boost. Riding
out through the back of the property was a perfect release. There
were trails to follow, very lush with ferns and Spanish moss.
There was a deep ravine as well, home to the coyotes we heard
at night in the fields behind the house. I often sighted coyotes

while riding. Like the ravine in Toronto, one could get lost here, surrounded by green trees and vines, immersed in earthy smells, bushwhacking on the edge of one of Canada's largest cities. In one more way, history was repeating itself. It would turn out to be in more ways than one.

It didn't take long for the coyotes to notice Punch, and vice-versa. The small white dog must have looked like a tempting meal, and they ventured closer and closer to the house in the evenings, sometimes in a pack. One night, I was saddling up my young mare and I noticed Punch trotting purposefully out through the back field straight towards the ravine. The next thing I noticed was a small pack of coyotes on the edge of the woods. They were definitely going to meet Punch, and the little terrier was in danger. I hadn't finished tacking up and jumped on my young inexperienced horse with the saddle barely done up. With the halter and shank, I headed her out to the back at a canter, yelling at the coyotes.

By the time I got there, the pack had surrounded the little dog. He was holding them off as they circled and attacked repeatedly, and had blood on his mouth, ears and back. I scared them off, and Punch returned with me, uncontrite. We had to keep an eye on him constantly as he and the coyotes continued their standoff, eyeing each other across the field and making forays into each other's territory.

We were riding both horses along the trail closest to the ravine one afternoon in November. There was a light rain as we made our way along the edge of the dark gully. Both dogs were with us, trotting in and out of the woods, when ahead of us on the trail appeared a lone coyote. In a flash the little Jack Russell was after it. They disappeared down the trail and into the shadows. There was no way we could follow on horseback or on foot. After calling him for an hour, we had to admit we were defeated and rode in silence home, sure we would never see the dog again. We put the horses away in disbelief. People had told us coyotes lured prey into their lairs to kill them, and here it was. It had actually happened. Six hours later, Punch arrived home, bloody once more, but surprisingly intact. He had once more, unbelievably, outwitted the coyotes.

Elizabeth was in her element in the Fraser Valley. The carefully laid-out grid of paved roads divided the fertile land into hundreds of small acreages with an astonishing variety of hobby farms. There were vineyards and cranberry bogs. Ostrich and alpaca farmers were the newest trend, but farmed deer were also making an appearance. Sod farms with specialized equipment took several layers of turf off the land each season. In the late summer, the fields were full of workers, many in bright *saris*, as East Indian families banded together to bring in their crops. The constant warm rain added to the sense of lush richness of the place. It was a stark contrast to the difficult circumstances the Nova Scotian farmers had often had to tolerate, with the uncertain heat and unforgiving soil.

And of course, everywhere there were horses—beautiful horses.

At the clinic, things were relatively quiet. It was winter in B.C., and the rain had set in. Most of my calls were in and around Vancouver, and I spent a lot of time on the road in the rain. Again, as in Toronto, the clients had accepted me well. And again, as in Toronto and Nova Scotia, the subject of the little alcohol wipes came up. Dr. Moore had observed me using the small swabs to prepare injection sites and one day said to me, "Don't you know those things just smear the dirt around? They don't sterilize anything."

I laughed to myself. I stopped using the swabs for good and have never had any injection site infections. However, I've used the story many times as an anecdote, proving how even experts disagree.

One dreary Friday afternoon, I had just finished a Vancouver run and was leaving Southlands, sitting in gridlock traffic in a cold winter rain. The receptionist from the clinic called me on my two-way, asking, "Are you still near Southlands?"

"Yes, I am. What's up?"

"Get back to the riding centre. There's a horse with a possible broken leg!"

I turned my truck around and got there as fast as I could. A fracture was the ultimate equine emergency. The horse and rider had been cantering at the far end from the arena complex. Misty, dark-green trees surrounded the sand oval, and a late-afternoon fog made the setting almost spooky. I drove up onto the track beside the floundering animal.

The situation was dire. The young girl standing holding her distressed horse in the drizzle awaited my verdict. She had been galloping and heard a loud crack from the right front leg of her middle-aged gelding. He was sweating profusely, a common sign of pain. It took me only a couple of moments to assess the pastern and feel the crunch of the fractured pastern bones.

"He will have to be euthanized," I said solemnly. "It's the only kind thing to do."

I administered the solution after she had said her goodbye and taken his tack off.

The procedure went smoothly enough. But it was the sight of the young woman, tears mixing on her face with the rain, as she walked away from her beloved horse, with saddle and bridle over her arm, into the fog, that stayed with me for a long while.

🐎 🐎 🐎

I was still working along in good faith at the equine hospital, but there were two big problems. The simplest one to explain was that Dr. Moore was quite obviously overstaffed. I had gathered from some of our conversations that if he could have called off our agreement he would have before I arrived. In a way, my arrival had created a problem for him, as it was now difficult for him to provide me with full-time employment.

There was also the subtle problem of my role at the clinic. We usually had several abdominal surgeries a week, and I was under the impression that Dr. Moore wanted to take on another mature vet in order to have someone else to do surgery when he was away. Granted, that would have taken some dedicated teaching time, something hard to come by in a busy practice. I hoped to be introduced to abdomens quickly so that I could start to develop the skills needed to deal with colics. Perhaps it would start with opening, closing, and assisting, but there would be a logical progression from that point on. We were preparing a colic one day and had just transported it to the surgical suite. Our technician was clipping the abdomen of the large animal lying on its back on the table.

"Would you like to scrub?" Dr. Moore asked.

"Sure, great," I nodded enthusiastically and went to the surgeon's scrub sink to lay out my cap, gown and size 7 1/2 gloves.

"No, I mean scrub the horse," he said without apology, turning back to the sinks.

I was stunned. How could I be in this position again? A technician could easily have scrubbed the surgical site. It would have been more than obvious to Dr. Moore that I had jumped at the chance to assist, and it would have been simple enough to let me do so. What was wrong? Had I somehow failed to get across that I was an experienced surgeon? I needed and expected to be included.

I retreated a bit that day. There were more small slights, but I had learned to expect them. I couldn't ignore it any longer when a horse shipped in with a bad cut on a hind leg. Dr. Moore was some hours away, and I radioed him to tell him of the horse's arrival.

"I'll go ahead and sedate and start to clean and debride the wound," I proposed.

"No, just leave it till I get there," he replied.

I felt defeated. I bandaged the leg, gave the horse a pain-killer injection, and left the clinic.

"Why didn't you stick around?" he asked the next day. I didn't reply. He would never understand, and it was better to keep my mouth shut. I now knew that I was not to make medical decisions on my own.

"Anyway, we have to talk," he said, leading me into his office.

"We really can't carry a fifth vet much longer," he said. "Could you do small-animal locums to get through the winter, and we'll see what the next busy season brings? We could still give you two days a week."

It was like a strange déjà vu. After transplanting myself from coast to coast, I would need small-animal work to get me through the winter once again. It was funny to me, but stranger still, it felt almost like a relief. I had to admit that I had not been able to stand toe to toe with him emotionally or professionally, and the strain of being back in the assistant's role was beginning to show. I thought I had a realistic view of what could be changed in this particular situation, and this domineering veterinarian was not going to change for me. The dynamic was not at all good for my spirits. I could take all the courses in the world to update my surgical techniques, but I would again be the nurse. I had to face the fact it was the way our personalities would always interact. I had misjudged—and put myself right back in the situation in which I had found myself in Toronto. Despite the years that had gone by, I was not up to maintaining the hard shell that would enable me to endure another apprenticeship. Perhaps this time I was just too old.

I went home and called my sister and Paul, to run it by them. I was not willing to struggle for the respect I felt I was entitled to and might never get. I went back the next day and quit my job.

🐎 🐎 🐎

The rest of the winter, I was inundated with requests for locum work, providing relief for both small-animal and equine veterinarians who needed time off. I was so busy with part-time work I could have worked seven days a week. There was no high-powered equine work in my life, but I often didn't have to be on call, either, in these positions, so it balanced out. I had a freedom, both in time and responsibility, I hadn't experienced in years. I also had the pleasure of meeting many veterinarians and sharing practice tips with all of them. I was offered seven jobs in the next six months. Two of them I particularly wanted to take, but I was hamstrung. My original non-competition clause prevented me from working full time for any one practice in that area for five years, and despite various letters and phone calls, it was not negotiable. The job I had been offered had not worked out, yet I could not take another. The weak point in my legal argument was that I had decided to leave Dr. Moore's practice. I was stuck. I had lots to do and enough money coming in, but I was definitely coasting. I could see, though, that it was a much-needed break.

One of the vets I worked for that spring specialized in reproduction. He was well versed in the newest techniques for artificial insemination and frozen semen and was beginning to work on embryo transfer when I started working for him. I became a regular there, and in breeding season often went to the breeding shed on my days off to follow the mares and learn new techniques, as little of this had been done in Nova Scotia.

As I had learned in Toronto, breeding with frozen semen can be tricky. It is incredibly labour intensive and not always successful even when done right. I wanted to become proficient in dealing with the mares, straws, and equipment, as this was clearly where the future of breeding lay. Embryo transfer was even trickier. A show mare can be bred to a top stallion, then the seven-day-old embryo flushed out of her uterus and collected in a Petri dish. It then has to be implanted in a mare of less value, the recipient, who will carry it to term. This can involve looking through several litres of fluid to find the tiny embryo and can meet failure at every turn, including rejection of the embryo by the recipient mare. It took me several weeks to feel comfortable with all the techniques and equipment.

It ended up being another giant step forward, as I knew I was playing catch-up for being six years on my own with limited equipment and numbers of mares to work on. As with dentistry, I was now riding the wave of a new level of equine medicine.

I felt privileged to have so many beautiful mares to work on. And because I worked on and off for several vets, I now had been in almost every barn in the Fraser Valley. Although it was totally different than what I had envisioned when moving out there, I was having fun. I had no regrets about leaving Dr. Moore.

When I did have time off, Elizabeth and I explored British Columbia. One outstanding summer weekend, we went kayaking in the Gulf Islands. Based out of Salt Spring Island, we discovered the different ocean world of the West Coast. The islands of Salt Spring and Galiano were enchanting; with an eclectic mix of artists and aging hippies, they have a flavour all their own. You could get there only by ferry or light airplane. The highlight of that particular weekend was seeing a pod of three killer whales migrating near shore at sunset. We sat on the rocks and watched them break the surface of the calm, silky water over and over. It is a magical sight unique to that part of Canada.

On another weekend, we travelled to Vancouver Island and made our way to Pacific Rim National Park to go whale watching. The town of Tofino is on the northwest end of twenty miles of dramatic, windswept beach. Its tourist industry revolves around the natural beauty of the area, the last old growth of temperate rain forest in the world, and whale watching. There are people there from all over the world. We elected to go out in a large Zodiac raft filled with two outboards rather than the larger, two-storey wooden craft offered. Running up that coastline in six-foot swells to see several humpbacks that had been spotted miles away, we were treated to an adventurous boat ride not for the faint of heart. The area is both wild and mystical, rich with native lore, art and culture. I felt totally in awe of the beauty I saw everywhere around me.

Easter was late that year, and spring was already well established in the Fraser Valley. The daffodils had come and gone. People were gardening and mowing, and the apple trees were in bloom. I had been invited, with another younger woman vet, to give lectures on sports medicine at a clinic in the interior near Kamloops. The clinic was for three-day event riders, and the practical portion was how to ride cross-country courses with young horses. Both of us had a young horse far enough along to take to the clinic and we were invited to ride gratis. I was extremely excited and rented a horse trailer for the weekend. I had the trusty Dodge dually. We headed out of the Fraser Valley at four on Good Friday afternoon, trying to get ahead of the rush of long-weekend traffic. It was sunny and beautiful, and many people were already on the road with boats and campers. Both of us were to lecture the next morning during the classroom sessions to be held before the four groups of riders began. We had lots of time to get there by early evening and meet people. But the Coquihalla had other plans.

The Coquihalla is nineteen miles of dramatic highway cut into the mountain. It goes straight up — or down, as the case may be — and can be intimidating, especially in bad weather. We were caught off guard shortly after we headed out in the sunshine. By the time we got to Hope, the traffic had gotten really heavy, and the sky looked threatening. A few drops of rain fell on the windshield of the truck, a standard transmission with no four-wheel drive or chains. Within half an hour, still climbing steadily with three lanes of socked-in traffic, we were in a snowstorm. Susie turned on the radio. They had closed the gate at the bottom of the Coquihalla, preventing more traffic from starting up, but we, along with many others, were stuck.

The surface of the highway was covered with frozen, rutted slush, and traffic was barely crawling. Transport trucks and cars started pulling out to the right until both right lanes were stopped. Those of us still trying to move up on the left were in trouble and, as my wheels started to slip and buck, I made a decision to pull in to the right between two transports. I had barely enough momentum to keep moving, but I managed to get the end of the trailer clear of the passing lane. I was on an angle across two lanes, and gradually all the car traffic crawling behind me up the mountain was forced to a halt as well.

We sat, thousands of cars and trucks stuck in the darkness, as the snow built up on our hoods and in the truck boxes. I had two large horses behind me, standing on an angle in the dark with no water and no place to unload. There was no way out of the mess we were in. We wrapped ourselves in horse blankets and sat, trying not to panic. It was really cold. The horses were doing surprisingly well, still eating hay and not pawing or objecting in any way. My companion and I, not well acquainted, sat in silent misery in the cab.

It took hours, but finally we saw help coming. A convoy of snowplows was winding its way up by moving cars or going between them. A salt truck followed, and some cars were moving out, following them. Gradually, more and more cars moved out, and by midnight some of the transports started out. I was one of the last to try it. I had to back out of the two feet of snow built up around the truck onto the frozen, packed lane that had been opened, still on a sharp uphill grade. With my standard truck heaving and the wheels slipping and grabbing we started to make our slow ascent up the steepest part of the Coquihalla. The horses stood stock-still. It took what seemed like forever to reach the top. There were still many miles of nasty, icy roads ahead of us. We pulled into the show ground at around seven a.m., two feet of snow on the roof of the truck. We were not only emotionally and physically spent, hungry, thirsty, and cold, but we were also worried about the horses.

Both of us elected to do our lectures at nine. Other people took care of our horses while some fed us breakfast and hot coffee. My shakes were disappearing when I stood up in front of the forty or so riders. By noon when my group rode, I felt able to join in, and my horse and I had a fantastic weekend learning to jump down banks and do sandy slopes and water. The drive home was uneventful. I have never been able to describe the experience in a way that came close to the reality of being on the mountain that night in a sudden blizzard with the two horses.

Elizabeth and I had discovered a secret riding trail through a tiny, little-used park that felt amazingly like a haunted forest. Just on the outskirts of Langley, it boasted a few massive, first-growth cedars, with the dark, twisting, up-and-down paths of cedar bark snaking around and over the impressive roots. Moss hung from and coated the spooky, long-armed trees. The forest embraced us happily and hid us from the swirl of the busy expressways and rat race so close by. On a rainy day, with wax jackets on, we often were the only humans in the park. Our companions were the giant banana slugs, the slinking coyotes, and our horses. Some of the trails were so steep that the horses slid down the moist bark on their hocks. It was a treasured escape for both of us.

Elizabeth had dropped in to a nearby show stable soon after we found our wonderful rental house. It was around a "city block" from our farm and would be an ideal place to work. She got along instantly with the talented jumper pro who ran the barn and soon noticed that everything was done in top form, from the schooling program for the clients and their horses to the horse care itself. After a quick interview, Elizabeth was offered a job riding there. It seemed another case of being in the right place at the right time, as they had just lost their professional rider. Throughout our time in the Fraser Valley, Elizabeth continued to thrive on the atmosphere and instruction there, schooling young hunters every day and getting to the occasional show. Backing their young stallion was an effort well rewarded by seeing him win classes at Spruce Meadows his first time out. Unbelievably, she could ride her horse to work every day via a narrow, paved road connecting the two farms. Lined with hedges, twisting and turning past secret driveways and paddock fences, travelling the Telegraph trail felt as if one had been transported to England. What a commute — while thousands sat on the slick Trans-Canada Highway, Elizabeth puttered along on a loose rein!

Life was surprisingly lonely outside of work for both of us. It wasn't that we weren't accepted; it was just that no one was interested. It seemed as if people had just had enough of other people and newcomers. If the imposing gates and alarm systems didn't drive that home, the guard dogs did. Friday nights were a highlight, with a trip to the grocery store or perhaps a dinner on a café patio. We both missed our families. Time went by slowly outside of work. Both of us knew we had to have a break after the stress of leaving Nova Scotia, and the rest and the new routine were healing. But after a few months of homesickness and dealing with the disappointment of moving 5,000 miles for a job that scarcely existed, I was keeping up a braver façade than I felt. It turned out Elizabeth was doing the same, though she loved her job. We were both Ontario girls.

🐎 🐎 🐎

Breeding season was starting to slow down when I got my first call from Jim. He sounded upset. I hadn't heard from him in a long while.

"Are you interested in the practice?" he asked. I was blown away. I hadn't heard from him since last Christmas, as we had kept in touch infrequently over the years. I was up on his life enough to know he had purchased land in Nova Scotia and he and his wife wished to move there. I heard he was selling the practice but didn't know another vet had just set up in town. Jim now felt his practice was not going to sell easily or for nearly as much as he'd hoped.

"I'll think about it," I replied.

"I'll send out the last two years' financial statements," he said, encouraged, adding, "I think you are the only person who could make it work. There are still a lot of people here who remember you." It had been nine years.

It was exciting food for thought. I knew we would never be able to afford a farm in the Fraser Valley even if I had been released from my contract with Dr. Moore. Both of us were homesick for family and friends in Ontario. Despite my years in Nova Scotia, I deeply felt the Ottawa Valley was home. I took the financial statements to an accountant as soon as they arrived. I was tremendously excited, but did we have the strength to make one more move?

"The price is a bit high," he said. "I'm not sure the practice profit would support the debt you'd have."

I still had a nest egg from Nova Scotia to put in, but the figures didn't work out. I was discouraged. I didn't have enough to put in to buy the practice. I called Jim with a negative answer. He sounded as disappointed as I was.

Several days later, he called back. "Just come home. I want you to have it. We'll work something out," he said.

"What do you mean?" I asked.

"We'll make it work," he assured me. "I want to be out east for Christmas."

Because it was Jim and only because it was Jim, I believed him. Elizabeth had no trouble agreeing to Ontario as home. We decided to buy a stock trailer, rent a large moving truck, and take the horses and furniture home ourselves, in a convoy. It took only two weeks to organize. It was August. We had been in British Columbia a little over a year when we pulled out.

The trip home was another adventure. I had decided to call ahead and ask vet clinics to recommend overnight digs for the horses in each different city. Usually it was easy to find a stable owner who would permit us to put them out in their ring overnight. We stayed at the track in Regina, at a vet's stable in Thunder Bay. For each of the six days, we loaded them and drove twelve hours. At night, we looked after ourselves and the two dogs and one cat last. Each day, the horses accommodatingly jumped onto the open-sided trailer with two large box stalls. Our little train of truck, trailer, and the big diesel moving van trekked across the country. Slowly, as a result of one phone call, we were going home.

The end of the trip was the yard at Anne's farm. The two tired horses moved about the grass paddock slowly, stiff and sore, as we all embraced each other. This time I had no doubt that, thanks to Jim, I really was home. With an overwhelming feeling of relief, I let myself believe I wouldn't have to try so hard any more. I started work the next day.

SIXTEEN

HOME IS
WHERE THE HEART IS

AS GOOD AS IT WAS to be back, things were challenging at Brentwood for the first few months. For one thing, most of the staff had jumped ship, unsure how things would go with a new owner. The ones who had known me had long since moved to other jobs, and the few that stayed on were uncertain.

During the first few weeks, I had to staff the hospital with old friends. Elizabeth and I provided a framework of stability and filled in all positions as needed from receptionist to kennel assistant. The computers were old and crashed often, and the clinic had lost something since my first time there in its heyday. There were dustballs in the corners and the windows leaked. It was obvious that Jim had been departing emotionally for a while. It was as if the spark had gone, or perhaps the magic of the place. But then, it could have been rose-coloured glasses that had created the fond, nostalgic aura of magic I believed the old place held.

Kate, the technician who had stayed on, worked very differently than I did, and an unfortunate power struggle ensued. This made surgery days unpleasant. One day we were preparing to anaesthetize a cat for a spay and declaw. When I told her I would like to anaesthetize and intubate the patient, she assured me that she had always done this for Jim and could use the student to hold the animal. When I approached the animal five minutes later, it was indeed intubated and lying on its back, being clipped for the spay. However, it took me only a minute to see its tongue was grey-blue and it wasn't breathing properly.

"This patient is in trouble—get the tube out, I'll re-intu-bate," I barked.

Kate paled and quickly deflated and pulled out the cuffed endotracheal tube. A quick look told me it was full of bile-stained saliva and had been in the esophagus. Blowing it out quickly, I reinserted it into the trachea and started ventilating the little animal with the re-breathing bag. Within seconds its colour returned to pink and within a minute its heart strengthened. I decided to carry on with surgery when all the vital signs were normal, and, because the kitten was young and strong, it did well. It was embarrassing and traumatic for Kate, who definitely learned that day, the hard way, the futility of a power struggle. Things were more peaceful after that, but we were still uncomfortable working together.

The computer system was starting to crash more and more often and at critical times. Sometimes on Saturday mornings when we would have many people lined up to buy pet food, words and numbers would start rolling randomly across the screen as if to say "too much!" Other times, deposits were printed out reversed or with missing transactions—causing confusion and frustration at the end of a long day. Within two months, I knew I would have to spend unexpected thousands on a new computer system.

Another challenge was the lack of equipment to do horse work. In the years since I had been away, the equine business had been let go, and the tools had suffered similar attrition over the ten years. I had left all of my equipment in Nova Scotia. There were a few rusty tooth floats, an ancient, broken, portable x-ray, and a mouldy stomach tube, but not much else. It was a far cry from the equipment I had to work with in the Fraser Valley. Supplies could be immediately ordered, and within two weeks, I had a rudimentary equine set-up. Unfortunately, the two most expensive items would have to wait. Both a portable x-ray machine and an ultrasound machine cost thousands. How could I get going without them? After I had been back a few weeks, inundated with horse work, I decided I had to find a way and managed to find both machines, used. Luckily I found out I could lease even used equipment, a practice quite common in the medical field. It provided me with a way to buy them over time and in addition would create full payment write-offs for my business. This was a great new management tool for me. There was so much still to learn about running a business. Even after my experience in Nova Scotia, I still felt like a novice.

Cattlemen wandered in all fall asking for products they had always bought at Brentwood. With regret, we sheepishly had to tell them we had discontinued carrying their medicines, as we could no longer look after their livestock. After many years with Jim, it was a difficult adjustment for them, and as it turned out, created some resentment in the farm community.

One Saturday, I attended a local auction, very much enjoying the outing and the popular Lanark fall ritual. It was partly bargain shopping and partly a celebration of the end of harvest season and a good opportunity to visit with friends. I was always looking for antiques, although my house was already too full of them. It turned out to be a perfect Thanksgiving weekend with a blue sky, warm breeze, and brilliant orange leaves complementing the brown hues of the harvested fields. Lines of pickup trucks signalled the spot. The secretary's booth and hot chocolate stand were busy, and the lines of farm machinery were gleaming. It was an excellent auction with wonderful, well-maintained farm equipment. As I walked along a display of tools lined up on the lawn, I saw one of my favourite farmers. I had done a lot of work and many calvings for him in my first career at Brentwood. Expecting a warm response, I greeted him. "Beautiful day to be out, Moe."

"Funny to see you here—I thought you'd given up on the farmers," he muttered.

"It's been good to be back in the Valley," I stammered, trying again.

"Guess you're pretty busy, then, looking after horses and horse people," he said.

I did not know how to respond. After a pause I said, "I did

not feel I could help you properly, as I haven't done cattle for so long. I'm really sorry."

We both looked away at the same time, but it was hard for me to accept that the goodwill I had had with these fantastic, salt of the earth, Lanark farm people was tarnished and our relationship damaged.

By late fall, Elizabeth and I still had not found a place to live. We were renting a tiny, non-winterized cottage on a lake near town and the many drafts were becoming evident in the bitter cold. Our horses, in a field nearby with not much but a water trough and sparse fall grass, were starting to feel sorry for themselves, despite two daily feeds and weatherproof blankets. Now, a skim of ice had to be broken at the trough each morning when we showed up to placate them and apologize for their rough accommodations. I was starting to feel desperate, as I had anticipated finding a hobby farm to rent long before this.

One morning in late November, we woke up to find that winter had started early. Ten inches of fluffy snow had fallen overnight. The trees and beautiful split-rail fences were decorated in pristine white coats. Although it melted quickly, it gave us a taste of the Valley winter that was to come. That day brought a much-needed break on the housing front through the visit of an old friend.

Gracie McLeod had been a client with Brentwood for years, but she and her husband had given up horses. She appeared at the clinic with no animal that day and asked to speak to me.

"I have been thinking about it, and I think our farm would be perfect for you," she said. My heart leapt. Their special, very private property was within ten minutes of the clinic. Even better, it had a wonderful, eclectic house with personality and potential and a classic Lanark log barn, well set up for five or six horses.

"Come for dinner tonight and we'll talk about it," she said.

I tried not to be too optimistic, but I knew it felt right. It seemed as if fate had once again intervened at a critical time. I was prepared to act fast. Mrs. McLeod had explained that they had purchased a winterized cottage on the Rideau River and wanted to move quickly.

A tour of the hobby farm confirmed my feeling that Lady Luck had smiled on us yet again. The long laneway led to a secluded, park-like enclave, and the perennial beds just peeking out from beneath the new snow promised a beautiful spring display. The shingled house had a Maritime feel, and I could see immediately how it could feel like home.

Mr. McLeod had just done extensive barn renovations, and the structure was sound, with only some chinking to finish in the log barn. The horses could be moved right in. A long walk out to the back half of the property revealed first a mature oak and maple forest with winding trails, then cedar groves with a large beaver pond at the far end of the path.

"We ski and skate out here," Mrs. McLeod said. It all seemed too good to be true. It only took a week to arrange a price and private mortgage. December first was decided on as the closing date. On that day, many friends showed up to help paint the entire house from top to bottom, and the move was easy on the second.

I found myself hoping, as I took things out of boxes and unpacked them, that my rambling days were over for a while. Although she didn't have the same memories of Brentwood or the Valley, Elizabeth seemed to be falling in love with Lanark, too. This move might signal the end of a long path home.

🐎 🐎 🐎

My first real test with the horse community came in early December. The work was difficult and dramatic, and for people I did not know. I had never had a problem such as the one presented to me this bitter, cold day. The emergency call came in on a Saturday afternoon. Three Percherons had fallen through the ice of a swamp half a mile behind the horse farm of a young horseman, and the whole local community had gotten involved in trying to rescue them. Would it be possible for me to come and help?

I took the icy trail to the back property on the back of an

ATV with my gear on my lap. A distressing sight greeted me. Though one horse had been rescued, two remained trapped in the shallow, icy pond. They had struggled so much that one lay exhausted with its head and neck on the ice and the rest of its body submerged. The sky was charcoal grey and foreboding with the threat of snow and cold wind. One of the huge, grey beasts stood, but broke the surface of the ice with each attempt at a step forward. There were fifteen men, a tractor, hay bales, and rope scattered about. Some neighbours left with the walking animal and promised to come back with hot coffee and reinforcements.

The first prone horse finally had a rope girth secured over its withers and behind its front legs, at great sacrifice to the farmer who had carried the rope under and around the animal in the cold water. The rope was attached through the halter to the tractor and the pull to solid ground began. After much bucking and thrashing and more broken ice, the frozen swamp finally held. The horse skidded on its knees a dozen feet before it got its footing and stood. It was dried with hay, covered with a blanket, and led slowly back.

The last mare was losing strength, and hypothermia and muscle cramps were getting the best of it. She was getting too weak to fight. I knew that we didn't have too much longer to save her from the terrible cold. Again, a second man managed to get ropes under and around her mid-section, with a separate one tied around the neck and halter. A bed of hay was laid forty feet along on the ice and the tractor once again attached to the horse. With nothing to lose, the animal was pulled forward until the ice held and it slipped along over the bed of hay. Occasionally fighting to stand, she finally reached shore, but could not get up. I administered a mild sedative to stop her from thrashing, and the weak but still magnificent Percheron was trussed and rolled onto a stone boat for the ride home. The tractor rolled slowly down the now dark path in the gathering snow with its precious cargo in tow. On reaching the barn, the man backed the tractor into a shed, and she was rolled onto a bed of straw.

Frantic attempts to warm and revive the mare were

working. Heating blankets and blow dryers, brandy and sugar were all used. I hooked up an IV and ran warm fluids into her. Six hours later, she stood, but the down side and leg were obviously severely damaged and painful. She lived, though two weeks later all the skin sloughed off her left hind leg and haunches. Rick, the owner, did the long months of nursing faithfully, and I did not see her again for a long while. I was gratified to hear she was in foal the next summer.

Around this time, the sole staff member I had inherited from Jim announced she was going back to school in January. Our rapport had never been great though we had achieved a reasonable peace once our power struggle had resolved. It seemed the best for both of us. I needed another technician desperately. A veterinarian I was speaking to said, "You might try Erin Smith; she has recently stopped working at Dempster's clinic—tired of the drive, I guess. She lives near Brentwood and I think you two would get along. I told her you were looking."

An interview of this obviously competent woman revealed extensive experience and more than a little spark. After many questions back and forth about skills and responsibilities, I offered her a job. There was no doubt in my mind she was of the old school, both in work ethic and sensibilities, having worked in a farm practice.

"Dr. Martin told me we would be a great match," she said, "as I generally don't have to be told anything twice!"

I laughed, my reputation for liking people quick on the uptake having obviously preceded me. Perhaps, alternatively, it was a reputation for a certain lack of patience. Whatever the case, I felt Erin and I already had a certain understanding, and with her country background and mixed practice experience she seemed a logical part of the team. We rolled into the New Year setting up our new computer system together. I was constantly impressed with what Erin could do, juggling the front and back and sorting out glitches in technology at the same time. With both the home and business fronts getting sorted out nicely, I could breathe a sigh of relief. At least it seemed okay to breathe and just enjoy Christmas with family and friends.

One of the greatest things about being home in Lanark was that my sister Anne had two wonderful girls, and I loved being an aunt. My nieces, Kate and Court, were already avid horsewomen at five and seven years, and showed the unflagging devotion of true horse lovers, showing up in the barn day after day. They just kept getting more excited with learning about horses and riding all the time. Neither flies nor heat nor hard work could turn them off, and I loved teaching them all I had learned, as did Anne.

It was a joy to be their doting aunt, and I bought them a beautiful white Welsh pony the first summer I was home. She was hidden in a log shed and presented with a big red bow around her neck. Still small enough to ride double, the girls put her through her paces perfectly that first night, bareback, out on the beautiful spring green lawn. With smiles a mile wide and joyous laughter, they trotted bumpily around the huge maple trees on the front lawn. They really seemed to appreciate their special gift and opportunity. Did they somehow know then that their "Aunty" would be a lifelong supporter in their chosen sport?

"Fancy" was well trained and knew her job, but would unceremoniously dump any child on her ear if she got too cocky. We had a lot of laughs as the kids learned to ride her and went on to show her, always game to climb back on if they ended up on the ground. There were lots of ribbons at the local fairs and shows the first year, and, as it turned out, many more horses and ribbons to come. I was happy to take a backseat role in the teaching and just be there for the fun when I could. How wonderful to have a family sport and hand it over to the next generation with love and just see it keep on growing!

SEVENTEEN

NOEL'S NINE LIVES

BUSINESS WAS BRISK at Brentwood our first spring. The phones were busy, and it was difficult for all of us to get our work done and juggle phone calls. We were often in desperate straits in the waiting room, especially on Saturdays when the clients were too often getting poor service or waiting far too long, as in so many cases since my return. Then the right person to rectify the situation walked in the door.

Jill, an experienced veterinary receptionist, bred German short-hair pointers and had a lot of experience with horses as well, having been a Pony Club commissioner. After twenty years with two other clinics, she had moved to our area. She was businesslike and to the point and could do our bookkeeping as well. I snapped her up. She needed no training and took over the front as the busy spring season began. The time of year for the birth of puppies, kittens, and foals, as well as heartworm testing season, keeps a small-animal vet running in May. Added to that rush, the horse clients dust off their mounts after a long winter, and phone in, needing annual checkups and vaccinations. The business of horse breeding starts in May in this valley, and we anticipated a rush of activity in that sphere, as well. All systems were in place.

Marg Zwicker was one of our steady clients. Four foot eleven inches tall and round, she reminded one of a jolly Mrs. Santa Claus, complete with the twinkling eyes. She came in almost weekly with her tiny, but also very round, Shi Tzu, Lady.

Living alone and loving the attention we gave her, Mrs. Zwicker always found a small medical complaint to give her a reason to visit. Often she brought cookies, rich shortbreads being her specialty. Her husband had died two years ago and she did not drive, so getting a taxi to and fro was part of her routine. Lady often needed her nails trimmed, as she didn't walk much, but she might also come in for runny eyes or a slight cough. Over time, she had developed some bronchitis and a mild case of collapsing trachea, common in small-breed, overweight dogs. Stress could cause her to become cyanotic, her tongue turning blue as she was deprived of oxygen, and we had to be very careful working with her. We were often reminded by Mrs. Zwicker that "She's all I've got." Lady got fed three times a day with a spoon. She lived her life on Mrs. Zwicker's lap.

Erin and I had worked out a great system of shared responsibility, emphasizing each of our strong points. I soon learned she could be trusted to do all the anaesthetic procedures safely, and I would work on one animal after another as she prepared them. One of the first difficult lessons we learned that spring had to do with the dangers of altering routine or equipment. We had a six-month-old tortoiseshell kitten to spay in the spring. She belonged to a new client who had just moved from the city so I did not know her well. The cat had been a Christmas present, thus her very apt name, "Noel."

Her pre-anaesthetic checkup was good, and all went well until I moved her into surgery myself. Erin had not had time to check the pop-off valve in the surgery room where we had our gas anaesthetic machine, something she usually did. This valve is critical in letting excess pressure out of the gas system. She thought I would certainly have done it but I had the surgical set-up on my mind and proceeded to drape the kitten and lay out my packs, after putting her on the oxygen gas mixture. Moments later, Erin came into the room and, with a glance at the fully inflated re-breathing bag, realized something was wrong. One quick movement and she was at the machine letting off the valve and the pressure. We'd hardly had time to speak about it before we realized our patient was in distress. Noel's gums were white and she could not breathe normally. My heart was racing and

I managed to croak, "Set up the x-ray machine. I'll bag her—I think she may have pneumothorax!"

Pneumothorax is a condition where air leaks out of a tear in one or both lungs, creating a positive pressure in the chest, where a vacuum should exist, and severely inhibiting breathing. I had caused the problem with excess pressure from the gas machine. Pneumothorax is life-threatening and demands immediate emergency procedures based on draining the excess air out of the chest.

I yelled for Elizabeth. An x-ray showed one lung was torn and collapsed and was surrounded by air. We flew into emergency mode, Elizabeth ventilating the little animal to keep its blood oxygen up. Erin clipped and prepped the chest, while I gathered gloves and a chest tube. In such a situation, adrenalin is high. Everyone was flustered and very worried, but teamwork prevailed. After one hour, Noel was stabilized. With the small chest tube in and a bandaged chest, she was breathing on her own. I felt she was out of the woods and decided to call the owner. Not only would I have a most difficult explanation to make, I would also have to spay Noel at another time. I sat with my head in my hands gathering my thoughts. Nervously, I dialled the client's work phone number and got her immediately. Not long into it, however, the conversation took an unexpected turn. I opened my mouth to start.

"We had a problem with Noel's anaesthetic," I began, hesitantly. "She had a breathing problem and we had to clip her chest and do emergency procedures—but she's okay. She is bandaged and will be here for a couple days." I managed to get all this out before Mrs. Mains interrupted me. I had not had a chance to tell her that her cat had not been spayed.

"Oh, I know why she had problems breathing," she exclaimed, "One of my children fell on her last week. I was worried about broken ribs."

I had been rescued and am not proud to say that I took the coward's way out. Perhaps I shouldn't have, but I made a split-second decision to capitulate, so relieved that she wasn't angry.

"I'm sure it will be fine in a month or six weeks, let's give her time to heal and spay her in a couple of months. She doesn't go out, does she? She won't get pregnant?" I asked the client.

"No," replied the owner, "that will be fine." When Noel went home with a shaved patch on her chest, the client was surprisingly unruffled. Erin and I, however, were shaken, and it took us several weeks to relax and recover from the traumatic anaesthetic experience. We have double- and triple-checked every hose and valve since.

Around the same time, we had another very uncommon anaesthetic experience that really cemented our ability to work as a team in an emergency. When an animal has a rare adverse reaction, teamwork and speed are critical, and it turned out we had the right combination of personal dynamics and skills to jump into action when needed. It can be the undoing of the relationship between a veterinarian and his or her veterinary nurses if resuscitation does not go well even once. Confidence both in the process and your fellow team members is one of paramount importance.

The scheduling of a male puppy neutering is considered routine, and so it was with Benson, the eight-month-old chocolate lab presented to us one Tuesday. Although he was a bit smaller and quieter than a usual chocolate boy, he was in good spirits and all his vitals checked well. "What a love," Erin declared as he licked her face while we induced his anaesthetic with the first intravenous dose. As soon as he was on his side with his endotracheal tube in place, we noticed his colour—it was blue-grey. I checked the valves urgently and gave him a breath.

"I'm sure I have the tube in place," I said. "I saw it go in the trachea!" Hurriedly, I bagged again, but noticed his chest still did not expand properly. We checked the tube placement by pulling it out and replacing it. It was correct, all right, but we still could not get his chest to expand normally. The same sick, panicky feeling that had happened with Noel's emergency started to well up. My heart beat rapidly, and all of us were turning red. "Please set up the x-ray plate, Erin. I'll bag." I tried desperately to improve his colour as his heart weakened. The x-ray shocked us. The young dog's chest was full of golf ball-sized tumours, likely lymphoma, so full the lungs had lost elasticity and could not expand with my attempts at ventilation. It was unbelievable that Benson was not thin or coughing and that the outward lymph nodes were normal. He had likely been presented to us just before becoming a very sick puppy.

It was all incredibly uncommon and unfair. The clients were lovely, and I did not want to break the news to them. It took all our skill to breathe for and recover Benson while the iv we had given him wore off. With sadness, I had to call them in to look at the terrible radiographs. They elected to have a few more days with Benson before bringing him back to put him to sleep. None of us wanted to see him suffer. I have never seen a case such as this again.

We had not heard from Mrs. Zwicker for a few weeks, which was most uncommon. One day, her daughter called to say she had had a mild stroke, but was at home recovering; it seemed that only her speech had been permanently affected. She booked an appointment to drive Mrs. Zwicker over with Lady, as Lady's toenails needed a trim. Her daughter mentioned Lady was not active and didn't seem to be herself, but guessed that she had missed her owner's attention during her hospital stay.

When they arrived, it was clear that as Mrs. Zwicker's health had deteriorated, so had Lady's. Mrs. Zwicker cried as she got hugs all around. We could see she had slowed speech and a new droopy look to the left side of her face. We could barely pry her beloved pet out of her arms to examine her. I think their separation had taken a toll on both of them. Lady appeared lethargic and had occasional fits of coughing. We were told that she had hardly moved around in the past week and her famous appetite was not the same. With chest radiographs it became apparent that she was suffering from congestive heart failure as well as the collapsing trachea. Each breath had become an effort, and Lady was also becoming dehydrated.

The cycle of birth and death is part of our everyday life at Brentwood. We see puppies and kittens in appointments followed closely by animals with cancer or terminal diseases. Often the loss of a pet is the first loss a young family suffers, and we are trained to guide people through this very difficult experience. As well, since we look after an animal from youth to the end of its life, part of our mandate is to help a client decide when his or her pet is suffering and there is no hope for recovery. At no time is this counselling more difficult than in the situation I now faced. Often seniors who have lost their spouse feel their pet is their only link to that beloved partner and their past. In fact, it may be their most important emotional touchstone. I certainly knew that Mrs. Zwicker's health was profoundly tied to Lady's well-being.

"There are a few things we can do for her," I began, "but we may not be able to give her a long time, because she has two serious problems."

Mrs. Zwicker, sitting in a chair in the exam room with her daughter's hand resting on her shoulder, seemed to get even smaller. She tried not to cry anymore, chin quivering. "How long will I have her?" she asked.

"We will treat her congestive heart failure and rehydrate her as well. Let us have her here in the hospital today. Unfortunately there is no easy treatment for her narrowed trachea," I said, deeply concerned about stressing both patient and owner.

With all the trust and confidence in us she could muster, Mrs. Zwicker left her dog. Several injections of diuretic were needed to relieve her pulmonary edema, and a slow intravenous drip improved her hydration. At the end of the day, Lady was allowed to go home with cautions that she might have to come back tomorrow. The morning phone call indicated she had eaten a bit, so we cautiously proceeded with oral medications. Mrs. Zwicker's daughter, who was staying longer, assured me that they would be given. Several days passed with no word about Lady. We cautiously hoped for the best. On day five, I received a panicky phone call. Lady couldn't stand and appeared to have collapsed and was in distress. By the time they pulled up and rushed her in, her tongue was blue and she had wet herself. Mrs.

Zwicker was helped to a chair in the waiting area and sat quietly while we put Lady in an oxygen chamber. I walked slowly up to the front. "We can give her additional diuretics and bronchodilators," I said. She stopped me.

"I know what's best." I could barely hear her. "She's not coming home."

I was relieved for Lady and, selfishly, for myself. Mrs. Zwicker had made the decision that needed to be made by her alone, without persuasion. But at that instant, I would have given anything to have been able to take away even a small portion of the pain I saw in that diminutive lady's eyes. "I cannot see her again," she whispered, "but I would like her ashes back."

I nodded slowly, and then helped her to the car. Several weeks later, her daughter dropped in to say Mrs. Zwicker had died. She had been happy that she had never had to leave her home. She knew we would want to know that Lady's ashes would be buried with her mother. None of us could express our feelings adequately or thank her enough for coming in to tell us. I experienced an unexpected emptiness as I walked to my car that day, knowing I would miss both of them for a very long time. Mrs. Zwicker had become so special to all of us it was truly like losing a family member.

🐾 🐾 🐾

Once in a while, we had an accidental false alarm at Brentwood, usually a loose animal that had escaped from its cage. I would be awakened by a call at an ungodly hour and instructed to meet the police. Luckily we had not had a break-in up to this point, but these calls were annoying, and we were charged for them. This bitter cold night was no exception. As I entered the building with the two police officers at three in the morning, I saw a small black cat near the back door. I had left at suppertime and noticed the wild female cat in our indoor dog run, in yet another metal cage. A barn cat, she could not be easily handled and had been put in the wire cage to recover from her hysterectomy to avoid stress to her and us when the owners came to get her. She was to be picked up early in the morning of the next day. The top door of the Dutch doors had been left open for air circulation, and the one-inch square mesh of the smaller cage should have been secure. I had experienced a moment's doubt about the open top door of the run and, as it turned out, should have followed my instincts and closed it.

How would we ever catch the terrified animal in the large clinic with its many nooks and crannies? She would surely panic as we approached. As one policeman and I approached, she bolted for the bathtub room, crouched low to the floor. As we cornered her, she leapt to the edge of the slippery tub, then, defying gravity, started climbing the wall. The policeman yelled, "I'll grab her, I know animals," unwittingly doing exactly the wrong thing in an effort to help me. Before I could speak or suggest we use gloves or a snare, he had encircled her with two hands just below her front legs. Everything was happening too quickly, and the little cat, her head unrestrained, nailed him with her teeth. Her canines completely penetrated the base of one thumb, and he let out a yell and dropped her. We cleaned up his wound and started again to search for our feline escape artist in the darkened clinic. We spotted her near the front, where she had darted under the reception desk. At that point, the other officer, having stepped outside for a cigarette, opened the front door. Blackie saw an opportunity. In a flash she was out the door into the night. I gulped. Why had I not called off the search after we had the first mishap? Some settling down time would have helped, and I could have thought of a better plan. Adrenalin had taken over, and now it was too late.

We had lost someone's cat. Though she was wild, they had obviously cared enough to spay her. I called them in the morning. The owners came every day and called for her, but Blackie was nowhere to be seen. We put food outside, but after two weeks it was still there. We had all given up hope as the weeks went by and turned into a month. Despite the fact that she had been a barn cat, the owners were attached to her and were very worried. It was an unsettling feeling for all, not knowing what had happened to her.

Two months had passed when I went to get some hardware from a store, three buildings down the road. As I walked from my car to the front door, I saw a black cat out of the corner of my eye. Something told me it might be Blackie. On enquiring, I learned she had shown up there one day two months ago and they had been feeding her. A recent spay scar and a little white star on her chest confirmed her identity, and she was returned to her owners, much to the relief of everyone.

EIGHTEEN

JAMES THE THIRD

JAMES THE THIRD was my amazing flame-point Siamese cat. With the uncanny smarts of a dog, he had ridden across Canada twice in the front seat of the car, appearing to enjoy the scenery. Like his two predecessors, he had deep orange "points" and vivid sapphire-blue eyes that looked right at you. He could carry on a conversation. He was, at times, regal and at others annoying, as he wakened the household with bloodcurdling yowls at five a.m. He could play mind games with guests, hissing at them to keep them off his chair, allowing toddlers to carry him around upside down. You couldn't pill him "no how."

James had a couple of great years on the new farm. He often travelled far afield and was several times returned by neighbours annoyed with his yodelling. One November night, at the beginning of hunting season, he did not return. It was too cold for him to stray far, so we knew something was amiss. When the next afternoon brought no sign of him, I knew he was in trouble. We called neighbours and vet clinics to no avail. After stomping through the woods calling didn't work, and with worsening weather, we started a phone-call and poster campaign. After a week, we had all but given up. What a terrible feeling it is not to know what has happened to your animal. And there were fishers out there.

A child's voice on the answering machine gave us our only lead. "I think I saw your cat on Quarry Road," the little voice said, leaving no number or address. Well, at least it was *something*.

Elizabeth spent two days driving slowly up and down the dirt road five kilometres from home. On the last day before snow, she turned her head right and saw something white hop at the back of a hay field, far from the road. It was a quick movement in the grass that could have easily been missed, but something told her it was James. Running across the field calling him, she heard the unique voice, weak but recognizable. She scooped him up, hind leg dangling, and paged me, breathless.

"James is alive, I found James!" she exclaimed, thrilled.

"I'll meet you at the clinic," I replied, turning my car around.

The cat's leg was badly fractured and he had lost half his body weight. His tail had been shattered by the same careless, cruel shot that had broken his leg. There was a large healing wound in the cold, hairless tail. I doubted it would heal fully, as the circulation was so damaged. I decided to amputate the leg in a week when he had gained some strength, and give the tail a chance for a few weeks. Though battered and dehydrated, he seemed as happy as we were, purring on the treatment table as we put in an IV. The surgery went well, and the crooked tail healed and regrew hair. Though a shadow of his younger self, he has survived many years on three legs—body rearranged, but spirit intact.

Each spring, horse owners dust off their mounts and breeding horses and prepare for a busy show season or a new foal. For many breeders, it is a time to dream of producing a beautiful animal or a top-performance horse. For riders, there may be a dream of sunny spring trail rides or of winning a red ribbon or championship at a show. It is a time of optimism. One of the most enjoyable parts of this annual ritual for breeders is choosing a stallion with which to breed your mare. In this world of technology and science, artificial breeding had become the norm in the horse world. Top-class stallions from all over the world are available to more and more owners through the use of cooled or frozen semen.

Although I had learned a lot in British Columbia, I decided to take an update on artificial insemination in Colorado, where world experts provide short courses several times a year. I wanted to start out back at Brentwood armed with the most up-to-date credentials and knowledge possible. Using cooled or chilled stallion semen, the veterinarian has a larger window to follow the mare's cycle and predict the time of ovulation and to order the breeding dose from the stallion owner. The cooled semen is sent by courier or airplane, picked up by the mare owner, and deposited into the mare, where it can live up to forty-eight hours.

When using frozen semen, the mare owner must arrange for a portable canister of liquid nitrogen containing several sealed straws of semen to be shipped to the veterinarian, where it can wait safely frozen until the appointed time comes. The canister contains hazardous material, and not only is there danger from a spill, but any problem with the contents or temperature could cause the semen to be lost and the straws ruined. These straws are purchased by breeding dose, and each stallion owner charges a different amount for these doses, usually quite a lot, and often non-refundable. Each breeding dose is determined to be a specific number of straws depending on the potency of and preparation required for that animal.

In addition to this intensive work at the stallion's farm, the mare owner is highly involved in the mare's preparation. The veterinarian must visit the mare many times, ensuring she is free of uterine fluid and infection and following her cycle with a transrectal ultrasound probe. Mares must be trained to accept these invasive procedures and some need to be tranquillized initially. There is also that final consideration in the frozen insemination process—frozen semen is fragile and can be damaged by preservation at such low temperatures. Although it may look and move fairly normally under a microscope, its strength and ability to penetrate an ovum are compromised. This means the veterinarian must insert it as closely as possible to the time of ovulation, even if it's in the middle of the night. This can mean the vet has to visit and examine the mare many times around the clock, all on top of a very busy spring schedule. It is certainly a project that can't be undertaken half-heartedly.

Armed with my updated knowledge and equipment, I contracted to breed three mares in our area with one famous dressage stallion. A group of friends from several different stables, all dressage aficionados, had decided to buy doses of frozen semen together, and I agreed to receive and maintain the canister. All three animals were to come to a central barn near the clinic. The Jameses' farm had lush, green pastures, ideal for improving cycling in the patients. All were pre-certified free of infection and in good reproductive health according to their own veterinarians. Our project began in early May. Two mares were young, but one large chestnut warmblood had had many foals and had a uterus so large and pendulous it was hard to reach it all with my probe. This exam was carried out standing on my toes on a hay bale with my arm fully inserted in the mare. Day after day, we scanned the mares, waiting for their cycles to start. After a few days, all the mare owners agreed to synchronize the mares with hormone treatments so that they might cycle predictably and close together—saving work, time, and money for all of us.

Mrs. White, who owned the older mare, acknowledged we might have some difficulties with her fertility, but we optimistically began the process, not knowing what was ahead of us. We were committed.

After ten days of hormone treatments, the work began in earnest. Each day I met these patient owners at the farm and examined their even more patient animals trans-rectally. Finally we agreed that one owner would come and handle all three mares once daily. The tolerant animals were led into a set of wooden stocks, evacuated of manure, and ultrasounded for a maturing follicle over and over again. We were running out of things to talk about.

Finally, two seemed ready to breed; a large, soft follicle was present, and we stepped up the exams to three times daily so as not to miss the optimum timing. The old mare just did not seem to respond. Perhaps her age was against her, and she would need more time and priming. We were ready to proceed with the other two mares, and I called in extra help for the big event. Others were needed to thaw the straws in a water bath and to wash the mares. My old friend Mary, a nurse, volunteered to help. At midnight, we all gathered and set up to thaw and inject the precious material. Each dose was to be four tiny 5-ml straws, thawed, gathered into a test tube, drawn into a pipette, and injected the two feet into the cavernous uterus. From there, the trip to the fallopian tubes could be another two feet of traversing the torturous uterine wall. If the ovum did not rupture, the weakened semen could not wait long before dying. By midnight, both mares were inseminated. We all went to bed, agreeing to meet at seven in the morning and hoping for the best.

The exam the next morning found only one mare had ovulated, meaning the second was not co-operating and would have to be redone. The follicle remained present and un-ruptured, and she had not responded as predicted.

"We will examine her again this afternoon," I said. "Or perhaps we should plan now to wait for ovulation and inseminate just afterwards."

Four more precious mini-straws would have to be used, and we could not afford to miss her again. Often insemination would work after ovulation if it was close enough timing, and the owner agreed. We had no choice but to keep on. My other work was starting to suffer, and then there was the third, older mare. We had not been able to start her and must continue to be vigilant for a silent cycle. I started cancelling other calls in order to meet my commitment to my number two and three mares.

By the following day, I had number two mare inseminated and, breathing a sigh of relief, booked the appointment to do an ultrasound check for pregnancy on both of them seventeen days later. Mare number three eventually co-operated, and by the end of a week, I had all three finished. My sense of accomplishment was to be short-lived. The required seventeen days passed and then some, and I had ultrasounded all three mares; none were in foal! We all gulped. Hastily I tried to explain the possibilities for failure of pregnancy. With a sinking feeling, I called for a repeat of the game plan but decided to call the stallion owner for advice.

"We have been finding he didn't freeze well this year," the representative said. "Use two times the number of straws—that's eight per breeding dose." I gulped—we barely had enough straws left to do all three mares a second time. An immediate feeling of pressure came over me. What had been sent for three cycles would now do only two. How could I improve on what I had done the first cycle?

We earnestly planned, discussed, and rehashed events to prepare for the next breeding. Different hormones were tried, more frequent rectals done, saline flushes post-breeding, and hormones administered. Midnight meetings became tenser, and still the unpredictability of ovulation continued to bewilder us. The three mares all ended up on different days and schedules. Bleary-eyed, I pulled myself up at 6:00 a.m. each day, finishing them at midnight. Now, grim and determined to succeed with this, I let all my other equine and small-animal work suffer. Frozen semen would not get the better of me. At the end of two more weeks, all the mares were bred and all the doses used. We waited.

By the July first weekend, the farm owners wanting to go on holidays, we needed to check our patients and get them home. No one planned to try a third time. Each owner had spent hundreds of dollars. Thankfully, I had educated them before starting this process, and all understood there was no guarantee.

We gathered to do the ultrasounds on the holiday weekend. I found myself anxious about starting, willing it to be over with at least one successful result. Everyone looked at the small screen. Mare one was finished, and with no black vesicle on the screen, the ultrasound told us there was no pregnancy. Then mares two and three were finished. Not one mare was pregnant. Despondent, I packed up my gear, knowing the owners had had to pay for the straws in any event, which was not always the case. I could barely speak. Rumours circulating about the stallion's fertility did not help any of us feel better. The mares went home. Luckily, these three reasonable, well-educated breeders did not refuse to pay their accounts at month end and I felt incredibly appreciative, even contrite.

In October, I received a call from Mrs. White, the owner of the large, older mare with the abnormal uterus.

"She has not cycled again," she said. "Should we check her for fluid or infection?"

I drove out to her farm, worried. What if the repeat manipulations had caused an infection? Hoping for the best, I inserted the ultrasound probe. Perhaps her ovaries had just shut down when the summer got hot, which is known to happen when breeding season is over.

"Good God, she's in foal!" I just about fainted. "The small vesicle must not have been visible on day sixteen in this big uterus. I should have ultrasounded her twice."

Although both other mares were checked, I had no further pleasant surprises. It was ironic that the most unlikely patient had caught — but breeding horses is full of such unpredictable events. Many years later, I can still say that even with experience and all possible factors favourable, with healthy mares and good semen, there is a large measure of luck in all of it. I now warn owners that breeding mares is not for the faint of heart or pocketbook.

They named their filly Elena, a small tip of the hat, I suppose, to her vet.

🐎 🐎 🐎

Breeding season was well over with when I got called to examine two neglected horses with the local S.P.C.A. officer.

"We have had numerous complaints from the neighbours of these folks," he said. "Better go check it out. Have to take a vet along," he added gruffly.

We drove along a back road to an affluent-looking hobby farm, with beautiful landscaping and two nice cars in the drive.

Nothing could have prepared me for what I saw behind the tall, completely solid cedar fence. I have always considered animal and child abuse to be forms of mental illness — one I cannot comprehend, my first visceral instinct being to wish the perpetrators had to suffer at least a modicum of the same treatment. Nothing had prepared me for the scenario I was about to encounter.

We knocked on the door and the man of the house motioned to the barn area, but indicated he had no wish to talk to us or accompany us.

"Yeah, there's two horses out there, I think," he said. With that, he slammed the door in our faces.

Walking around the fence, we saw a small barn surrounded by a barren half-acre paddock with badly chewed fencing. There were no animals in sight. We entered the barn, ducking our heads and trying to see in the dim light. The floor had three feet of dried manure piled up, so my head was near the beams. I saw a couple of overturned feed buckets, and not a bit of hay in sight, before I registered that there were two horses in the far corner.

I gasped. The two Appaloosas were skeletal. I could see their spinal bones clearly, and their grotesquely inverted necks barely held up the bony heads with defeated eyes. There was not one ounce of flesh on the horses. It was a miracle they were alive. I cried. There was no water on the premises, and no sign of feed or hay on the property.

"He said it was the children's responsibility to look after them and they had lost interest," explained the officer. "A neighbour caught sight of them somehow."

"I don't know if they can be saved," I choked, shaken. I fought the urge to scream or to run.

"We must get them out of here today, and even then it may be too late."

"I know. I'll call a trailer for them and get the police."

The couple responsible for the neglect appeared to have simply wiped their hands of the care of the horses when their kids stopped going to the barn. They almost denied that they were there. The children were eight and ten years old.

One of the poor animals was destroyed, but the other grand fellow was saved. "Bob" lived with another of my kindest clients for ten more years. With star status as a revered survivor, he had enough carrots, apples, and love to make up for his abuse and heal his soul. Mine, however, was not the same for a long while.

NINETEEN

THEY JUST DIDN'T
NOTICE . . .

A YEAR HAD PASSED, sometimes in a blur, and the clinic was so busy I had to give serious thought to hiring another veterinarian. I had been on call seven days a week, and the pace was hectic. Often I got called back to the clinic for small-animal emergencies after going home, or called out to a horse emergency when starting a surgery. The town was growing rapidly, in fact experiencing a boom. New streets and houses were going up almost overnight. The workload showed no sign of diminishing.

We placed an ad in the professional journal serving our area, trying to describe our practice facilities, staff, and equipment as well as possible and setting out the terms of the job being offered. It was completely different trying to describe the atmosphere or practice philosophy. Each practice has a subtle and unique culture and unspoken rules and ethics, and we would just have to hope for a personality match. Many complex professional issues, such as policies on records, leniency on dispensing and finances, and—perhaps the most difficult—attitudes towards euthanasia, can be hard to negotiate with the wrong person.

To complicate the situation further, I was offering a job position in a mixed practice, but not a traditional mix with livestock. The fact that we did small animals and horses only served to put us in a very small group that tended to have very few applicants. In addition, those applicants had to be willing to be on call, something fewer and fewer new graduates are willing to do. Into this mix of factors, one could add location preferences, and the number of potential employees would drop further. Thankfully, our area was a popular one in which to live.

Although I had mentioned that experience was preferred, no experienced vets applied. In fact, only three people applied at all. Knowing that on call was a big deterrent, I was prepared to negotiate on this in the interviews, with lessening it being a bargaining chip. I dove into the interviews optimistically and was surprised at what I discovered. Rather than considering that it would be a privilege to get a job with Brentwood, the graduates felt *I* would be very lucky to get *them*. And the salary demands reflected this self-assurance. There seemed to be little awareness of the very necessary teaching, guiding, and mentoring that would be needed the first year out of school. Not to mention that the generally slower speed of work of a new graduate results in lower billings, with the result that the practice must carry the new vet for a while. What this really meant was that all the risk and responsibility would still lie on my shoulders, and I could anticipate adding teaching time to my busy schedule. Hopefully, taking the plunge and hiring a new graduate would be an investment in the future.

One candidate seemed suitable, friendly, and confident. She was keen to do all three of our target species. Ottawa was home, so it would hopefully be a comfortable match. The contract was ironed out, uniforms and nametags purchased, newspaper ads placed to announce the new vet in the town, and the new relationship began.

Cheryl had had some experience with horses and was keen to get more. Although not from a horse background, she was smart enough to get the lingo fast. Besides, no equine person had applied. Her small-animal skills seemed sound enough, and I felt I could train her in the rest over time. She was bubbly and enthusiastic. As the first few weeks went by, I found I wasn't as patient as I had thought and I often had difficulty steeling myself to repeat the same instructions over again. I went home at nights vowing to be more like Jim and shuddering at the fact that some times I reminded myself of Dr. Moore. I was anxious to get Cheryl up to speed quickly so that the pets and clients had minimal disruption.

Several weeks into her new job, Cheryl had to perform a horse euthanasia for a rather difficult client. The "old favourite," Cherokee, had been ill for a long time with Cushing's disease, and repeat episodes of laminitis had caused him to have chronic foot pain. It was time to end that pain, as winter was coming on and the frozen ground would make walking difficult. There was no way I could go out that day, though that was requested. Reluctantly, the owner agreed to have Cheryl go on the call, as that was the appointed day, the burial site had been prepared, and everyone had said their goodbyes. This could not wait. Cheryl had euthanized several other horses, and the procedure had gone smoothly.

After about an hour, Cheryl came back pale and obviously shaken.

"That did not go well," she said. "I must have hit the carotid artery instead of the jugular, because he went down convulsing; it was like he was galloping on the spot." She burst into tears.

"There was not enough help, and it took me several tries to get the vein again with his head moving. It was awful!" It was a situation I might not have gotten into, as assessing the need for sedation in advance or clipping the long hair over the vein are things one learns through hard experiences such as these. I felt sorry for her.

It was not half an hour later that I received an angry phone call from the horse's owner. She ripped up one side of me then down the other for having sent Cheryl to do this critical job. Her complaints were many, but the most strident was the fact that her final image of her pet was of this stressful debacle. I apologized profusely, understanding her point, but also trying to point out these things could happen to any of us, especially with thin, dehydrated animals. Indeed, it *had* happened to me. I was left feeling frustrated that I could not shelter Cheryl from all the hard experiences I had had no matter how I tried to anticipate everything I needed to tell her.

The horse people were merciless. I understood it would take patience on their part to allow Cheryl to learn, but had no idea how little they had. Even discounted bills didn't appease them. And then there was the talk within the horse community to combat. Cheryl started to feel nervous going out on calls, although many went well. She was definitely more comfortable staying in the clinic. I was left wondering how to make it all work out.

One cold night, she had a late call for a colic, the most serious equine emergency. Although a blanket name for any abdominal pain, the word colic strikes fear into every horse owner. In some cases, it will be caused by a simple problem like gas buildup or impaction; in others, a twist of the bowel will cause rapid worsening of the pain. Without surgery, some of these animals die. The skill is in deciding which animals need surgery in time to send them to the vet college before it is too late to save them.

"MacDonald," the old gelding in question, had had several impaction colics due to poor teeth and indigestion. His owner, Mrs. Tailleur, was a scientist and an experienced horsewoman, having seen many vets perform. As the horse was inactive, he always tended towards too-dry manure. Cheryl went through the routine examination of vital signs and decided it didn't look too serious. His gut sounds were diminished, and she did a rectal exam of the senior citizen, feeling the expected impaction. It was still small and should be easy to treat. A stomach tube would have to be inserted via one nostril, and mineral oil and warm water pumped into the animal in a large enough quantity to soften the mass.

After several fruitless attempts, the horse started to throw his head and struggle. He could not be convinced to swallow the tube. On the last try, the left nostril started to bleed profusely and Johnny snorted blood vigorously all over Cheryl, Mrs. Tailleur, and the stall wall. The amount was sensational, and soon large clots were hanging out of the horse's nose.

"We'll have to sedate him and try the other nostril; he must get this oil," Cheryl said. "The bleeding will stop soon," she tried to reassure the unconvinced owner.

After sedation and a nose switch, the anxious young veterinarian tried on the other side. Despite changing the head position and stroking the throat, the animal would not swallow the tube and started gagging. Now the oil would have to be administered by dosing syringe. The lack of co-operation continued, and Cheryl wore half of the gallon of oil on her coveralls. Frustrated, she cleaned up and left, telling the owner to continue with the oil and walking the horse throughout the night. Thankfully, Johnny did pass manure the next day, but it was the last straw for Cheryl.

The next day, she approached me at a quiet time and said she was throwing in the towel. I certainly had no trouble knowing how she felt, remembering my own cattle troubles.

"I think I'll be better off in a city practice," she said, "and I'd love the no 'on-call.'" I realized it was probably for the best. It was unfair for her to be subjected to such pressure. I was alone again.

I changed my tactics. I felt it was critical to get someone in place who was comfortable with horses, preferably before the next spring's busy season, with its demands. Perhaps if this person could do horses well, he or she could do all the artificial insemination, and I could slowly train him or her to do small animals. I advertised the position differently.

Again, no experienced candidates applied but the fellow I did hire had good recommendations and credible horse experience. Richard started out with a splash and had a shiny suv leased and fully stocked for the road within two weeks. He really looked the part. However, we got into a totally different set of problems when it came time for him to wear his small-animal hat. It got so that I was afraid to be away from the clinic.

One day, I came back to a very distraught Erin after having spent a morning in surgery with this fellow.

"I had to re-tube all the animals," she said. "He didn't get one tube in the trachea." She ended her long list of complaints by saying, "Please don't leave me alone with him again."

I kept an eye on what was booked and made sure it was easy enough, but I still felt nervous when I was on the road.

On another occasion, I came back to find several staff members upset. Voices shaking, they surrounded me in the staff room.

"You must not keep this fellow," Jill said. "I wouldn't let him touch one of my animals, so how can we recommend him to the clients?" She had a point. I wrung my hands. What had happened?

"Dr. Carrera gave vaccines to a small dog whose file was clearly marked ALLERGIC/NO VACCINES," Jill said. "Only because Erin was here and the puppy got oxygen and antihistamine did it pull through. It could have been a disaster."

I threw my reading glasses on the floor in exasperation. I knew I couldn't ask our clients to entrust their precious animals to a vet we wouldn't trust with our own. Voices in my head questioned my ability to choose and interview a vet correctly. How had Jim been so tolerant with me all those years ago? I was finding it hard to be a good and patient mentor and found I had difficulty getting through the mistakes. I just knew that everyone at the clinic, including myself, was suffering the strain of being constantly on edge.

With a sinking feeling I knew I had to follow their wishes and let the vet go. We were well within the three-month trial period, and despite Richard's good promise in the stables, there had been little interest or aptitude in treating our smaller pets. The job was clearly not meant to be "equine only," and the fellow had to go before damage was done. It was one of the hardest meetings I have ever had to do.

"But I have just leased a vehicle and an apartment," he protested. "You must give me longer."

"I will pay first and last on the apartment," I said. "That's the least I can do. I'm sorry, but you'll have to clear out your car." As a last effort at goodwill, I muttered, "I am sure you can get a job doing horses only."

After that, I gave up on trying to find a perfect match. I guess I felt that when someone was meant to fit in, he or she would come along. A lady veterinarian who did a great job on small animals agreed to work two days a week for us with no on-call. Although I was still on call seven days a week, I could now go out on farm calls those two days without worrying. It was a good solution for a time, and the practice continued to grow.

Not a summer goes by that we don't have a case of maggot infestation in a dog or cat's skin. The heat of summer causes skin rashes to become painful, developing discharging sores called hot spots, and if the dog has a long or thick coat, the results can be disturbing and repulsive. When Rip was pulled across the waiting room floor by his collar, unable to stand, we had no idea that what was about to confront us was the worst case of maggot infestation any of us had ever seen.

It was readily apparent to me that the old dog was in trouble. His mucous membranes were purple and the high fever confirmed toxemia. He was close to being in shock. I examined his coat, wondering where the awful smell was coming from. On parting the hair, I could see many moving fly larvae burrowing under his matted fur. When I rolled Rip over, his scrotum and anal area were alive. Shockingly, there were holes in the skin and maggots were actually travelling in and out of them before my eyes.

"This dog's in danger," I said. "He is close to toxic shock." I tried to explain to the owner what had happened.

"He has been outside, he lives tied to a doghouse," they replied, visibly upset. "We had no idea this could happen."

"We see it in the summer, with the heat and long coat — they get hot spots, and the smell attracts the flies."

"Please try to save him," the traumatized owners pleaded.

None of us could cope emotionally with the reality of what the dog was suffering. I walked out of the exam room door, shaken. There was also the difficulty of coping with the smell.

"Cancel all the appointments," I said to Jill. "This is top priority. I don't know if I can even save him."

I called a staff member at home. "Please come help us and bring your clippers. We need all the help we can get right now. This is a real emergency."

We had set up an iv and started fluid and antibiotic therapy within moments. The animal was in extreme pain, and yet sedation was risky and possibly life-threatening. As we started to clip, we realized there was no way he could withstand the pain. I would have to sedate him. The drugs flattened Rip, but the fact he was oblivious was, in reality, a relief.

As the hair was clipped back starting from the shoulders, the coat started to peel back in a layer of mats that were all connected. With each new handful of hair, repulsive white wormlike creatures were revealed. They were in the mats and in the purple-coloured holes in the damaged skin. They were dropping on the counters and floor. Erin started to gag despite her facemask.

"I have never seen anything like this!" she muttered. "Is this neglect?" I paused, not knowing what to say.

"These people really care about their dog," I replied. "They obviously have been too busy to groom it, though, or they would have known before now about the mats and this situation."

"Lots of outdoor dogs never get groomed," another staff member said. It was hard for all of us to believe this dog was loved.

We worked on him for three hours. Two people clipped the thick coat and then the legs. Two others washed the painful skin and flushed insects out of holes with water and disinfectant. We laid cool cloths on the burning skin. We sprayed the wandering maggots that seemed to be everywhere with insecticide. Still more emerged from the skin. It was a nightmare that seemed to go on and on. The old dog hung in there and fought for his life despite the odds being stacked against him. The rotten smell permeating the clinic got into our clothes and hair and noses despite our masks. We all wondered whether it would have been kinder to euthanize the dog.

We had collected a garbage can full of hair and writhing maggots.

"He seems to have a will to live. Let's hope for a miracle," I said, trying to buoy up the team.

At ten, we wrapped up the sleeping patient in a blanket and loaded him into my car. I was reluctant to leave him alone for the night. The next twenty-four hours would tell the tale. His temperature was down to 103 degrees from a life-threatening 105 by the time I had him home. I called the owners to say he had made it this far.

"His colour is a bit better, and the antibiotics are kicking in," I said. "Tomorrow morning will tell us what to do next; there are still risks such as kidney failure in a dog his age."

The next morning, I awoke from a restless sleep to see Rip looking at me from his crate. He fully intended to have breakfast, it seemed. He looked like a different dog. The miracle I had hoped for really had taken place. He was still a bit shaky walking with his IV line in, but the dark-red skin lesions were already a less inflamed pink, and the holes in the skin looked like they were going to heal quickly. I called the owners.

"The best place for him will be at home," I said. "Pick him up at five after I take the IV out." When the owners arrived, there were tears and hugs all round.

"We feel terrible," they said. "Please tell other people to clip their dogs in the heat. Please don't let this happen to anybody else."

I decided to spare them a lecture. They had learned a very hard lesson and almost lost their dog.

"There will be a lot of after-care," I instructed them. "You will have to bathe the skin faithfully and keep him in the cool garage. Apply this ointment twice a day to all the wounds."

"He'll be an inside dog, now," they said as they headed out the front door with their pet.

🐎 🐎 🐎

My experiences with Cheryl and Richard underscored the difficulty I would have many times over in hiring a veterinarian. It is difficult to wear two hats; the small-animal clients must be completely comfortable with their vet, as the horse owners must be confident in theirs.

I realized I was a dying breed. Now commonly called dinosaurs in our profession, we were raised to believe we could, or had to, do it all. Like the old rural doctor, we were expected to handle everything presented to us. The new era of specialization had led to a very different type of graduate coming out of veterinary school, often suited to cattle or horses or reptiles or pets exclusively. It would take time to find a fit for our practice, but we were settled for now and I was proud of the team I was building and of the clinic.

🐕 🐕 🐕

The "Katrina Dogs"—survivors of Hurricane Katrina—arrived at three in the morning. We had waited since six the evening before . . . myself, reporters, and volunteers willing to take the traumatized animals home and foster them. They would have both emotional and physical wounds. There were coffee cups and cigarette butts on the front steps, and people were getting impatient, restless, running out of things to talk about. A rescue group from the city had travelled in convoy to New Orleans, with vans, RVS, and cars, and responded to the urgent need to get the unclaimed dogs and cats out of the city after the hurricane. Months had passed, and many remained unclaimed; charity was running out. The local rescue group I most often dealt with had agreed to take sixty animals and perhaps more later. I had agreed in turn to do my part and receive them at my clinic for a screen before they went to the foster homes. I could detect ill health and dehydration, as well as parasites the new owners would need to know about. Perhaps I could prevent or detect a serious problem or disease outbreak.

The convoy of tired drivers pulled around to the back in the chill November air. We had the back of the clinic opened up for the screening, and several local high school students were there to help me. We took temperatures and looked for mange and malnutrition. We carefully handled and lifted the exhausted and shy and sometimes defensive animals, so short on trust, and fed their more exhausted human drivers. Emotions ran high, stories were told, and some fosters blatantly tried to claim the cutest dogs. One very shy dog got away into the night and was lost for several hours after surviving a 3,000-mile journey. The total situation was intensely dramatic for all involved.

There was one kind, middle-aged woman who arrived with the convoy that was actually far from home. She had driven an RV from Michigan to New Orleans pulling a second small house trailer and filled it with crates and animals. She had linked with the rescue group, who came back to me, and had driven well past her home to deliver her charges. They had gone many days with little sleep, driving and stopping only to feed, water, and walk the dogs. She was almost over the edge. On her lap when she pulled up, almost unable to stand herself, was a small kitten. At first I didn't see it. The lady walked stiffly towards me in the night and started to cry. She thrust the strange-looking creature into my hands. It had burnt ears and a burnt tail. I'll never forget the urgent voice I heard next.

"This is not a throwaway kitten—she lived through the fires ... she must be saved. She represents the people and city of New Orleans. I did not travel all this way to have someone give up on her. Can I trust you to save her? Can you assure me she will not be put to sleep?"

I knew there was no answer possible but, "Yes, you can trust me. Yes, I will save her."

The lady relaxed. Cinders enjoys a home with one of my staff members to this day, a living, loving tribute to the human–animal bond.

TWENTY

NATURE IS
NOT ALWAYS KIND

REPRODUCTION CAN HAVE its difficulties in any species, including humans. I had long had my hand in breeding, starting with guinea pigs at the age of ten. As animal lovers, many of us become enamoured with one species or one special breed, and some of us become involved in breeding animals long-term. This labour of love takes far more time, devotion, money, and work than a layperson can imagine. A dog breeder must work to learn about his/her breed, develop his/her own lines, then show the dogs and market the puppies. A lot of heart-break can occur along the way as litters are lost, diseases like hip dysplasia manifest, or puppies are returned. Breeding animals can be an emotional roller coaster, and only the most resilient stay involved long-term.

Our clinic was slowly establishing a relationship with several new breeders in the area. They are slow to give you their confidence and are generally very knowledgeable and even challenging clients. In addition, information from the Internet, seminars, and long experience means we veterinarians sometimes have to run to keep up with them. It can be well worth it as we all learn together, or very difficult to maintain when there is a difference of opinion.

When the dog owner plans a breeding, the timing of whelping is critical, and there is a lot at stake. Many have a waiting list for pups. In some cases, Cesareans are planned on an elective date at an arbitrary time after the last breeding, usually day sixty-two or sixty-three. This can be made easier if the bitch tells us she is ready to whelp. Especially the brachycephalic breeds, those with huge heads such as bulldogs, are not allowed to give birth on their own.

I had a breeder of Gordon setters in the practice who had had wonderful results with a certain line of dogs, especially with their temperaments. She decided to breed her favourite older dog, a middle-aged seven-year-old, one last time. Although I was concerned, the bitch was fit and had never had whelping problems, so I optimistically stood by for the call, making sure I would be in town at the time. I doubted she would need a section.

Day sixty-two passed with no indication Delilah was going to go into labour. Although she was quiet, her exam gave us no cause for concern and her vital signs were normal. We let her go one more day. On day sixty-three, the owner and I were both worried. She was a little depressed, and no activity had been seen from the pups that day. There was no elevated temperature or discharge to confirm an infection, but it seemed to both of us something was wrong. We decided to do a Cesarean late in the day and hastily set up the surgery, even calling in extra staff. An x-ray had indicated there were eight pups and there would be jobs for three or more people just resuscitating them after the mild dose of anaesthetic they would get. All was in readiness: hot water bottles, oxygen, thread for the umbilical cords. As I made my first cut the owner sat in a nearby room waiting anxiously.

Within moments of opening the abdomen, I realized Delilah was in trouble and potentially so was I. The uterus was a poor colour and thin-walled, and the abdomen had some abnormal fluid in it indicating the start of a septic process. I called for my other veterinarian, working at the front, to cancel appointments and glove up. It was unlikely the pups were alive. My suspicions were confirmed when I handled the uterus. My fingers immediately went through the wall as I attempted to lift it and some hairs from a dead pup appeared on my gloves.

"Go tell the owner we're in trouble," I said to Erin. "The pups appear to be dead and the uterus unhealthy. We will have to spay her to save her; we'll do our best."

Returning, she said, "Mrs. Harris had not wanted to spay her, but do it if you must."

The bitch's colour was poor and I was worried about her anaesthetic. Keeping the inhalant gas as low as possible, we turned up the fluid rate to try to prevent her from going into shock. It took all our skill, as two experienced vets, to remove the damaged uterus and eight dead pups, tying off all the large bleeders. The abdomen had to be rinsed thoroughly with warm saline, as so much material had spilled into it.

As she recovered, the poor dog continued to struggle for life. She was cold and her oral membranes were pale and she did not wake up for the longest time.

"I would not take her home," I said. "She should go to the emergency clinic for overnight surveillance and not be left alone. There's no one here," I added.

Mrs. Harris started to cry. The events had caused a kind of shock reaction in her as well. Rather than going home with eight lovely new pups, she had her much-loved, favourite dog in a life-threatening situation, hundreds of dollars spent, and potentially many more to spend saving her pet. Having gone this far, we had to do what was best for the dog.

"This has never happened before," she said, "and I've bred older dogs."

"I don't know why it happened. Perhaps the pups died first of a bacterial or viral infection, or perhaps she had uterine inertia due to her age or a low calcium level," I replied.

"I feel like I am in a nightmare, but I'll go," she choked out.

"Start warming up the car while we get warm blankets around her, and we'll carry her out," I offered, getting the stretcher.

Delilah did live, but Mrs. Harris decided not to breed another older dog again. Within months, however, she cheerfully came in to book hip radiographs for certification on a lovely new bitch she had purchased. This time she was sure everything would work out fine.

☙ ☙ ☙

I worked for a large thoroughbred breeding farm on and off, especially for emergencies, as I was the closest veterinarian. That spring, they had twenty mares foaling and many of them had already given birth by May. They were almost finished with the exhausting overnight watches and the worry about too-cold nights. By early spring, I could admire a band of lovely mares and foals out in the spring sunshine as I drove up the laneway. We had already begun the business of checking these mares for infection and rebreeding them to one of the farm's two stallions. The manager was a knowledgeable man, well supported by two helpers. He was worried about one of the last mares, also an older animal that had had a very large foal the year before.

It turned out doing Cesareans weren't the only tragedy I had to deal with that spring, as I now encountered the worst foaling challenge of my career. One night, the manager called to say something was wrong.

"Final Rally has been trying to foal for an hour," he said. "Something's wrong! I washed up and put my arm in. I think the head's back." I told him I was on my way. Within half an hour I was up and dressed, had driven to the farm, and was in the stall. The mare was on her side already tired from pushing. The manager and his two helpers were well prepared with soap, hot water, towels, and ropes. They waited anxiously for my examination. I lay on my side in the straw, straining to reach the foal against the mare's intense labour.

"The head and one front leg are back, and it's a very large foal," I said. "We will have to sedate her and give her an epidural to get it out." At that point I had no idea of the ordeal ahead of me and still hoped the foal was alive. Once I got its head up, I would be able to tell for sure.

I injected the mare with an intravenous sedative and could see her immediately relax and take a bit of a rest. In order to stop her involuntary straining, I would have to clip and surgically prepare a site on the top of her tail for an epidural anaesthetic.

This local anaesthetic would stop her labour so I could push the foal back and try to elevate its nose and head into the birth canal. I would work on the left front leg later.

I lay in the fluid-soaked straw on a blanket and tried repeatedly to get the head up. It was frustrating work, and the vagina was already dry and swollen. It was hard to push the foal back far enough, as I was working uphill against gravity. Repeatedly I got a hold on its ear and worked my way to the lower jaw, only to lose it. Finally, I got a loop of baler twine, which I had taken inside on my hand, around the lower jaw. By pushing back on the forehead and pulling on the twine from outside, I swung the head around and up. A touch to its non-reactive cornea told me it was already dead. I told the despondent manager.

"I knew something was wrong, just had a feeling," he said. "How will we get it out?" He could see I was already tiring.

After trying repeatedly to feel my way to the knee of the left front leg, I knew I needed to take a break. I was making no progress. This is a critical stage, when a veterinarian, while still working, must formulate a contingency plan.

I described to Joseph, a tall, strong, twenty-year-old standing by, how to try to pull up the missing leg. He stripped to the waist and washed up. Lying on his side, he tried to feel what I was describing and started working on the leg. I went to call the office. Bruce, the other farm helper, sat in the corner holding the mare's head down.

"I need more people and equipment," I told Erin. "Please come out with two of you prepared to set up an iv for the mare. Bring lots of fluids and more anaesthetic. I'll also need the feto-tome."

I knew that if all of us could not get the front leg up, we could not pull the foal. The mare's vagina was very swollen and dry, and our room to work was diminishing. She was pale and cold and needed fluids to help prevent shock. Erin and Elizabeth could get that set up while I worked. The clinic would now be empty of staff except for the one person on the phone.

I returned to the stall, grim-faced.

"Let's work until they get here," I said, "then if there is still no progress, I will have to cut off the foal's head to get it out."

"Are you sure it's dead?" Joseph choked out.

"I am 100 percent sure," I said, still upset at the prospect of what was to come. I had been through the embryotomy procedure in calves, where the baby has to be dismembered to be removed. It seems to be against all that nature intended.

By the time my team arrived, we had to re-sedate the mare to keep her down and set up the IV fluids. She had started struggling a bit. To let her up could be dangerous, as her hind leg strength and coordination could be comprised by the epidural. She would have to stay down, so I hog-tied her front legs. We lubed her vagina with oil and prepared the fetotome.

This archaic-looking piece of equipment is a three-foot-long steel tube with two separate channels coming first out one side of the rounded end that looks like a mushroom. I threaded the serrated wire used to cut through the tissue out one end and back into the other channel, leaving a loop, which would go over the foal's head and settle just behind the skull on the other side. The wire was attached to handles and with a sawing motion it would to cut through any tissue in its way. Lying on the now sodden blanket and working one-handed, it took a few moments for me to get the wire placed around the head. But then it took Joseph only a few moments to saw through the neck, and I pulled out the head of the beautiful foal. Its eyes were opaque, signalling that it had been dead for a while. I breathed a sigh of relief.

"It was black, with a beautiful stripe." The barn manager choked back tears. Even for the most experienced horseman, this is a hard thing to see. We moved on, knowing that giving in to the emotion of the moment would only make it more difficult to complete the job.

I returned to the business of getting the front limb up. To retrieve the foal and pull it out the birth canal was critical. I felt the knee and pulled it repeatedly up and towards the backbone. Eventually I could work down the little leg to the ankle and foot. Cupping the foot to protect the uterus, I heaved the knee up, then the neck back and pulled for all I was worth. The foot came, and finally we had two long legs to work with.

The foal was drying out, and I decided to pump warm water into the uterus to lubricate it and try to float the remains out. In twenty more minutes, three of us had the poor ruined foal out of the mare. It was large and stretched terribly as the hips came through, causing me to think it might give in the middle.

"It was a beauty, a large colt," I said, then turned my attention to the mare. She was pale and a bit shocky. I was well aware her uterus could also prolapse after such a difficult pull, and re-sedated her just enough to prevent straining and struggling.

"Increase her fluid rate and re-warm the fluids," I said. "We'll hold her down until she is stronger."

By seven that night, she was on her feet, eating hay slowly. I had given her painkillers and knew by the look in her eye that she intended to live. I found myself wishing that would be her last foaling ordeal but I knew that unlike the dog, Delilah, Rally would be rebred. Few brood mares have the luxury of retirement. For the record, she never caught in foal again, despite many tries. Finally she did get sent to a retirement home as a companion, as I had hoped. Her will to live, evident through that terrible day, kept her going well into her thirties.

We often debate about nature, its wisdom and its cruelty. Both of these animals would have died with their young inside them in a natural setting. Despite its wonders, Mother Nature can sometimes use a helping hand, and I felt good to be able to help them. Suffice it to say, most dogs and horses have their young happily, instinctively, and unassisted—thank goodness for that.

TWENTY-ONE

EMUS, CAMELS, AND YAKS

I HAD BEEN BACK at Brentwood for three years and felt really happy. Sometimes I made a slip and called the clinic home, telling a client I'd "meet them at home." I felt more and more like my previous boss and mentor as I started to unconsciously adopt his habits, calling at eight to see what was on for the day or zipping into the parking lot and turning the clinic upside-down. Returning had been a great decision, and I was very proud of the clinic and its staff of very caring people.

We had added a new woman to our staff to train at both the front and back. Young, and with two children, she juggled a busy life, but was always cheerful and brought fun and enthusiasm to her job. Charlotte was excited about learning, ready to work hard, and always up for a good joke. She had different and humorous opinions on everything from books to celebrities that kept conversation flowing. We had all entered a comfortable phase in our professional and personal relationships that few workplaces achieve—celebrating birthdays, highs and lows, without living too much in each other's lives.

By year three, Elizabeth was taking care of all the horse bookings and questions, as I simply could not continue to work and also answer my many phone calls. In general, this was well accepted. Although many equine clients come and go, the ones that stayed enjoyed and used our support staff well. I often took helpers on the road, so we were seen as operating as a team. Everyone except Erin tried to go on horse calls and get a break from the clinic and phone.

One day Elizabeth said to me, "I've just had the most interesting call from way above Lanark. I don't know what to think."

Elizabeth wasn't easily thrown, but this call had left her quizzical.

"This lady says she's bought a zoo. She has many types of animals up there and wants to meet with you to talk about being her vet. She doesn't seem to know a lot about horses but says she has four to castrate."

"Okay," I said, "I'll give it a go and take help. It should be fun, and it's beautiful up there."

"I'll call her back then and book a whole afternoon," Elizabeth replied. "It's over an hour's drive to get there."

When the day came, I decided to take Charlotte, who was comfortable with horses. The May day was beautiful, the drive would be fun, and I felt really up as I packed the car. It had been far too long since I had driven the back roads of Lanark!

"Don't forget Tetanus shots and antibiotics," I said. "Who knows if they have been vaccinated." The clinic was humming as we pulled out of the parking lot, having no idea what to expect.

Our drive was a mix of lightheartedly enjoying the scenery—vivid green fields and rolling hills peppered with stones—and analyzing the latest television shows in detail. The dirt roads became more winding and narrow as we approached the farm. It was a perfect day for such a call, a bit cool and windy to keep the flies down and make it easier on the horses as they underwent anaesthesia.

As has always been the case before a castration, the horse is examined, then given a sedative. A few moments later, an intravenous general anaesthetic is given, and four handlers assist a slow "sit and fall" procedure that ends up with the animal on its side. The twenty or so minutes following are enough to do a minor surgery before the horse wakes up. Often the horses sweat a lot from the particular drugs used, so avoiding a hot day is better for them. We help them to their feet and back to their stalls to wear it off. Occasionally, depending on their breeds and temperaments, dominant and high-strung horses being more challenging, they are difficult to get down or up—meaning that only very experienced horse people must take part in the anaesthesia.

The couple were aging city people, both having been involved in the arts and music scene in Montreal. They were in their late fifties when they decided to follow a dream and build a house in the backwoods. Shortly afterwards, a small zoo in the Eastern Townships of Quebec closed, and they decided to purchase half the animals and give them a forever home in the Lanark Highlands. What awaited us on the call was unique and unexpected. A camel stood on a hilltop as we drove up the laneway. A group of spotted goats, the likes of which I had never seen before, ambled across a distant field and three yaks stood in a circular wooden pen.

Mrs. La Perriere introduced herself and her husband at the door to the house. Classical music could be heard coming from within. She had brown hair threaded with grey down to her waist, knotted loosely behind her back, and her husband had an impressive shock of white, flowing hair and round glasses. Both had worn-out sweaters and jeans on, but still maintained an intellectual air.

"Call me Kay," she said. "I will give you a tour of the farm and animals. We have had to fence the yaks, as they kept wandering over to the neighbours', but the rest of the property is not fenced, and we want the animals to feel free."

At this point I started feeling slightly concerned. The horses were nowhere in sight, and I felt it was a fairly sure bet that they had not been gathered up prior to our coming.

"The horses have not been handled much," Kay said. "In fact, two have not had halters on." It was reminiscent of breaking Ziggy many years ago, but these colts were much larger and more opinionated. I proceeded gamely on.

"Let's put the yaks in the barn," I offered. "It might be best to put the horses in the round pen to halter and castrate them."

After half an hour, we had the yaks in the ramshackle barn. Inside were two stalls, both filled with large emus. As I negotiated the pile of manure, ducking the low beams, I inadvertently backed up too close to a half stall wall. With a thud, an emu pecked me soundly in the back of the head, almost drawing blood. I stumbled away.

Kay proceeded across a field with a bucket of grain. "The horses are almost always over this hill," she said. Shortly thereafter, she appeared with one horse eating from the bucket, three others and the camel following. It took some doing to get the four of them into the round pen and haltered, but within an hour of arriving, we had the unsuspecting animals gathered up and hot water and equipment ready.

The wind had come up, almost irritatingly, so my gloves and syringes were blowing around a bit, as was the dust, and it became a bit harder to hear. Mrs. La Perriere stood by calmly, obviously not intending to help. Charlotte and I attempted to get near the first horse. We had to at least check its heart and colour before I administered the first dose of sedative, if indeed I could even get an injection into him.

I was four feet from it when it bolted out of Charlotte's hands and across the round pen mixing with the other horses. She caught it again with the bucket, almost getting trampled by the hungry herd.

"Throw the rope around a sturdy post," I advised her. "I'll try to come back to him."

Thankfully, this time the sedative was given successfully, and within twenty minutes, we had one colt gelded and his tetanus toxoid administered.

The first colt, a very nervous Arabian, got up very roughly, staggering and falling several times. This was going to be very different than the four Clydes I had had to do many moons ago on the clinic lawn—not surprisingly, just as different as these clients were to the elderly Lanark horseman of that day.

After two of the other colts were anaesthetized and lying on the ground recovering, we were tired and had dust in our mouths, eyes, and clothing. Our gear was dirty and scattered about. Thankfully, the fourth colt would not be caught, and we elected to call it quits for the day. Mrs. La Perriere promised to work on handling him before we returned.

She and her quiet husband appeared satisfied and paid cash, promising to call us back before black-fly season to do the fourth colt. Several days later, Elizabeth received a call and relayed to me that the owner had decided to let the fourth colt stay a stallion. They wanted at least that one to lead a free and natural life. I sighed, hoping he, too, did not visit the neighbours. A farm with no fencing is not the best place for a stallion, even in the quiet Lanark Highlands. We wished them all the best with their stock.

Charlotte and I had so many stories to tell from our "James Herriot" day that, despite any knocks we took doing the rough-and-tumble job, it was well worth it. Our day in the highlands meeting Mother Nature had been a fun and different experience from the everyday work of the now more urban clinic.

ᖇᖇ ᖇᖇ ᖇᖇ

Autoimmune diseases are uncommon but not rare in veterinary medicine.

Always to be taken seriously, autoimmune disease is the manifestation of a complex process whereby the body turns on itself, usually targeting specific tissues or cells. If red blood cells are the targeted tissue, now recognized by the scanners of the body, white blood cells or lymphocytes, they will be rapidly destroyed, resulting in a profound anemia. If the joints are targeted, the disease manifests as severe polyarthritis; if it is the muscles, then it will be myositis or inflammation of the muscles. In rare instances, widespread tissues are attacked, resulting in a syndrome like lupus in humans. A.I.D. is severe, acute, and life-threatening if not diagnosed and treated immediately with a steroid that suppresses the overactive immune system.

Cinnamon was a regular. A golden retriever mix, she had come from the pound after being abandoned. She had a wonderful new owner, a retired schoolteacher, who had devoted great effort and expense to cleaning up her chronic skin problems.

"Cinnie hasn't been feeling well for a few days," reported Gerdie. "She hasn't eaten at all today and not much yesterday."

I examined the sweet dog, concerned by her distressed appearance. Was she in pain? A lot of possibilities ran through my head as I examined her. Did her face look strange and possibly swollen? I was alarmed at her temperature.

"She has a fever of 105 degrees!" I exclaimed. "What is going on here?" I ran through the possibilities. Viral, bacterial, and autoimmune diseases can all cause a high fever. Was there a clue? Pneumonia, or perhaps an abscess? At the worst, I suspected septicemia or a blood-borne infection, possibly from an internal abscess or peritonitis.

Cinnamon grunted as I palpitated her sides. Under the hair I found a small tooth mark, likely the result of a fight with Gerdie's other dog, and an area of discoloured skin. Reddened and sore, I suspected it would go purple next.

"I found an abscess! It's poisoning her," I said. "We must start her on antibiotics and fluids and plan to lance it as soon as she is stable." Gerdie nodded. We agreed she'd stay in hospital. I explained she would have a drain in her side coming out the bottom of the incision.

The next morning, the reddened area on her side was indeed larger, hotter, and darker red. I planned to anaesthetize her. Her fever was down to a respectable 103 degrees, probably, I surmised, as a result of her IV antibiotics and an aspirin-like drug that I had given her. I thought I was on the right track.

I laid out my endotracheal tube and checked the anaesthetic hoses and surgery table. All was in readiness for what should have been a routine procedure. However, as Erin gave the IV induction agent and the little dog went to sleep, I found I could not open her mouth more than one-half of an inch. It was absolutely frozen shut! I could hardly believe it and now had grave anaesthetic concerns. I must get a tube into her somehow. My mind raced.

Somehow I got a very small tube into her airway, giving me a moment to think. Her head did indeed seem swollen and slightly asymmetrical. Did she have an abscess behind one eye, causing difficulty opening the mouth due to pain? No, it would still have opened under anaesthetic, if not when awake. Myositis, extreme inflammation of the temporal muscles was the only other plausible diagnosis. Had this all started when muscle destruction resulting from the abscess on the side of her body coded her body to attack the denaturing muscle proteins? Or had the autoimmune myositis come first, attacking her head and her flank? Whichever, I started clipping her for an exploratory examination of the abscess and a muscle biopsy of her head.

"Have you heard of the new test they do in the States for anti-muscle antibody?" my associate vet asked, looking interestedly over my shoulder. "It would take ten days to get back, and we'll probably have to treat her for autoimmune disease anyway, but it would be good to confirm it." Of all the diseases in this family, myositis is actually the most rare. As Cinnie woke up, I debated whether to wait for the results or just start Cinnie on high doses of prednisone. We were all very concerned about her; she was one of our favourite little patients. She looked terrible, waking up shaved in several places, with a large tube coming out from under the pocket on her side.

"Let's go ahead with the prednisone," Gerdie said when the possibilities were explained to her. "On thinking about it, I feel she's actually been sick for longer than I realized, maybe even a couple of weeks."

"We're not out of the woods," I explained. "Autoimmune disease can be difficult to treat, prednisone has side effects, and unfortunately it can go into remission, then come back."

"We've got to try," she responded.

Cinnamon was awake but groggy when I gave her the first high dose of iv prednisone. By the next day, her head seemed slightly less swollen, and she had a brighter look in her eye. By day three, we had more progress, and she had advanced to eating gruel. By week two when we got the tests back confirming auto-immune myositis, she could open her mouth a couple of inches wide and went home on hand-fed soft dog food. The appearance of her head, however, was bizarre. All of the muscles on top of her skull had atrophied after the severe muscle inflammation, and she now had a hollow, pointy appearance to her head above both eyes.

"I can live with that," Gerdie said. "Just don't take her off the prednisone too soon!" I had discussed the gradual reduction of the dose of steroids over three months, and the owner was obviously terrified.

"We'll watch her blood values and see if both of you can live with the side effects," I said.

A month later, when the hair had grown back on her side and her mouth was opening well enough for her to eat hard food and yawn, we started reducing the dose of the life-saving drug. Cinnie was on the mend and playing with Gerdie's other dog. All went well as we successfully withdrew the drug without a remission, but Cinnamon to this day has a head only a mother could love. Her muscles never regrew, but she can catch a treat in the air now with a satisfying "chomp"!

🐎 🐎 🐎

Charlotte had had a job offer in the city some thirty miles from her home. After much internal debate, she approached me one night almost in tears. We got along well, so she was very concerned about hurting me.

"I have a job offer I can't refuse," she said. "It's a lot more money, and I will get to do much more at the back of the hospital as a vet tech."

"Can I counter?" I said, upset at the prospect of losing such a valued staff member. The clients loved Charlotte.

"I have already accepted," she grimaced. "I'm sorry. This is my two weeks' notice."

I accepted her resignation with regret, wondering why she hadn't come to me if she wanted a change of position or a raise. I found it difficult sometimes to guess what was coming at me next regarding what the staff members were feeling or unhappy about. There is truth to the statement "It's lonely at the top," and I was finding it hard to always be the boss. Sometimes it would have been nice to just be part of the gang.

We planned a going-away party for her last Friday at Brentwood. It was to be held at a nice local restaurant, and I would bring a gift and a going-away cake. We all moped about for the two weeks, the atmosphere visibly restrained. On the Thursday night before the party, Charlotte phoned me, again in tears.

"I have changed my mind," she said. "I did a trial day and it just wasn't a fit; besides, I hated the drive. Can I come back?"

"Of course you can—you haven't left," I said, trying not to show how happy I felt. "The party will go on. We'll celebrate your not leaving!"

She was embarrassed, but agreed to it. It was a good excuse for team building and a bit of leg-pulling.

I made a call to the bakery early Friday morning. "Can you change that cake for me, or is it too late?" I asked. "I need one that says, 'Welcome Back Charlotte.'"

Even the lady at the bakery got the joke. "It's no problem. We should be able to do that."

We had a great luncheon on the outside patio. Charlotte was presented with many humorous, scratched-out, and revised cards. The crowning touch was the cake, worthy of a deep blush and a mandatory photo. We were all back to routine on Monday. It was the first time I had seen someone quit a job and never leave.

🐫 🐫 🐫

It was Saturday afternoon, and we had just locked the front door. It had been one of those Saturdays when every moment had been filled to overflowing. We had been running to get it all done. Fit-ins, emergencies, lab work, and food sales all combined to make a short break or even lunch impossible. I sighed as I packed up my records. "I'll do these Sunday," I said to Charlotte, "I'm too tired now."

I had just started the car when my pager went. The lady on the phone informed me that the clients were already on the way. Their dog had attacked a smaller one belonging to a very elderly lady. They were pulling into the parking lot as I hung up.

The young couple was frantic. They helped the tiny, white-haired woman up the steps carrying her small Maltese-type dog in a very bloody towel. Her face was set and white, as if she were in shock. In the exam room I folded back the towel. The little white mixed-breed female was panting and looking right at me as I examined the deep gashes on each flank just ahead of her hind legs. She was in terrible pain, but did not offer to bite. I felt a crunch in her pelvic area.

"It looks serious. There may be a pelvic or hind leg fracture, and these wounds may penetrate the abdomen."

I escorted them to my office, finding a seat for each of them. They were all crying now, and the young couple informed me the police were on the way. Someone had reported the incident.

"Please stay with Mrs. Weiss. I'll give her dog painkillers and start fluids. I will need to take x-rays and clean the wounds," I said, leaving them.

Mr. Hill came to speak to me while I was working on Trixie. His wife stayed with Mrs. Weiss, waiting. "She has Alzheimer's," he said. "She doesn't drive. Her neighbour said they would come get her later. We feel awful . . . we don't know what to do with Jack . . . this is the second time . . ." his voice trailed off.

"Please hold this," I said, not able to devote my attention to him. "I have called in a technician, but I need help with the clipping."

I was extremely concerned about Trixie. She continued to look stoically at me, but I had seen no movement in her hind legs. After Erin arrived, I left her washing the deep cuts and went to speak to Mrs. Weiss.

"I am concerned she may have a broken back. As soon as the painkillers have worked, I will take an x-ray," I said.

A deep moan, almost a wail, started emanating from the tiny lady as she rocked forward on the couch. Her distress was painful to see. Mrs. Hill, sobbing, put an arm around her. "Her husband died last year, and she lives alone," said Mrs. Hill. "We must call her son in Kingston."

I carried on with my vet work in a well-trained, automatic manner, yet I felt shaken by the situation. Two policemen appeared and went into my office, and I heard low voices.

Trixie let us move her to the x-ray table and take the two views I needed of her back and pelvis. I gasped when I saw the images on the monitor. The fourth and fifth lumbar vertebrae were completely out of line. It was the worst broken back I had ever seen. I steeled myself to go back into my office.

I asked the Hills and the police to go into the waiting room and I sat down by the frail woman. "I will bring Trixie in," I said, "but it is really bad, her back is broken." She didn't speak. "She'll never walk again," I added.

I wheeled the IV stand in and sat Trixie on her lap. We sat silently for a while then she started cooing to her little pet. "You'll be fine, the doctor will help you." Trixie mercifully slept in her lap.

After a long time, perhaps ten minutes, had passed, I said, "You know what must be done."

"She can't live like this." Mrs. Weiss nodded. In a moment of clarity she said, "I've had dogs all my life; these things happen. Go ahead."

I went into the hall and told the Hills and the officers they could leave. I would drive her home. No neighbour had appeared, and yet it seemed all right. The clinic would be more peaceful, and I wanted to take my time. I locked everyone out. Erin left, almost in tears, and I pulled the injection of euthansol. Walking back into the office, I sat down, and it seemed we both rested for a while. The clinic was now dark and quiet. The late afternoon sun was coming in through my office window.

"When you are ready, you tell me," I said.

"Go ahead."

The final moments were fine, a blessing really, and it felt so appropriate to just sit with her for a while after. The light was dimming as we got up and I put Trixie in the back of the clinic.

"I'll take you home and come back for her," I said. "I'll bring you back her ashes in a beautiful urn."

We left the clinic, and I helped the heartbroken lady into the passenger side of the cold car.

"Where do you live?" I asked, easing my foot off the brake.

"I'm not sure," she said. "Somewhere near the hospital, I think." A fog had covered her face.

"It's okay," I said, feeling perfectly calm, "we'll find it, it's a small town."

We drove around for half an hour watching for familiar landmarks. Finally she exclaimed, "There it is!" The worried neighbours appeared as I pulled in. They had thought the police were bringing her home.

"We'll stay with her until her son comes," they reassured me. "She shouldn't be living alone anymore."

"Would you like tea?" Mrs. Weiss asked me. She looked calm and accepting. Perhaps she was unaware of what had happened.

"I must go home," I said, feeling overwhelmingly tired. I felt a sudden need to see my own dog. I left feeling drained by the busy day, by the tragedy I had witnessed, and by the overall loss she was dealing with, especially that of her own self. Her dog, her husband, soon her house—all gone, but the loss of her memories of them seemed cruelest of all.

TWENTY-TWO

GETTING BACK UP

AS LUCK WOULD HAVE IT, the veterinarian I had been waiting for just walked in the front door one day. No well-thought-out ads were placed, no strategies employed. It was at the generous suggestion of a neighbouring clinic that Dr. Leanne Best sought us out. Having applied there for a mixed animal position, she admitted cattle were not really her thing, and the veterinarian interviewing her wisely sent her to us, believing it would be a perfect fit, which it was.

Our practice was maturing, developing a sense of longevity and stability. We were in a nice rhythm with sharp, conscientious staff. Most of us inherently shared the same value system, and thus our unique practice culture had developed. Even more than when we had so actively sought a young veterinarian in the past, we needed someone who "got us."

"You could be a hard group to break into," one of my friends had said to me. Yet with Dr. Best, there didn't seem to be any effort to the transition. She just slid in and starting working with us.

Having a new veterinarian working for me was a delicate balance. One must be able to give appropriate space for a young professional to grow and to resist trying to control every case. On the other hand, the interests of the clients and patients must be protected during the learning curve. Being a mentor means finding just the right balance between these factors and also developing the co-operative spirit that enables each to give and receive information. Lastly, I had to believe I had enough and current information to give. I knew I did. I finally had someone I could truly mentor in the most legitimate sense.

The only moment Dr. Best really needed me, I was out back of the clinic looking at a lame horse. Things in the clinic were running smoothly. It was a surgery day, something everyone enjoyed. Leanne was spaying an overweight labrador, a task not for the faint of heart. While working in the deep, fat-filled abdomen, it is easy to have an ovarian pedicle slip and a bleed start.

Erin came out of the clinic with a flustered look and a shaky voice. "We need you in surgery, hurry," she muttered in a tense voice.

I ran through the treatment area, not stopping to scrub, and donned a pair of surgical gloves.

"Open the incision," I ordered, as I saw her struggling with blood-soaked gauze. It was evident that the abdomen was filling up with blood.

"Turn up the fluid rate!" I barked. "We'll need retractors and sterile towels to pack off the bowel." In a few moments, the offending ligature was located and the bleeding stump tied off more tightly. The dog recovered easily and had no ill effects from the worrisome event. She went home innocently wagging her tail, as labs are wont to do. Leanne never had the same problem again. Somehow it seemed to cement our working relationship. I was just glad I was at the clinic, not on the road.

We soon developed a supportive style much like Jim and I had had. Dr. Best would cover for me if I was late or on the road. She would willingly change the day's schedule around if it became apparent my whole routine small-animal day had to be scrapped for a complex equine call. "Let's just make it work" became our motto. It was refreshing to be able to say "what do you think?" and "do you mind?" and "can you handle more?" to affirmative responses. Dr. Best even agreed to start up and monitor our Web site, knowing we had to join the technology generation. It was met with a great response.

Shortly after she started, Leanne saw a seventeen-year-old cat as an emergency late one afternoon. The owner was difficult, tending to be taciturn and negative. The cat was not eating and had distressed breathing. She was in a life-threatening situation, but Mr. Timmins did not want to let her go. Leanne explained to him the several serious processes that might cause these clinical signs — all probably fatal — the most common being congestive heart failure. He flat out refused euthanasia; so, frustrated, Leanne came to me.

"The little cat is suffering and cyanotic," she explained. "I told him we did not have an oxygen cage, but he also refuses Ottawa. Could you talk to him?" I met the same stonewall. I realized Mr. Timmins would rather have Shadow die at home than make this terrible decision.

"The last time I saw you was twenty years ago," he said, still conveying an air of negativism I was soon to understand. "You said my dog was going to die of cancer, and it didn't even have cancer. Why should I believe you now?"

I stammered, beet red, "Both of us believe Shadow may die during the chest tap to remove fluid, or have a heart attack soon."

"I want you to try; the kids are all upset."

"Then we'll pre-oxygenate her. I'll test blood in the meantime to see if there are other problems with kidney failure that could mean we shouldn't proceed."

He agreed skeptically, saying, "I just want to take her home tonight and not with a great big bill."

I gulped. The situation was certainly awkward and stacked against us, but I carried Shadow to the back and started to work on her. When the blood work came back, it was perfect, giving us no reason to halt. And the oxygen had helped her very much

"Okay Leanne, lets proceed," I said. "You might as well learn to do a chest tap."

After clipping and preparing her sites, we injected a spot mid-chest on both sides with a local anaesthetic. Shadow was being surprisingly tolerant. Erin held her gently in a sternal position while I inserted a small plastic catheter into her chest. It, in turn, was attached to a valve and a longer tube, and in this way I removed 180 ml of pinkish fluid from her left thorax. Leanne repeated the process perfectly on the right, and soon Shadow was breathing easier.

"Let's give her a diuretic and send out that blood for a thyroid test," I said. "Mr. Timmins said she had lost a lot of weight lately."

Hyperthyroidism is a common disease in older cats. It can be linked to heart disease, and Shadow's x-ray, taken after the fluid was cleared, showed she had an enlarged heart. Perhaps she had something further we could treat. When the test came back the following day, it confirmed her thyroid hormone was way up. If corrected with a daily medication to shrink the enlarged thyroid, the condition can be reversed and the cat will gain weight. As well, the strain on her heart would be less. Shadow was now at home doing well and had started eating and grooming again.

We added pills for hyperthyroidism to her daily regime of cardiac medication. Her owner was practically beaming "I told you so" when he picked them up. The family successfully administered three pills every day, twice a day, to their little cat for a year before she died one day at home. They truly had the last word and taught Leanne and me a lesson on giving up too soon that we have never forgotten. Sometimes you can beat the odds. The words "Remember Shadow" carry a lot of weight at our practice when someone feels like giving up too soon.

There were many cases of different and interesting surgeries that I had to expose Dr. Best to. One day it might be a urethrostomy on a male cat who had had several urinary blockages, another day a surgery to repair an eyelid. Our pattern was to do them together once and then Leanne would do one on her own with me available for questions and help. By the end of six months, I felt she could tackle almost anything I could. Things were going well on the equine side as well, and so I felt blessed. I was learning my share, too, from my colleague just out of school.

We had had some great staff parties, all building strong bonds of friendship. A spa day and a cooking class were hugely popular, but the most fun of all was a zany staff car rally. With a "redneck theme" proposed in advance, everyone was to show up at the clinic in costume at the appointed hour. I knew I had invited trouble with a best theme car, but had little idea how everyone would go to town.

Dr. Best and her husband turned up as Lulabelle and Clem complete with rollers and a phantom pregnancy; she looked like a different person. Their car had a camp stove hanging off the back bumper. Others filed in, in coveralls or work shirts with ball caps and blackened teeth. Perhaps the best costumes were two part-time ladies in red and black flannel with tool belts and work boots giving out business cards entitled "Fix it chicks — Get 'er done." We were off.

I had planted clues at ten stations, creating our own mini-Amazing Race. There were trick directions to get there, times to adhere to, and questions along the way. I had eighteen people running the roads of Lanark for four hours picking up everything from pumpkins to road kill. They were not all pleased with me, as some got lost and had to backtrack many times. Retrieving condoms at village stores and flags from buckets in rapids were only a few of the pranks. Points were deducted for phone calls home for help, where I anxiously awaited the post-event party. I had tried to make the trip worthwhile, with good prizes, and the most competitive teams made it to all stations and back on time. It was a good exercise for everyone on how to keep your cool with your team. No one thought they would ever want to enter the real Amazing Race after experiencing the Brentwood Car Rally. As with all our parties, it was fodder for conversation for days and a chance to blow off steam.

My interest had been piqued at a conference where the newest veterinary "must-have," a digital x-ray system, was the hot topic. I came back to the clinic excited about the prospect of getting one. For years, veterinarians and doctors have developed radiographs using a film and wet chemistry system similar to photography. This system had been reliable enough, but plagued with problems of quality, not to mention being smelly and messy. Should we consider another brave leap into the age of technology? Leanne thought we should. I carefully worked the figures—could we afford it? I decided to take the plunge

A laser imaging system translates the image of the animal into a digital format, making it possible to view it on a computer. Of course, these New-Age images could also be emailed, lightened, darkened, and magnified, as well as put on the animal's computer history. It would be fun as well as progressive. Our days of playing in the smelly darkroom were drawing to a close. Now, we would just have to deal with electricity failures, software glitches, and a steep learning curve. We unpacked the many large boxes three weeks later, and I can say I have as yet not lost the thrill of seeing those x-rays pop up on the computer screen. We have the extra positive experience of seeing our clients' delight when asked if they would like a printed copy to take home. A foot-dragger in the past, I was now a technology convert.

Aero was a beautiful and stately six-year-old male German shepherd, a classic Rin-Tin-Tin fellow. One day, he was presented to me with a three-week history of straining to urinate. His owner could see that his problem was worsening quickly. I thought immediately of small bladder stones moving out to block his urethra. These small crystalline calculi can form in the bladder, then move out and get lodged at the os penis. This is a bone in the penis of the male dog, limiting the diameter of the outflow tract. I snapped an x-ray of the bladder, pelvic area, and penis. To my great surprise, no calculi were visible. They would have shown up as iridescent white pearls.

I decided to sedate Aero and pass a urinary catheter. Although he was usually gracious, the next procedure would really push his limits of tolerance. Once sleepy, the 100-pound dog was easily slipped sideways onto the floor into a position of complete lateral restraint. I lubricated a long rubber catheter, but could not pass it. What was going on? I would have to do a dye test next. At that moment, I discovered a walnut-sized lump between his hind legs. It had been well hidden in hair and by the thick skin, but I kicked myself remembering many past resolutions to do a thorough physical exam. I called Aero's owner, Gladys. "I think

I've found the cause of the problem. We'll have to biopsy the lump I found. It appears to be growing around or pushing on his urethra." She readily agreed, even though an anaesthetic would be needed, but then asked cautiously "What will we be able to do about it? And what will we be able to do to help him pee while we wait for the results to come back. Shouldn't you just remove it?"

"I won't know if I can until I get him under," I said. " I'll get the catheter in and leave it there so the bladder can drain. He'll have to wear an 'E collar.'"

It didn't seem to be a good solution to either of us. Not only would Aero be dripping urine constantly in her meticulously clean-carpeted house, but the exuberant dog would be bumping into the door frames and furniture with his own personal lampshade on his head. I sighed, feeling stuck. Clearly I didn't have the answer to this one yet. I only knew I had to deal with "the lump."

"No promises, but I'll see if I can remove it," I answered, "first thing tomorrow morning." Aero's bladder being drained, he went home overnight.

When I got the big dog anaesthetized and on his back the next morning, I could clearly feel the lump. I did manage to pass a very small catheter and discovered that the urethra appeared to go right through the middle of the hard mass. Not only did I have that complication, but I would have to cut through the penis, a very vascular tissue prone to hemorrhage and full of nerves, even to do the biopsy. The prospect of totally removing the mass seemed unlikely. I set about optimistically. Working with a magnifying loop and watching for nerves, I dissected carefully through the spongy tissue using electrocautery to try to control the bleeding. The white, grisly mass did seem to attach to the urinary tube, but I tried my best to detach it and leave the urethra intact. After Aero was sewn up, I called Gladys.

"I will leave the catheter in place, and he'll have to stay here overnight to recover, but I think I got it all. I can't guarantee there are no microscopic cells left. In five to seven days, we'll know what it is," I said.

By day three post-surgery, we were all frustrated, thankfully not knowing how far we still had to go. Aero had his E collar off many times a day, had chewed at parts of his incision, and now there was extensive bruising evident under his tail and down his inner thighs.

"There is ongoing slow bleeding," I explained. "We must keep him quiet and monitor his blood values." Despite her reluctance, the owner agreed to keep him mildly sedated.

After a week, I got the pathology report back describing the tissue from the troublesome lump. It was a rare urethral tumour and had only been recognized and written up once in North America—in a German shepherd! I called a urinary specialist. They told me in no uncertain terms that I could not have removed all the cancer cells and that Aero should have a complete penile amputation and perineal urethrostomy—a drastic procedure that would leave him urinating from a hole under his tail. Heartsick, I called Gladys. He had just started healing.

"Aero will have to have another big surgery—one that I will call in a specialist for," I said. Not surprisingly, she started to cry.

When I told her the cost, she simply stated, "I'll go into my savings. All I care about is that I'll have my dog in the end. Will he really be able to live that way?"

I assured her he would. I had done many urethrostomies on cats and knew there was a chance of complications like scar tissue around the opening, but it was unlikely. We booked the Board-Certified Surgeon to come to our clinic.

When Aero was finished, he had a smooth abdomen and a two-foot incision. A two-centimetre pink opening of mucous membrane under his anus showed where he would void. Dr. Phillips had done a masterful job.

Aero continued to challenge us with his aftercare. He was getting less and less magnanimous about medical interventions. Gladys had to drag him into the clinic, and several days he dragged her back out. For three weeks solid, we cared for Aero every day as his exhausted owner went to work. By this time, she had observed every urination around the clock for six weeks. In time, his long incision healed well and his urethrostomy worked perfectly. It did everyone at the clinic proud to see him lift his leg on our front step — and always elicited a laugh from his owner, as he marked his territory with gravity, not knowing he was aiming in the totally wrong direction.

My nieces were turning out to be great riders. Several years of showing ponies had made them tough and determined horse-women. Although Anne no longer rode, she was a great teacher, and they had jumped many a jump by my fiftieth birthday. I had only one request for my half-century celebration: I wanted to go on a cross-country ride with them. Sophisticated preteens, they were definitely more interested in showing than riding across fields and ditches and jumping solid obstacles, but they indulged me. It was, unbeknownst to me, the last time I would talk them into such a bold, fast-paced ride over solid obstacles.

The day was as perfect as only September days can be, with the leaves turning, and a fresh, fall crispness in the air. Elizabeth had decided to join us, and, steaming mugs of coffee in hand, we all loaded up and trailered to the best cross-country facility in the area. Our four horses were perfectly turned out, and, with cross-country tack and boots on, they looked splendid. Their coats were gleaming with dapples, and the brass on the bridles was shining. I remember thinking how amazing it was to be there with my most special people and four beautiful animals. For all of the people and animals involved to be healthy and fit and together to fulfill my birthday wish seemed almost too good to be true.

We set out with enthusiasm, the horses on good behaviour, as if they sensed that the day was special. Elizabeth picked up a canter over the first expanse of mowed field, and we were off. I didn't look back, just waved my arm and shouted, "Follow me!" grinning at Elizabeth. The kids were close behind and shouted their approval over the first fence, a large X made of very heavy poles. The course was dry and well maintained, with perfect sand footing and imaginative obstacles and combinations. We were out an hour and a half, cantering through the shimmering light of forest trails and popping into surprise clearings with leaps up onto banks or down into water. Plank coups came up quickly, and fences built like giant wooden lounge chairs or sod-topped stone walls had the horses jumping happily and well. We cantered around corners and up small inclines side by side, stirrup to stirrup, until the horses were sweaty and as satisfied with their outing as we were and ready to go home. A birthday I will never forget, it surpassed my expectations in every way, filling me with an indescribable joy of living, riding, and horses. Perhaps I could yet hope to celebrate my next decade the same way!

We have moved along now. Leanne is married. Erin's children are teenagers, and Charlotte's are in school. The practice continues to grow. Leanne's presence has brought me the sense of space and time to allow me to start writing down my stories. We all learn every day, and we are often surprised by what we do and see. I still feel privileged to be able to help animals and seldom take it for granted. Veterinary medicine is a passion I was lucky to discover; the continual process of learning and growing it grants me is only a small part of its greatness. If I continue to be as blessed as I have been throughout my life, there will be many more stories to tell.

I am back in the stands, waiting for fate to decide on William's destiny. The sky had clouded over a bit, and the crowd huddled together as if the day had cooled off. The jockey limped off the centre field to a smattering of applause. But when William's ears appeared above the black barrier, the crowd went wild with a thunderous roaring. He hopped into the waiting trailer and that was really all there was to it. People started to file out. I dried my tears, feeling drained.

I think about William and what he taught me about myself. The changes and losses I have experienced in my life have made me stronger. The passings I have witnessed and even enacted for others in my career have made me more compassionate. I readily admit to being moved by what animals do for people over and over again. It hits me at the most unexpected times and always reminds me of William. Whether racing, jumping, pulling, or teaching, they serve and tolerate us. Whether on our laps, guarding, playing with, or indulging us, they epitomize love. More than just giving to us, they give us the benefit of the doubt. How could I consider it any less than a privilege to have served them?

I experienced a deep sense of happiness, not only that William was alive, but that I was. That day in the stands, I was bestowed with a deeper understanding — not just of what animals have meant to me, but of myself.

That was William's gift.

One Veterinarian's Journey in Photos

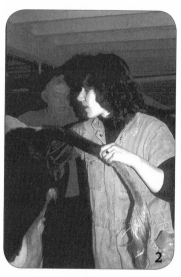

1 The South Shore. 2 Shouldn't you be a nurse? 3 Carry on Currier and Ives! 4 Pachyderms visit OVC.

5 Gaining confidence. 6 Calving woes. 7 Floating teeth at the farm. 8 A sick sheep . . . 9 Gentle giants. 10 House moving.

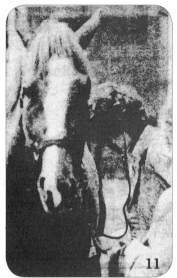

11 Able to show? **12** Starting
to help. **13** Punch and Enya.
14 Elizabeth tests herself.
15 Follow me. **16** Teamwork.

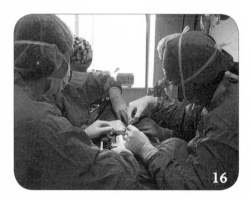

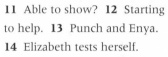

17 James the Third.
18 Welcoming new life.
19 In her element.
20 Back in Lanark.
21 Fiftieth celebration.

GLOSSARY

ACETABULUM   The cup-shaped socket of the hip joint that receives the head of the femur.

AMNION   The innermost fetal membrane; a thin, transparent sac that holds the fetus suspended in the amniotic fluid.

ANAESTHETIZE   Administration of a drug or agent used to abolish the sensation of pain; to achieve adequate muscle relaxation during surgery; to calm fear; to decrease consciousness.

ARTHRITIS   Inflammation of a joint; usually accompanied by pain and swelling, and frequently changes in structure.

ARTHROSCOPIC SURGERY   A surgical procedure to look inside a joint; carried out through an arthroscope.

ARTIFICIAL INSEMINATION   The implanting of live spermatozoa into the genital tract of the female carried out by human/veterinary doctors or technicians.

ATROPHY   A decrease in the size of an organ or tissue.

AUTOIMMUNE DISEASE   A disease state characterized by a specific antibody or cell-mediated immune response against the body's own tissues.

BARBITURATE   Classification of drug used to depress the nervous system; used to induce apathy and sleep, and, in high doses, general anaesthesia.

BITE ALIGNMENT   The position of upper and lower teeth in relation to each other when the mouth is closed.

BLOOD GLOBULIN   Large circulating proteins that protect against infection.

BLOOD UREA LEVEL   Nitrogen in the blood in the form of urea, a waste usually filtered out by the kidneys.

BOG SPAVIN   A term used to describe the accumulation of synovial fluid in the tarsocrural joint of the hock.

BRACHIAL ARTERY   The main artery inside of the front leg.

BREEDING FOLLICLE   A fluid-filled structure on the ovary that grows, softens, and ruptures to release the ovum (egg) each estrus period.

BRONCHODILATORS   Agents used that cause dilation of the bronchi, thereby facilitating breathing and removal of secretions.

CALF-JACK   A T-shaped metal instrument that fits below the cow's vulva with a winch that attaches to the calf's legs to pull it out.

CASTRATION   Removal of the testicles.

CHLORAMPHENICOL   A broad-spectrum antibiotic with specific therapeutic activity against gram-positive and gram-negative bacteria.

COLIC   A syndrome caused by severe pain due to disease of an abdominal organ.

COLITIS   Inflammation of the colon.

COLLAPSING TRACHEA   A narrowed part of the trachea restricting airflow (found in obese and toy breed dogs).

CONGESTIVE HEART FAILURE   A condition that occurs as a result of impaired pumping capability of the heart and is associated with abnormal retention of water in the lungs and liver.

CRYPTORCHID   Retention of the testicles in the inguinal ring or abdomen.

CYANOTIC   A bluish discoloration of the skin and mucous membranes due to reduced concentration of oxygen in the blood.

DECOMPRESSION OF GAS   An essential part of the treatment for acute gastric dilatation in dogs and horses; done by stomach tube or tap.

DISIMPACTION   Manual/surgical removal of feces from an impacted colon.

DIURETIC   An agent that increases urine excretion or the amount of urine; an agent that promotes urine secretion.

ELECTROCAUTERY Cauterization of tissue by means of an electrode that consists of a red-hot piece of metal and either direct or alternating current.

ELECTROLYTES Usually refers to the amounts of sodium, potassium, and chloride in the blood.

ENCEPHALITIS Inflammation of the brain.

ENDOTRACHEAL Within the trachea.

ERUCTATION Oral ejection of gas or air from the stomach.

ERUPTION TIMES Appearing or becoming visible, as in eruption of the teeth.

ESOPHAGUS The muscular tube that carries swallowed foods and liquids from the pharynx to the stomach.

ESTRUS The time during the reproductive cycle when the female displays interest in mating.

EUTHANASIA The deliberate ending of life of an animal suffering from an incurable disease; an easy or painless death.

EXTRACTION TECHNIQUE The process or act of pulling or drawing out.

FALLOPIAN TUBE The tube or duct that extends laterally from the lateral angle of the fundal end of the uterus and terminates near the ovary.

FEMORAL ARTERY The chief inside artery of the hind leg.

FLEXOR TENDONS Tendons of the superficial and deep digital flexor muscles, situated behind the metacarpal or metatarsal bones.

GASTRIC TORSION Rotation of the stomach predisposed by large meals followed by exercise.

GASTROENTERITIS Inflammation of the lining of the stomach and intestine.

GELDING A castrated male horse.

GIGLI WIRE SAW A very strong wire saw used in orthopedics; also suited to performing fetotomies on fetal foals.

HALOTHANE A colourless, heavy liquid administered by inhalation to produce general anaesthesia.

HEAVES Asthma in horses; also known as chronic obstructive pulmonary disease (COPD).

HIP DISPLASIA A developmental problem of the canine coxofemoral joint, in which the ball of the hip does not fit into the socket.

HYPERTHYROIDISM Excessive functional activity of the thyroid gland resulting in elevated circulating T4 and a high metabolic rate.

HYPOTHERMIA Low body temperature.

HYSTERECTOMY Surgical removal of the uterus.

IMPACTED The condition of being wedged in firmly; constipated.

INCISOR REDUCTION Reducing the height of the incisor teeth mechanically.

INHALANT ANAESTHETIC A substance that can be taken into the body by way of the nose and trachea; that is, through the respiratory system.

INJECTION REACTION An adverse reaction caused by a chemical agent (drug or vaccine).

INJECTION SITES Locations where medication is placed, as into the subcutaneous tissues, muscles, or blood vessels.

INTRAVENOUS FLUIDS Fluids injected into a vein to replace and correct both fluid and electrolyte imbalances.

INTRAVENOUS CATHETER A plastic tube placed in the cephalic, jugular, or saphenous vein when intravenous fluid or drugs must be infused in large volumes.

INTUBATE To insert a tube into the trachea.

KETOSIS The accumulation in the body of the ketone bodies: acetone, beta-hydroxybutyric acid, and acetoacetic acid.

LAVAGE Irrigation or washing out of an organ or cavity.

LUPUS Autoimmune syndrome where various body tissues are attacked by an animal's own immune system (including liver, heart, skin).

MALPRESENTATION Faulty fetal presentation.

MARSUPIALIZATION Conversion of a closed cavity, such as an abscess or cyst, into an open pouch by incising it and suturing the edges of its wall to the edges of the wound.

MASTITIS   Inflammation of the mammary gland.

MIDLINE   The fascial line that divides the body into right and left halves ("linea alba").

MYOSITIS   Inflammation of the muscle.

NEONATAL   Pertaining to the period immediately after birth.

NEUROLOGICAL   Pertaining to or emanating from the nervous system or from neurology.

NEUTER   As a verb, to desex an animal.

ORTHOPEDIC SURGERY   That branch of surgery dealing with the preservation and restoration of the function of the skeletal system, its articulations, and associated structures; particularly associated with the correction of deformities or fractures of the musculoskeletal system.

PARVOVIRUS   A group of viruses similar to adeno-associated viruses. They are pathogenic in animals and humans and cause severe diarrhea and damage to the bowel wall.

PERITONITIS   Inflammation or infection of the serous membrane lining the walls of the abdominal and pelvic cavities.

PNEUMONIA   Inflammation or infection of the lung.

POLYARTHRITIS   Inflammation of several joints. More common in very young animals because of the frequency of navel infection and bacteremia and the immaturity of the arthrodial tissues.

PROLAPSE   A falling out or dropping down of an organ or internal part, such as the uterus or rectum.

PULMONARY EDEMA   An effusion of serous fluid into the pulmonary interstitial tissues and alveoli. Preceded by pulmonary congestion.

PURULENT   Containing or forming pus.

RADIOGRAPH   To obtain records of internal structures of the body by exposure of film specially sensitized to x-rays or gamma rays;.

RESECTION   Excision of a portion of an organ or other structure.

RHINOPNEUMONITIS   Herpes virus causing inflammation of the mucosae of the nasal cavities and the lungs.

SALMONELLA A bacterium, several species of which are pathogenic; some produce mild gastroenteritis and others a severe and often fatal food poisoning. Symptoms in an animal are uncontrolled muscle activity, lack of consciousness, and paddling.

SEIZURING A condition in which muscles seize up; caused by toxins or abnormal electrical activity of the brain.

SEPTICEMIA Systemic disease associated with the presence and persistence of pathogenic microorganisms and their toxins in the blood.

SHEARED MOUTH The state of the molar teeth when occlusion is poor, leading to wear in such a way that the teeth pass each other like the blades of a pair of shears.

SHOCK A clinical syndrome in which the peripheral blood flow is inadequate to return sufficient blood to the heart for normal function, particularly the transport of oxygen to all organs and tissues.

TEETH-FLOAT An instrument for the filing or rasping of a horse's premolar and molar teeth. Handles are twenty-four to twenty-eight inches long with a broad head into which an interchangeable rasp can be screwed.

THERAPEUTIC RIDING A program designed to enhance the well-being of individuals, particularly those who are handicapped.

THORACIC EMPYEMA Accumulation of pus in the thorax or chest around the outside of the lungs.

TOXEMIA A condition resulting from the spread of bacterial products in the bloodstream.

TRANSRECTAL ULTRASOUND PROBE A probe reflecting sound waves to create images of soft tissues, usually ovaries and uterus.

TUBE WORMING Passage of a one-centimetre diameter tube via a nostril to the stomach to administer deworming medication.

TWITCH A restraint device for horses whereby the nose is pinched/held in a rope, chain, or vice to facilitate medical or painful procedures.

UMBILICAL HERNIA Protrusion of abdominal contents through the abdominal wall at the umbilicus, the defect in the abdominal wall and protruding intestine being covered with skin and subcutaneous tissue.

URETHRA The tubular passage through which urine is discharged from the bladder to the exterior via the external urinary meatus.

URETHROSTOMY Creation of a permanent opening for the urethra in the perineum or groin.

WAVE MOUTH A condition in which the tables of the molar teeth have a wavelike appearance due to uneven wear.

WEANLING A young food animal in the period immediately after weaning and up to six to eight months of age.

X-RAY PLATES Protective metal container holding x-ray film.

REFERENCES FOR GLOSSARY:

D.C. Blood and V.P. Studdert, *Saunders Comprehensive Veterinary Dictionary*, 2nd edition (Bath, U.K.: Harcourt Publishers Limited, 1999).

Dennis M. McCurnin and Joanna M. Bassert, *Clinical Textbook for Veterinary Technicians*, 5th edition (Philadelphia, Pa: W.B. Saunders Co., 2002).

Taber's Cyclopedic Medical Dictionary (Philadelphia, Pa: W.B. Saunders Co., 1997).

About the Author

Dr. Helen Douglas was born in Nova Scotia, but has lived most of her life in her beloved Ottawa Valley. Helen's veterinary career has spanned more than three decades and has taken her from humble log barns in Lanark to Olympic show barns in Toronto and the Fraser Valley in B.C. It has encompassed a very wide and fulfilling range of animals and experiences, from treating injured deer and vaccinating feral cats in bags to breeding imported show dogs from England and warmblood horses from Europe.

Helen has travelled and practised extensively, including in England and the Bahamas, but has returned to the Ottawa Valley with the full conviction that there is nothing you might want out of life that you can't get in Lanark County.

She began riding in 1965 and plans to continue well past her fiftieth anniversary of first getting on a horse. Thus began a love affair that would last a lifetime and take her on horseback all over Canada, the U.S., Ireland, South America, and beyond.

Helen's avid interest in other cultures and travel has led her to Lesotho, South Africa, where in affiliation with the humanitarian group Help Lesotho, she volunteered in an orphanage for three months in 2008. She maintains her connection with them by assisting with their Web site and farm and sponsoring several children.

Reading, riding, swimming, and gardening are squeezed into her busy life as a country vet when at home in Carleton Place.

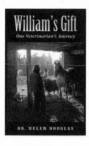